CONTENTS/TABLE DES MATIERES

Canada: The State of the Federation 1987-88

Edited by
Peter M. Leslie and Ronald L. Watts

Institute of
Intergovernmental
Relations

Queen's University
Kingston, Ontario
Canada

Canadian Cataloguing in Publication Data

Main entry under title:

Canada, the state of the federation

1985-
Annual.
Continues: Year in review.
Issued also in French under title: Canada, l'état de la fédération.
Vol. 1987-88 edited by Peter M. Leslie and Ronald L. Watts.
ISSN 0827-0708

1. Federal-provincial relations - Canada - Periodicals.* 2. Federal government - Canada - Periodicals. I. Leslie, Peter M. II. Watts, Ronald L. III. Title: State of the federation.

JL27.F42   321.02'3'0971   C86-030713-1 rev

The Institute of Intergovernmental Relations

The Institute, part of Queen's University, is the only organization in Canada whose mandate is solely to promote research and communication on the challenges facing the federal system.

Current research interests focus on the respective roles of federal and provincial governments in the economy, the place of Quebec in confederation, aboriginal self-government, and a wide range of policy issues affected by the structure and working of federalism.

The Institute pursues these objectives through research conducted by its own staff, and other scholars, at Queen's and elsewhere through an active and growing publications program and through seminars and conferences.

The Institute links academics and practitioners of federalism in federal and provincial governments and the private sector.

PREFACE

This is the third edition of the series *Canada: The State of the Federation*. The intention, as in previous volumes, is to survey recent events of importance to Canadian federalism and, in the light of these events, to comment on present-day and emerging issues affecting the federation. The previous editions covered the years 1985 and 1986, but because the second edition was delayed in appearance, this third edition is a double issue. It covers the years 1987 and 1988 in order to get back to our originally intended schedule of publication early each autumn.

This year's edition departs from the format of previous editions which examined developments in particular provinces and ranged over a variety of concerns. It focusses instead upon the two major current issues which have dominated the federal-provincial agenda during 1987-88: the Canada-United States Trade Agreement signed 2 January 1988, and the Constitutional Accord approved by the 11 first ministers on 3 June 1987. In addition, a feature introduced in the second edition, a chronology of events in the previous year affecting the federal system, has been continued, but covers the two years 1986 and 1987.

This volume was begun under the editorship of Peter Leslie. However, before its final completion he left the position of Director of the Institute of Intergovernmental Relations at Queen's University in August 1988 to take up a two-year appointment as an Assistant Secretary to the Cabinet for Federal-Provincial Relations in the Government of Canada. The editorial work was therefore completed by Ronald Watts who became Acting Director of the Institute on 1 September 1988. The co-editors would like to express their warm thanks to the contributors to this volume, and to the various members of the staff of the Institute of Intergovernmental Relations who have performed vital tasks in preparing the typescripts for publication. The main production work was done by Valerie Jarus, whose patience and meticulous attention to detail has been much appreciated by us both. We would also like to acknowledge the help of Patricia Candido in the secretarial and general organizational tasks. We are particularly grateful to Denis Robert, a Research Associate of the Institute, for preparing the summaries of each chapter in the other official language, and to Darrel Reid, Information Officer of the Institute and Chris Kendall, a

Research Assistant in the Institute, for preparing the chronology. We would also like to thank Michael Hawes who reviewed several of the contributions on the Canada-U.S. Trade Agreement, and Marilyn Banting who has helped by copy-editing. Douglas Brown, who joined the Institute as Associate Director on 1 September 1988, also did much to help in the closing stages, particularly with the distribution arrangements. As in previous years, the production of this book and the other Institute publications is very much a team effort, and we are glad to have this opportunity to thank all the members of the team.

Peter M. Leslie
Ronald L. Watts
October 1988

CONTRIBUTORS

Formerly with the Intergovernmental Affairs Secretariat of the Government of Newfoundland and Labrador, **Douglas M. Brown** is Associate Director of the Institute of Intergovernmental Relations at Queen's University.

Keith Brownsey is a Ph.D. candidate in Political Studies at Queen's University, with research interests in political economy and American politics.

A former Research Associate at the Institute of Intergovernmental Relations, **Sheilagh M. Dunn** worked with the Ministry of Intergovernmental Affairs of Ontario from 1985 to 1988.

Avigail Eisenberg is a Ph.D. candidate in Political Studies at Queen's University, with an interest in Constitutional issues.

Christopher Kendall is a Research Assistant at the Institute of Intergovernmental Relations.

Peter M. Leslie was, at the time he worked on this volume, Director of the Institute of Intergovernmental Relations.

Hugh Mellon is a Ph.D. candidate in Political Studies at Queen's University, with a research interest in the Atlantic provinces.

David A. Milne is a Professor of Political Science at the University of Prince Edward Island, and author of *Tug of War: Ottawa and the Provinces Under Trudeau and Mulroney.*

A graduate of the University of Regina and the University of Toronto, **Darrel R. Reid** is the Information Officer of the Institute of Intergovernmental Relations.

A graduate of Université Laval and the Université de Montréal, **Denis Robert** is Research Associate at the Institute of Intergovernmental Relations, with special research interests concerning Quebec.

A former senior public servant in the Governments of Saskatchewan and Canada, and a member of the Royal Commission on the Economic Union and Development Prospects for Canada, **Thomas K. Shoyama** is a Professor at the School of Public Administration at the University of Victoria.

I

Introduction

ONE

The Peripheral Predicament: Federalism and Continentalism

Peter M. Leslie[1]

L'auteur de ce chapitre effectue une analyse de l'Accord du lac Meech et de celui sur le libre-échange qui s'articule autour de trois objets principaux: 1) en utilisant une approche "centre-périphérie" il étudie les enjeux des deux accords et démontre leur interdépendance; 2) il s'interroge sur les possibilités d'en arriver, dans l'un ou l'autre cas, à un "meilleur" accord; et 3) il envisage les risques inhérents à un échec de l'un ou des deux accords.

Les deux accords comportent beaucoup de similitudes. Dans les deux cas il s'agit d'une décision capitale: le maintien du statu quo est pernicieux et les effets escomptés de ces accords seront à toute fin pratique irréversibles. Il fallait donc aller de l'avant avec prudence. Dans les circonstances, les accords obtenus répondent aux exigences de la situation. Les effets conjugués des deux accords sur la fédération canadienne causeront sans aucun doute un certain degré de fragmentation (Meech) et d'homogénéisation (libre-échange). Toutefois, un échec de l'un ou des deux accords provoquera des conflits fédéraux-provinciaux et inter-régionaux non moins préjudiciables pour le Canada.

To illustrate her case against free trade, Ms. Atwood refers to the purported habit of the beaver which, when afraid, bites off its own testicles and offers them up to its pursuer. We are obviously dealing with much more than public policy in this debate.

Globe and Mail editorial
1 July 1988

---

1 This chapter was written while the author was Director of the Institute of Intergovernmental Relations, Queen's University.

Canadians are indeed dealing with much more than public policy, as they debate the merits of the Free Trade Agreement (FTA).[2] They are arguing over the framework within which future policy will be made; and many are aware that the framework will shape government policy as long as Canada exists. It is not only opponents who say this. That the FTA will constrain future decision makers is a large part of its attraction, at least to those who resent past policies of economic nationalism; to them it is virtually an economic bill of rights. In Alberta one hears: "With this agreement, central Canada will never again be able to impose on us a National Energy Program!" Because the agreement changes the rules under which future governments will operate, its essence is truly constitutional; it may well have more potent constitutional effect than the Meech Lake Accord.[3] Partisan critics see both as sapping federal policy capacity—the FTA, abdicating vital powers to Washington; "Meech," ceding authority to the provinces. Others believe that Meech leaves federal power intact but that the FTA subordinates the provinces to an ascendant federal government. A third group sees Meech as decentralizing and the FTA as a counterbalancing, centralizing force.

Whether the combined effect of Meech and the FTA is centralizing or decentralizing is undoubtedly important, but not in itself. What matters is the social, cultural, and economic effects of (de)centralization. Thus the debate over the Meech Lake Accord is not really about the structure of government in Canada, but about possible *consequences* of structural change; it is about the rights that inhere in Canadian citizenship, and about the desirable or tolerable extent of interprovincial variation in public policy and citizenship rights. Specifically, is Quebec to have the powers and policy responsibilities that will enable it to move forward along a course very different from the rest of Canada, or indeed are all the provinces to have enough autonomy to go their own way regardless of the preferences of national majorities—of which the federal government is generally presumed to be the expression, and the agent? These questions are similar to those that animate the trade debate. That debate is ul-

---

2   The Canada-United States Free Trade Agreement, a far-reaching agreement leading toward the economic integration of the two national economies, is described later in this chapter. The FTA was negotiated in its main outlines by 4 October 1987; the final text was completed 17 December and signed 2 January 1988. In both countries implementing bills are now (late July 1988) before the national legislature.

3   The Meech Lake Accord, a federal-provincial agreement to amend the constitution in ways that will make it acceptable to Quebec, is summarized later in this chapter. The Accord was reached unanimously by First Ministers 30 April 1987 and given final form 3 June; it must be endorsed by all provincial legislatures as well as by Parliament before the relevant constitutional amendments can be proclaimed.

timately about tension between the values of prosperity and national independence, in other words about Canada's ability to fashion its own future within North America, economically, socially, and culturally.

It thus appears that both the Meech Lake and the trade debates are about relations between *centre* and *periphery*. Meech is ostensibly about centre-periphery relations within Canada, and the FTA about centre-periphery relations internationally—although I shall argue that no such neat distinction between the domestic and the international can, in practice, be drawn. The first and primary purpose of this chapter is, then, to survey both debates from a centre-periphery perspective, and to assess the significance of both agreements in this context. Their "interconnectedness," it will be argued, derives from a hierarchy of centre-periphery relationships, in which the domestic is embedded in the international or continental.

The FTA and the Accord are agreements reached at the executive level in 1987, but have yet, as of mid-1988, to complete the process of legislative endorsement or implementation.[4] While, in both cases, some opponents are aiming simply to defeat the measures in question, others say they are looking merely for improvements. For this reason it is important—and this is the second purpose of the chapter—to consider whether either or both could advantageously be reopened. On this matter it should be said at once that the obstacles to achieving a "better" Accord or a "better" FTA are formidable. The analysis will explain why.

A final question concerns the management of risk. In both cases, Meech and the FTA, a momentous decision is to be made; it is widely agreed that the action taken is likely to be irreversible. In the case of the Accord, this belief arises from the difficulty of achieving constitutional change under the 1982 amending formula, which the Accord proposes to tighten further in certain respects. On the trade issue, while the proposed FTA may legally be abrogated by either country on six months' notice, observers acknowledge that the costs of abrogation would be—at least for Canada—too great to make this a tolerable choice, once the agreement has been in effect for long. The apparent irreversibility of a decision obviously heightens risk; a natural reaction is to say, "Until you're sure, don't commit yourself." This would make sense if no negative consequen-

---

4 Both face significant opposition—the Meech Lake Accord in Manitoba and New Brunswick (all other legislatures have now approved it), and the FTA in Parliament, where the Senate has the power to block the implementing legislation and, it would appear, force an election. Since both the Liberals and the New Democrats oppose the FTA, any electoral outcome other than a renewed Conservative majority government would be likely to kill it.

ces flowed from rejection or indefinite postponement. However, there are risks inherent also in allowing either or both agreements to fall to the ground. In the case of Meech, the risk lies in a direct, though not necessarily immediate, challenge to Canadian unity, resulting from a new wave of nationalism in Quebec. In the trade case, risk—we are not talking here simply of opportunities foregone —derives from the fact that the *status quo* is not an option. Conversion to this belief was probably the single most important factor explaining the federal government's decision in September 1985 to propose the opening of negotiations; and even if one were to doubt that the government's assessment of the situation was accurate at the time, the ensuing two years of talks entirely eliminated the *status quo ante* as a viable state of affairs.[5] If Canada rejects the FTA, and standstill is impossible, then what course remains available to us? While consideration of that question lies beyond the scope of this chapter, it is important for us here to understand the nature of the risks inherent in collapse of the FTA, or of Meech, or of both. To do so is the third and final purpose of the chapter.

By the time these words appear in print, the FTA may already be approved or rejected; the fate of the Meech Lake Accord may already be clear. The intent is not to argue a case but to show how ultimate passage or ultimate collapse of the agreements will condition the future development of Canada in fundamental ways. It is possible to do this only from the perspective of the present, a moment in time when two decisions of immense importance lie before us. I have not attempted to guess what decision will be made, but to look for longer-term effects, acknowledging that approval or rejection are, in both cases, credible outcomes. With this in mind I have undertaken (here I recapitulate):

- to highlight what is at stake in the Meech Lake Accord and the FTA, and to show how the two are interconnected, by examining both within a centre-periphery context;
- to ask whether, in either or both cases, a "better" agreement is possible, or at least conceivable as a practical proposition; and
- to explore the risks inherent in failure of either or both.

---

5   Part of the argument here is that during the process of negotiation Americans became infinitely more aware of, and better informed about, Canadian trade and industrial policy. Previously, they had directed their trade remedy laws and actions mainly against the Europeans and the Japanese, and only in relatively few cases against Canada; now, they have collected reams of information about Canadian policies, and this information will form the basis for "dozens of countervail petitions—which may still be brought, of course, if the deal is in effect." See R.A. Young: "Breaking the Free Trade Coils," *Policy Options Politiques*, 9:2 (March 1988), 7.

Unfortunately it is not possible to take up these three subjects consecutively. Rather the scheme of the chapter is, in the next section, to highlight a few features of Canada's historical development from a centre-periphery perspective; then to comment, in the next two sections, on the Meech Lake and FTA debates, touching on the three subjects mentioned above; and finally, in a concluding section, to pull together the discussion.

CENTRE-PERIPHERY RELATIONS

The concepts of centre and periphery draw our attention to spatial relationships, especially ones based on economics. Most fundamentally, they are about functional ties that arise between major urban centres—places of industrial, commercial, financial, and administrative importance—and the more sparsely populated regions around them, where primary production is the main form of economic activity. On a larger scale, they are about economic ties between those regions where urban centres are large and numerous, and other regions where towns and villages are essentially outposts of the urban economy serving a rural population. However, while the words "centre" and "periphery" draw our attention to settlement patterns and to linkages among regions, they are about much more than this. They also imply that inequality is built into the complex set of relationships—economic, cultural, and political—that arise among regions or regional communities. Indeed, it is arguable that inequality is of the essence. Thus Rokkan and Urwin describe centres as "privileged locations within a territory."[6]

Inequality takes diverse forms: in the economic realm, exploitation; in cultural affairs, hegemony; in politics, domination. Subordination in these three areas is the essence of "the peripheral predicament," (again, I invoke the words of Rokkan and Urwin), a condition built up over time, from which it is increasingly difficult for a region to escape. Thus, the centre-periphery idea demands attention to historical context. The patterns we observe today have arisen over time, and they make no sense except as outcomes of processes of historical development. Moreover, centre-periphery terminology apparently implies a theory of the *cumulative causation* or "vicious circle" type, according to which existing disparities in condition or status tend to become ever more sharply etched. In other words, the theory tells us that conditions in the periphery tend to worsen over time, the periphery experiences increased economic insecurity and not infrequently a declining standard of living relative to residents of the

6   Stein Rokkan and Derek Urwin: *Economy, Territory, Identity: Politics of West European Peripheries* (London: Sage, 1983), p. 6.

centre. The periphery tends also to lose cultural distinctiveness and to suffer a decline in political power. The hallmark of peripheralization is *lack of control.*

In Canada's case the centre-periphery concept has a double reference, both internal and external. Among provinces or regions, south-central Ontario is heartland or centre, and the rest of Canada is hinterland or periphery. In an alternative formulation, the Windsor-Quebec City corridor is heartland while the north, east, and west are hinterland. Internationally, Canada is periphery or semi-periphery, evidently dependent throughout its history upon an external centre, core, or metropole—formerly Britain, now the United States. Indeed, as the work of Harold Innis has made clear, internal (interregional) relationships have always made sense only when seen in international context.[7] Thus Innis emphasized that the linkage between the internal and the external dimensions of centre-periphery relations has been very different, depending on whether the metropole (imperial power) was/is Britain or the United States. Innis pointed out that as long as Canada remained economically within the British empire, policies and political structures designed to strengthen that linkage did much to create or to accentuate an internal set of centre-periphery relationships. He observed that a centralized form of political organization was essential to the building of a transcontinental economy that bound together the St. Lawrence valley and the provinces of east and west. The nineteenth century economy, which was geared to the export of staple goods to European markets, required the building of east-west lines of communication; it demanded also a complementary set of national policies in immigration and trade. Thus a strong central government with extensive legislative and fiscal powers was essential. While the hinterland provinces chafed at the more restrictive features of the national policies, those policies did at least contribute to the rapid development of the Canadian west.[8]

As long as the principal markets lay in Europe, there remained a logic to the system. However, once Canada was brought into the orbit of the American empire (Innis' term), the effect was to weaken the control of the central regions

---

7 Nor does such linkage seem unusual; while the centre-periphery concept refers, on the face of it, to a pair or dyad—a centre and the surrounding periphery—it actually makes more sense to think of each pair as part of a complex set of dependency relationships, either a chain or a network.

8 In the Maritimes, they probably contributed to economic decline. If the grievances of that region have been treated less seriously in central Canada than the grievances of the west, that is probably because the implied threat to national unity was less severe. The population of the Maritimes is small, political discontent has not manifested itself through partisan revolt, and the poverty of its resource base has deprived the region of bargaining power.

over the periphery. As transatlantic trade declined in relative importance, especially after the First World War, central government dominance became more strongly resented, at least in the west. By then the settlement of the prairies had been completed, and the development of a north-south pattern of trade and investment strengthened the role of the provincial governments. Ownership of public lands was transferred to the prairie provinces in 1930, whereas hitherto they had been reserved to the Crown in right of Canada "for the purposes of the Dominion". The transfer was both consequence of changing economic circumstances, and contributor to the subsequent, continuing expansion in the role of the provincial governments.

In this context, Ontario-led attempts to resist the continentalist embrace through a set of nationalist policies, both economic and cultural, have heightened internal inequalities and fed the hinterland's resentment of domestic (interregional) centre-periphery relationships. The general point is that an economic development policy based on protectionism—an essential feature of the first set of "national policies"—has been and remains internally divisive. The less-industrialized regions see protectionism as openly exploitative; in this context, it does not matter whether protectionism takes the form of tariffs, import quotas, subsidies for manufacturing, export controls on natural resources,[9] or export taxes.[10] The latter were among the features of the National Energy Program (NEP) of 1980, the apogee and very symbol of Canadian economic nationalism, and (in western eyes) a blatant case of the periphery's exploitation by the centre. Especially in Alberta, the NEP was viewed as the culmination of a long set of policies—for example, in transportation—whose cumulative effect was to favour the development of manufacturing in Ontario and Quebec, and to prevent the establishment of an industrial economy outside those provinces. In this interpretation of regional politics in Canada, political power has resided in the most populated areas (it should be recalled that Ontario and Quebec together contain more than half the Canadian population), and economic power has resided in Toronto; the two have reinforced each other, to the detriment of the west. Thus, for Alberta, and indeed for all those provinces whose economies are based on resource production, the ideal arrangement is to obtain constitutional or other lasting protection against nationalist economic policies, while retaining or expanding the constitutional powers that will enable them to stimulate and direct the development of their own economies. Nothing could be more effective in producing this result than a Canada-U.S. trade agree-

9 The licensing of exports of resource products has been used over the years to give domestic consumers privileged access to potentially scarce primary goods.
10 An export tax holds domestic resource prices below international ones.

ment that binds and constrains federal economic powers, except to the extent that they may be used to promote regional economic development—but which also leaves provincial powers intact. The desire to ensure that provincial powers would remain whole is a major reason why even those provinces most committed to the idea of bilateral free trade nonetheless insisted on being integrally involved in the negotiating process. Their involvement contributed, perhaps decisively, to limiting the scope of the agreement that was eventually reached.[11] However, for them there remains the problem, perhaps not adequately faced by some provincial governments, that if Canada gives up certain of its powers over the economy, the powers in question must be abandoned equally by the federal government and the provinces.[12]

Ontario remains opposed to the FTA. This makes its negotiation apparently a case of the periphery successfully mobilizing against the centre. However, to see the FTA this way would be only partly accurate. The distribution of population in Canada is such that an initiative of this kind could never have been launched without substantial support from Ontario and Quebec. Here, two factors have been significant. One is that the dominant elements within the business community have shifted against protectionism and toward free trade, at least continentally, and their conversion has been supported and to some degree led by academic critics of economic nationalism. The second pertinent factor is that Quebec has split from Ontario on the issue, for reasons we shall now explore.

In the fashioning of governing coalitions in Canada, the position of Quebec has historically been pivotal; and over the past quarter century or so the province's position on both constitutional and economic issues has shifted considerably. Quebec is home to a culture that is marginal or peripheral in North America, and this has led it throughout its history to defend and to assert its legislative powers and policy role in all matters having some cultural relevance. Prior to the Quiet Revolution of the early 1960s, a period of cultural change and the political affirmation, Quebec was willing to accept federal predominance in economic policy. Indeed it supported the main thrust of federal policy, of which it was a beneficiary. It was autonomist in social and cultural affairs, and acquiescent of federal power in economic affairs, if not actually centralist. As long as this situation obtained, there was ample electoral support for national economic policies with a strongly protectionist character, especially since federal political leaders successfully "managed" the discontents of the hinterland regions through the exercise of the patronage and the disbursement

---

11 See chapter 4, below, by Douglas Brown.
12 On this, see chapter 2 in this volume.

of favours that compensated them to some extent for the costs that protectionism entailed. However, this scheme of political management began to fall apart during the 1960s, and the negotiation of the FTA a generation later marks its utter collapse. During the intervening years there have been at least two major changes in the domestic politics of Quebec that have reduced the strength of the protectionist or economic-nationalist coalition in Canada.

The first of these changes is that Quebec has come to view economic and cultural issues as no longer separable. Until the 1960s, the Quebec government had accepted linguistic stratification of the economy, with anglophones controlling all major business enterprises; perhaps this was inevitable as long as Montreal remained Canada's metropolis. However, with the advent of the 1960s, francophone Quebecers became persuaded that the culture was no longer viable unless all positions in the state and private sectors became fully open to them. Reflecting this, the province embarked on a programme of Quebec-centred economic nationalism that was one of the hallmarks of the Quiet Revolution. Henceforth it became a truism that control of the levers of economic power was essential if Quebec was to develop along lines consistent with its own culture. At first the provincial government was the instrument of this change, and, though it has become conventional to insist that the francophone-controlled private sector is fully capable of competing with all comers, no Quebec nationalist would dream of allowing the province to relax its control over any instrument of economic policy that it now possesses. Quebec economic nationalism is rival to Canadian economic nationalism.

The second change that is relevant here is that Quebec has come to view federal economic policies as inimical to its regional interests. Partly this is because federal policy itself changed. During the postwar period Canadian tariffs dropped, along with those of other industrial countries, as a result of multilateral negotiations under the GATT; in this more liberal environment, parts of Canadian industry began to compete successfully on world markets, while other sectors fell into decline. In many cases the declining industries were located in Quebec. Furthermore, in the face of simultaneously rising unemployment and inflation rates from the late 1950s onwards, at least until the mid-1980s, federal policy-makers became less confident of Keynesian policies for economic stabilization, and began to rely more than in the past on structural policies, i.e., policies aimed at strengthening particular sectors of the economy. Correspondingly, regional development also became more of a priority; one notes, for example, the creation of the Department of Regional Economic Expansion (DREE) in 1969. In this situation Quebec, like other provinces receiving regional development funds, demanded authority to expend those funds according to its own priorities and its own conceptions of a desirable economic future for the province. As its traditional industries weakened—industries such as clothing, footwear, rubber goods, and paper—Quebec began to see itself as a region disadvantaged by federal economic policies, which it complained were responsible for its outmoded economic structure. This feeling, whether justified or not, was one source of a new provincial activism in economic policy; the other was its desire to support the entry of francophones into leading positions within the Quebec economy, in firms capable of operating successfully in interprovincial and international markets.

The thrust of Quebec's own economic development policies has consistently been to build industries that need not hide behind tariffs or import quotas. While this aim has not prevented the Quebec government from insisting on continuing infusions of federal cash to support its high-employment traditional manufacturing industries, the province now appears ready to forego the protection of its old industries if it can obtain better access to international markets for its new ones. Or perhaps it has chosen merely to opt for non-tariff protective devices, for old and new industries alike, in the form of state development assistance. The relevant policies are only partially covered by the FTA and, generally, are less easily controlled by international agreements. Moreover, in many cases the provincial government is as well placed as the federal government to implement non-tariff, non-quota forms of protection, whether through mixed enterprise, government procurement policies, or various types of development assistance. Be that as it may, Quebec refuses to accept a position where it is merely an eastward extension of the industrial economy of Ontario; and that is how it now views the historical thrust of federal economic policies. If, in future, the province is to accept the legitimacy of continued federal leadership in economic affairs, it will have to be on the basis of new policies.

These changes in Quebec's perception of the regional structure of the Canadian economy and of the impact of federal economic policies were sharply reinforced during the 1970s, a period when the price of resource commodities rose sharply. Developments in the oil and gas sector illustrated the change most dramatically, but all primary products shared in the resource boom. This raised the hopes and the economic strength of those hinterland provinces that were most richly endowed with natural resources. It was also, except in Ontario, responsible for the elaboration of a set of provincial economic development policies in which production from natural resources, or production geared to the expansion of resource industries themselves, was the key element. While the western provinces, especially Alberta, epitomize most clearly this policy thrust, Quebec adopted a similar strategy; abundant energy production (hydro-electricity, a non-polluting, inexhaustible resource) was seen as Quebec's economic trump. In this context, the economic nationalism of the National Energy Program was viewed negatively by the Quebec government, as it was in the west, though obviously in Quebec there was nothing like the same intensity of feeling—for one thing, Quebec consumers benefited from low oil and gas prices, as did Ontario's.

The NEP was a vital factor in forging a provincialist coalition on the constitutional issue which came to a head in 1980-81, with only Ontario and New Brunswick supporting federal power. Only when the federal government made a vital concession on the constitutional amending formula, allowing provincial opt-out from any amendment infringing its legislative powers or proprietary rights, did the provincialist coalition dissolve, isolating Quebec in opposition to the *Constitution Act, 1982*. Quebec had a set of cultural concerns, and experienced a degree of cultural insecurity, that gave it additional objectives, distinct from those of the other members of the provincialist coalition. Those, precisely, are the concerns that are addressed today by the Meech Lake Accord. Meanwhile, on the question of economic nationalism, the FTA offers assurances that at least some of the federal dragon's teeth have been pulled. Its capacity to implement policies of economic nationalism—essentially, policies supporting indigenous manufacturing industry at the expense of resource industries, and supporting Canadian capital against foreign capital—has been sharply reduced under the FTA. These are policies which are broadly unattractive to Quebec, which has lined up once more with the other provinces that see resource production as critical to their economic development, in support of an international agreement that will restrict the future economic role of the federal government where the continental marketing of resources is concerned.

All these developments show how thoroughly today's economic and constitutional issues are intertwined in Canada, and how the political base for traditional arrangements has been eroded. It is less clear whether there is adequate political support for new arrangements that the Meech Lake Accord and the FTA aim to put into place. Another area of uncertainty concerns the consequences of these agreements rather than the preconditions for their legislative endorsement. The FTA apparently offers resource-dependent provinces some protection against peripheralization within Canada; but what about Canada's peripheralization within North America? The question is not rhetorical. As will be seen, on this, the arguments go both ways.

THE MEECH LAKE ACCORD

The Meech Lake Accord is a response to Quebec's objections to the *Constitution Act, 1982*, which was based on an agreement between the federal government and nine provinces—all but Quebec. It was widely felt at the time that, since the Parti Québécois (PQ) government was committed to achieving independence for the province, it would be impossible to obtain Premier Lévesque's assent to any set of constitutional amendments that maintained a viable form of federalism for Canada. For political reasons, the PQ could never be satisfied. However, it is important to recognize that not only the PQ was opposed to the terms of the act; it was denounced by the opposition Liberal Party as well, and was censured by unanimous vote of the Quebec legislature. Although Quebec is already "in the constitution," in the sense that it is legally bound by its terms— and the Quebec government has acknowledged this—Quebec has not given its assent to the 1982 act, as all other provinces have. The Accord was negotiated in order to end Quebec's moral exclusion from the constitutional order, amending the *Constitution Act, 1982* in ways that make it acceptable to the Quebec government, and strengthen its legitimacy among the population of that province.

The opportunity for achieving this objective came with the election of a federalist party, the Quebec Liberal Party under Robert Bourassa in December 1985. By that time, there had also been a change of government in Ottawa, with the Conservatives under Brian Mulroney committed to bringing Quebec into the "Canadian constitutional family with honour and enthusiasm."[13] The main outlines of the position the new Quebec government could be expected to take were already known from its election platform, but a fuller and more precise statement (indeed, the first official statement as government policy) came in May 1986 at a conference at Mont Gabriel, Quebec.[14] On that occasion the minister responsible, Gil Rémillard, set out five conditions that would have to be met if Quebec were to recognize the legitimacy of the amended constitution and to participate in matters such as future constitutional change, as a full and active member of the federation. Until then its role would be that of an observer only, as for example it had been in the negotiations on aboriginal self-government, a stance that made it all the more difficult (and in the end, impossible) to reach agreement. Participants at the Mont Gabriel conference, who included many of those who had been involved in previous constitutional negotiations and were to be involved in the discussions that ensued, agreed that the five conditions were as modest as any Quebec government could reasonably be expected to put forward. They also agreed that it was necessary for the governments to sound each other out informally, without launching formal negotiations, to see if some basis for an agreement existed. This caution and the degree of secrecy it implied were, it was argued, necessary in the circumstan-

---

13 Speech by Brian Mulroney at Sept-Iles, 6 August 1984.
14 An account of this conference, and the text of the speech by Gil Rémillard, Minister responsible for Canadian Intergovernmental Affairs, are contained in *Canada: The State of the Federation 1986*, edited by Peter M. Leslie (Kingston, Ont.: Institute of Intergovernmental Relations, 1987).

ces then prevailing. An open rebuff to Quebec at this stage would leave the country in a worse-off position than before, with a further loss of legitimacy in Quebec for existing constitutional arrangements.

In the interval between July 1986, when informal bilateral discussions began, and 3 June 1987, when the final text of the Accord was adopted, Quebec's five conditions were, in the main, agreed upon. However, they were not necessarily accepted in quite the terms in which they had been proposed by Mr. Rémillard or subsequently, by Premier Bourassa.[15] One significant fact, though, is that the Premiers did publicly commit themselves in August 1986 to deal first with Quebec's five constitutional demands, and to postpone consideration of other constitutional issues for a later round. This commitment was renewed at a meeting of First Ministers in November. It seems likely that the premiers agreed to this two-step process because the First Ministers did not think it would be possible to take up any other constitutional issues until the "Quebec agenda" had been settled. Thus Quebec's five publicly stated conditions received priority. By comparing them with the terms of the Meech Lake Accord, one may infer something about the substance of the negotiations.

(1) Explicit recognition of Quebec as a distinct society.[16] "We must . . . be assured," stated Mr. Rémillard, "that the Canadian Constitution will explicitly recognize the unique character of Quebec society and guarantee us the means necessary to ensure its full development within the framework of Canadian federalism." In keeping with Quebec's position that it was not interested in merely cosmetic declarations, the proposed *Constitution Amendment* (the main part of the Accord) recognizes "that Quebec constitutes within Canada a distinct society," and instructs the courts to interpret the constitution consistently with that recognition. The words "within Canada" clearly indicate (in contrast to the position earlier taken by the PQ) a commitment to federalism. Even so, it is unlikely that recognizing Quebec as a distinct society would have been acceptable to other First Ministers unless counterbalanced by other provisions that limit the significance of the general declaration. Thus, preceding the reference to "distinct society," there is a clause describing Canada's linguistic dualism, with explicit reference to official-language minorities in Quebec and

---

15 Bourassa spoke to reporters at the annual Premiers' Conference, held in August 1986 in Edmonton.

16 This and the four subsequent headings are taken verbatim from Mr. Rémillard's speech at Mont Gabriel.

elsewhere in Canada; the courts are also instructed to interpret the constitution consistently with this "fundamental characteristic of Canada." Although some commentators have insisted that recognition of Quebec as a distinct society would create a Canada with two unilingual areas, Quebec and the rest, it is hard to find any basis for this assertion, given the counterbalancing features of this clause. That is not all. The distinct society clause also contains an explicit statement that the division of powers, "including any powers, rights or privileges relating to language" is to be left intact.[17] Thus the significance of the clause comes not in overriding, "trumping," or substituting for earlier constitution[17] as a complement to them. It is a guide to interpretation in cases of doubt, where there is conflict between two or more clauses in the constitution. Quebec can certainly be expected in future to promote its distinct identity, indeed the Accord enjoins it to do so,[18] but it will have at its disposal approximately the same range of powers as other provinces do. In these circumstances it apparently did not appear harmful to other First Ministers to recognize Quebec's distinctiveness, even though some and perhaps all were evidently opposed to giving Quebec any special constitutional status not available to other provinces.

(2) Guarantee of increased powers in matters of immigration. Quebec's motive here was clearly indicated by Mr. Rémillard: "Cultural security translates into giving Quebec sole power to plan its immigration. In this way it can maintain its francophone character by countering or even reversing demographic trends that foreshadow a decrease in Quebec's relative size within Canada." In effect, Quebec was proposing to accept a degree of openness of access to English-language schools, as prescribed in the *Canadian Charter of Rights and*

---

17 Interestingly, this proviso was supported by, and may have been proposed by, Premier Bourassa, who had become concerned that, without it, Quebec might lose some of its power to legislate over language.

18 On the other hand, it enjoins Parliament and the provincial legislatures (obviously, including Quebec) to preserve—but not to preserve *and promote*—linguistic dualism. The first part of the relevant clause reads:
"The Constitution of Canada shall be interpreted in a manner consistent with (a) the recognition that the existence of French-speaking Canadians, centred in Quebec but also present elsewhere in Canada, and English-speaking Canadians, concentrated outside Quebec but also present in Quebec, constitutes a fundamental characteristic of Canada; and (b) the recognition that Quebec constitutes within Canada a distinct society."
It is known that to have imposed on provincial legislatures the obligation to promote the "fundamental characteristic of Canada" referred to in (a) was unacceptable to some of the premiers.

Freedoms, but sought in return another route to cultural security: control over immigration. The response to this demand in the Meech Lake negotiations was two-fold. The first element was a political commitment by the federal government that it will update a 1977 Ottawa-Quebec agreement defining federal and provincial roles in immigration, and will also guarantee that Quebec will receive a share of immigrants proportionate to or slightly higher than its share of the Canadian population. The second element was to give constitutional effect to any such agreement, with Quebec or any other province—but only to the extent consistent with federal laws setting standards and objectives for immigration, or identifying classes of inadmissible persons. Since immigration has always been, under the *Constitution Act, 1867*, an area of concurrency (both orders of government may legislate), the immigration clauses of the Meech Lake Accord prescribe how to divide the field, while leaving Ottawa with authority to override provincial policies in stated respects as demanded by the national interest. Quebec obtains power "to plan its immigration," but not sole power in the field. The policy role offered Quebec may also be claimed by other provinces should they so desire at any future time. In addition to these changes regarding the selection process, the Accord provides that responsibility for certain services to newly-arrived immigrants shall be transferred to the Quebec government, together with the fiscal resources necessary to pay for them.

(3) Limitation of the federal spending power. On this subject Mr. Rémillard was strongly critical of the federal government, but made few specific proposals. He described the spending power as a "sword of Damocles" hanging menacingly over any province that wished to plan its social, cultural or economic development. While he added that "this situation has become intolerable," it is not clear whether he was reviving the suggestion that consensus among provincial governments should be required before a new shared-cost programme could be launched. A proposal along these lines had been put forward by Prime Minister Trudeau in 1969,[19] and the idea had been discussed at several federal-provincial meetings since then. If Quebec actually did demand this (as seems likely, given some of the statements made by other Quebec government participants at the Mont Gabriel conference), it got nothing. In any case it is clear that if the constitution were to require evidence of a provincial consensus in favour of any new programme, before Parliament could spend money in areas of provincial jurisdiction, that would nullify the spending power.

---

19 The federal position paper, *Federal-Provincial Grants and the Spending Power of Parliament* was issued under Mr. Trudeau's name.

Mr. Rémillard was clearer in saying that a federal commitment once made should be adhered to. He denounced the terms of a bill then before Parliament,[20] reducing federal payments under the Established Programs Financing scheme (health care and post-secondary education), and he proposed that provincial consent should be required—on the same basis as applies to most constitutional amendments—before Ottawa can alter the equalization formula in ways detrimental to provincial interests. The Meech Lake Accord, however, contains no provisions on this subject. Parliament retains full control to reduce both conditional and unconditional payments to provincial governments. Commitments under the spending power have not been contractual in the past, and the Accord does not mandate that they be so in the future.

Although the spending power provisions of the Accord neither establish a provincial consensus mechanism nor lock Ottawa into existing financial commitments, they do go a certain distance toward meeting Quebec's objective. They do so by prescribing that a province not entering a new shared-cost programme is entitled to "reasonable compensation." In that case, however, the province must have launched its own programme, or taken initiatives "compatible with the national objectives." This phrase is subject to various interpretations as to meaning and to ultimate effect. Some commentators think that the federal government will no longer have any incentive to exercise leadership in the social policy field through the cost-sharing device; others believe that provincial autonomy has been destroyed because compensation can be obtained only if a non-agreeing province allows Ottawa to determine its spending priorities and to lay out all but the details of program design.[21] Those who are critical of the new spending power clause (section 106A, inserted into the *Constitution Act, 1867*) on the grounds that it has a centralizing effect, point to the fact that the clause explicitly recognizes the federal spending power for the first time. Of course, it had to do this, if any limits on the power were to be established.

(4) Recognition of the right of veto [amending formula]. Mr. Rémillard demanded for Quebec "the right to absolute or qualified veto, a right of veto which would permit Quebec to say 'non' to amendments that infringe upon its historic rights in this federation. It is a security we must have." At the Edmonton meeting of premiers in August 1986, Mr. Bourassa publicly proposed that any province with 25 per cent or more of the Canadian population should have a veto over all constitutional amendments; furthermore, such a veto should be

---

20 *Bill C-96*: Federal-Provincial Fiscal Arrangements and Federal Post-Secondary Education and Health Contributions Act.

21 For a discussion of this controversy, see Chapter 3 in this volume.

"grandfathered," so that a province that once had it, should keep it even if its population fell below the critical 25 per cent figure. Since Quebec now has about 26 per cent of the Canadian population, and that percentage is declining, grandfathering would be essential for Quebec under this formula. However, other governments found this unacceptable. The agreement that was eventually inscribed in the Meech Lake Accord retained the features of the 1982 formula. These are as follows: (a) most amendments can be made with the assent of Parliament and the legislatures of two-thirds of the provinces containing at least half the Canadian population (the "seven-fifty" formula: seven provinces and 50 per cent of the population); (b) where a province's legislative powers or proprietary rights are affected, it can declare the amendment non-applicable to itself; if the amendment is in the field of culture or education, the province is entitled to "reasonable compensation" for its continued assumption of financial burdens that, in the case of other provinces, have been shifted to the federal treasury; and (c) for certain classes of amendments, such as changes to the amending formula itself, the assent of all provincial legislatures, as well as of Parliament, is required (the "unanimity rule"). The changes made in the 1982 formula by the Meech Lake Accord are twofold: (a) to extend the right to compensation so that it covers all subjects within provincial jurisdiction and not merely education or culture, and (b) to increase the number of items on the unanimity list, responding to Quebec's demand for a veto—but only in the areas specified. The new items are: the powers of the Senate and the method of selecting Senators; the principle of proportionate representation of the provinces in the House of Commons; the Supreme Court (whereas previously unanimity was required only for "the composition of the Supreme Court of Canada"); the extension of existing provinces into the Yukon or Northwest Territories; and the establishment of new provinces.

(5) Quebec's participation in appointing judges to the Supreme Court of Canada. "We would like assurances," said Mr. Rémillard, "that Quebec will be a full participant in the process of selecting or nominating Supreme Court judges." To offer that assurance, it was necessary to provide for something more than mere consultation, as that could turn out to be *pro forma.* If Quebec was to be built into the process, a change in the rules, as well as informal practices, was required. A proposal considered in earlier rounds of constitutional negotiation had been to seek federal-provincial agreement, but to provide for a deadlock-breaking mechanism if agreement could not be achieved. Could that be done without, in practice, transferring the power of appointment to this body? There was no obvious way to avoid this result, except to establish a mutual veto: Quebec would nominate a list of potential candidates, and the federal government would make the appointment from this list, provided it included at least

one acceptable name. The same arrangement was applied to other provinces as well.

It is clear that the main features of the Accord were shaped by the initial formulation of Quebec's demands in May 1986. All other provisions could be described as intended pacifiers—clauses to meet concerns of identifiable groups, or of specific governments other than Quebec. The irony though is that some of those clauses are among the most contentious parts of the Accord. There is a commitment to hold annual First Ministers' meetings on the economy and on the constitution, with Senate reform and the fisheries "roles and responsibilities" being placed on the agenda, apparently forever. As earnest of the federal government's seriousness on Senate reform, the provinces are given the same role in the appointment of senators as in the appointment of Supreme Court judges. Finally, the linguistic dualism—distinct society clause is declared not to affect constitutional provisions on Canada's multicultural heritage or on aboriginal peoples.

The terms of the Accord have given rise to varying interpretations, as well as to considerable public controversy. Some of those interpretations and controversies are discussed elsewhere in this volume;[22] however, it is already clear from the evidence presented in the preceding paragraphs that (1) Quebec was successful in meeting its fundamental objectives, and (2) not all of the province's goals were met in quite the way it apparently had in mind at the out-

---

22 For a discussion of the impact of the Accord on the powers and position of the federal government, see David Milne's contribution to this volume, "Much Ado about Meech," (chapter 5). Other commentaries are contained in "Navigating Meech Lake," *Reflections/Réflexions* # 2, edited by Clive Thompson (Kingston, Ont.: Institute of Intergovernmental Relations, 1988) (articles by Beverley Baines, Ramsay Cook, Peter Leslie, and John Whyte); and in Peter M. Leslie: "Federal Leadership in Economic and Social Policy," *Reflections/Réflexions* # 3 (Kingston, Ont.: Institute of Intergovernmental Relations, 1988). An overview of the debate, emphasizing the difference in the character of the debate in francophone Quebec and in the rest of Canada, is provided in Denis Robert's "Un tour d'horizon du débat public," chapter 6 of this volume. See also chapter 7, by T.K. Shoyama.

set of the negotiations. The process of negotiation limited and qualified Quebec's demands, without rejecting them. No doubt it would be much clearer how and where the compromises were achieved, if the full opening negotiating positions on all sides were known. However, even in the absence of such knowledge, it is clear that there was considerable give and take, and that the negotiators' success lay in finding the common ground among them. What is now at issue, as the process of legislative endorsement remains incomplete, is whether the compromises made by the First Ministers are acceptable to the Canadian people as represented through the provincial legislatures.[23] Unfortunately proposals from one quarter to "improve" the Accord would, to other groups or interests, make it entirely unacceptable.

Among Quebec francophones, as Denis Robert's chapter in this volume makes clear, the main criticisms of the Accord are that the Quebec government's aims were too modest at the outset of the process, and that too many concessions were made in the course of negotiations. The distinct society clause, for example, is criticized for being vague and meaningless—it ought to specify, say the nationalist critics, that Quebec has full and unlimited power over language legislation, and that it will automatically override the *Canadian Charter of Rights and Freedoms*. Also, the spending power clause has been described as a "Trojan horse" that marks a retreat, not an advance, in terms of Quebec's control over its own affairs. On the other hand, to the Bourassa government and to the supporters of the Accord among Quebec francophones, it is the *irreducible minimum* ("minimum vital") needed to enable Quebec to continue to develop as a society that is distinctive by virtue of its culture, within the framework of Canadian federalism. The existing division of powers, as altered slightly by the immigration clauses, is retained and protected, with the marginal extra assurance that the courts will take account of Quebec's character as a distinct society within Canada, when they interpret the division of powers clauses and other parts of the constitution. (It is said they do this anyway.) Effectively, what

---

23 Gallup polls show declining support for the Accord. Shortly after its signature, 56 per cent approved of it and only 26 were against, but by April 1988 opinion outside of Quebec was about evenly balanced—26 per cent for, 27 per cent against and 47 per cent "don't know". It should be noted that 56 per cent indicated that they knew nothing or almost nothing about the Accord, and only 6 per cent considered themselves well-informed. Among the small group that considered themselves well-informed, opinion was more polarized in Quebec than among the population as a whole. Among non-Quebecers who classified themselves as well informed, 49 per cent thought that the Accord gives too much power to the provinces and 60 per cent indicated that they disapproved of recognizing Quebec as constituting within Canada a distinct society. *La Presse*, 28 April 1988, B1.

Quebec has attained, in the view of its francophone supporters, is the assurance that the constitutional framework will not be altered without its consent: the clauses on the amending formula, the spending power, and the Supreme Court are all intended to minimize this possibility. It is not all that could be desired by francophone Quebecers, but it reduces risk.

Anglophone supporters of the Accord, and its supporters among the francophone minorities, consider that it has the positive virtue of gaining Quebec's recognition of the legitimacy of the Canadian constitutional order; they view it as an agreement that helps Quebec without damaging the interests of Canada as a whole. Protection of the national (Canadian) interest is achieved by having hedged in each of Quebec's five basic demands with a set of qualifications or limitations. From this perspective, the Accord merits support because it gives Quebec the assurances it needs, while making minimal changes to the existing constitutional order. To them it represents, as for the Accord's francophone supporters in Quebec, the successful application of a risk-reduction strategy.

In other words, by a *national unity criterion*, the Accord is a major achievement. This is a criterion that places special value on minimizing the tensions that are observably endemic to Canadian federalism. Success is marked by reduction of various forms of conflict: regional, intergovernmental, and ethnolinguistic (for example, among official language groups, aboriginal peoples, and "multicultural" groups). By this criterion, and on the perhaps over-optimistic supposition that the Accord will eventually go through, one can feel better today than in pre-Meech days about the state of the federation.

If the Accord's opponents are successful in stopping it, they will have done so by mobilizing opposition on other grounds—grounds that are equally valid as yardsticks for evaluating the state of the federation. The most potent of these, in the context of the current debate, is a *rights (social justice) criterion*. This criterion focusses on the importance of protecting and extending citizenship rights, including minority language rights, on a Canada-wide basis. While supporters of the Accord do not concede that it may in any way infringe or deny individual rights, opponents see it as potentially threatening in this respect. This is especially true of certain women's organizations (probably the most potent lobby against the Accord), certain organizations representing official-language minorities, and organizations committed to the defence and further development of the welfare state in Canada (for which the exercise of the federal spending power is viewed as an essential instrument). Here the rights criterion overlaps two others, a *citizens' preferences* criterion and a *nation-building* one. Invoking these criteria, however, is not necessarily helpful in weighing the merits of the Accord.

A person may place high value on citizens' preferences, an eminently democratic criterion of judgment, without it being clear at what level of aggregation preferences are to be counted. Some of the more abstract or deductive discussions of the values inherent in federalism, such as Albert Breton's supplementary statement to the report of the Macdonald Commission,[24] indicate that citizens' preferences can be maximized in a decentralized federal state in which both the provincial and the federal governments offer services to the public on a competitive basis (i.e., they compete for public support). This line of reasoning would seem to support the claims of aboriginal peoples to a form of self-government, and the claims of residents of the Yukon and Northwest Territories to eventual provincehood. The interests of these groups are sometimes invoked in criticism against the Accord, which fails to advance the claims of aboriginal peoples and works against provincehood for the territories. These complaints have been received with some sympathy, but it is not clear that a "citizens' preferences" criterion supports them. The crucial question is whether the preferences that should be counted are those of Canadians generally (undifferentiated according to place of residence, language, ancestry, or whatever), or those of "subnational" groups. To put the matter another way, under what circumstances should national majorities override "subnational" ones? That, indeed, is one way of putting the question to which the Meech Lake Accord attempts to give a politically acceptable answer. No answer that is more principled, or that is abstractly derived, is informative.

The same conundrum bedevils any attempt to apply a nation-building criterion. "Nation-building" means deepening the sense of collective identity that may exist within an extended (non-local) community. This implies recognition of shared values and mutual obligation, and may be facilitated through (a) possession of a territory, (b) control over at least certain instruments of political action, and (c) control over public and "private" instruments of economic decision-making, especially business enterprises wielding a substantial degree of market power. To gain more secure control over such instruments of political and economic control, and to reinforce the community's sense of collective identity during a period of rapid and often disorienting cultural change, have been basic objectives of francophone Quebec, certainly as ex-

---

24 Royal Commission on the Economic Union and Development Prospects for Canada: *Report* (Ottawa: Minister of Supply and Services, 1985), v. 3, 486-526.

pressed through the provincial government, from the time of the Quiet Revolution onwards. The Meech Lake Accord offers assurance—for some, too limited assurance—that those nation-building instruments will not slip out of their grasp. By the same token, some of those people who are committed to strengthening Canadian nationhood see in the Accord a threat that Canadians' sense of shared identity may be fragmented, their political loyalties divided. Although I personally do not share the Canadian-nationalist critics' concern on this point,[25] the complaints and fears they express are not difficult to discern.

- To describe Quebec as a distinct society, even "within Canada," is fundamentally repugnant to some people; they just can't bring themselves to do it, and resent being asked to do so. There is nothing more to say about this.
- Although the Accord explicitly does not alter the division of powers except in the field of immigration, and does so in a way that mainly confirms rather than alters existing practice, court interpretation of the extent of legislative powers may be affected by the "linguistic duality —distinct society" clause, and by the section on the spending power. These two clauses, and the immigration clause as well, therefore give rise to concerns that the rights of Canadians will not be uniform across the country, that equality rights (especially as regards women) will be threatened, and that existing guarantees of minority language rights will be weakened. The distinct society clause may override the Charter. Moreover, say these critics, the bonds of nationhood will be weakened because the federal government will, under the spending power clause, give up an essential instrument of policy leadership and social development. The common element of concern, brought into focus both by the distinct society clause and by the spending power clause, is the system of values inherent in Canadian citizenship, which critics of the Accord fear may be weakened.
- The Accord alters the constitutional amending formula in ways that will make it marginally or significantly more difficult to adapt the constitution to future needs. All observers agree on the general thrust of the

---

25 My personal differences with the Canadian-nationalist critics do not derive from differences in goals, but from differences in understanding of the facts. First, I believe multiple identities are integrating rather than disintegrating (loyalties cumulate, they do not divide). Second, my understanding of the practical effect of the Accord is that it concedes far less to the provinces than most Anglophone critics believe it does. For example, contrast this position with that in chapter 7 of this volume.

changes; but they disagree on *how much more difficult* future changes will be. Critics see the changes as ruling out future reform of the Senate and the conferral of provincial status on territorial governments. More generally, the revised amending formula, the critics say, will cast up new obstacles to the future adaptation of the constitution in accordance with the wishes of most Canadians.

- The Accord involves the provinces, equally with the federal government, in the appointment of Senators and Supreme Court judges. In this, and in calling for annual first ministers' conferences on the constitution and on the economy, the Accord will complicate decision-making at the centre. It will create new repositories of provincial power within national institutions. It will confer legitimacy upon provincial criticisms of federal policy, weakening the moral authority of the national government to make decisions on matters which, under the constitution, it controls.

In a nutshell, the Canadian-nationalist critics are saying: (1) that in the Canadian federation, the rights of citizens must be pretty much the same everywhere; (2) that pan-Canadian majorities generally have legitimacy when set against the preferences of provincial majorities; and (3) that the federal government must be strong enough to act decisively on behalf of the whole nation, without involving the provincial governments in its decisions or—in the case of shared-cost programmes—involving them only through co-optation and financial inducements.

The implications of all this are that the Canadian centre must be able to control the periphery, an imperative that is all the more strongly felt in a context where Canada itself is perennially insecure about its own national identity. To elaborate: the federal government, acting under electoral impulsions from the most densely populated regions, must be able to ensure approximate equality of entitlement to public services in every part of Canada; it must be equipped to act as guarantor of Canadian social values against homogenizing forces from the international environment; and it must be able effectively to defend and support Canadian economic interests against the logic of the international marketplace. Here we must remember that for Canadians "the international marketplace" is not an abstract thing. It means, concretely, the power of American corporations, complemented and supported by the actions of the American government to reinforce or extend—here I cite Harold Innis again—"the penetrative powers of the price system". By this he meant that the extension of markets brings about the transmission of social values, which in turn determines how political power will be exercised. That is the kernel of the concept of peripheralization in its social, cultural, and political aspects. It also neatly describes what those Canadians who are nervous about the Canada-U.S. Free Trade Agreement are reacting against. Margaret Atwood's (surely fanciful!) account of the behaviour of the frightened beaver says it all.

THE FREE TRADE AGREEMENT

The FTA was negotiated under conditions that Canada did not and could not control. The most fundamental of these is that Canada is simply much smaller than the United States—about one-tenth in terms of population and rather less (one twelfth or so, depending on fluctuations in the exchange rate) in terms of GNP. Moreover, within North America the major centres of industrial activity and financial control are located in the United States. The vast bulk of Canada's population is concentrated, ribbon-like, near the American border. Even the largest urban agglomerations in Canada are functionally linked to still-larger centres in the U.S., in some cases more closely than they are to each other. While Canada's merchandise trade with the United States is generally in a surplus position, interest payments, dividends, management fees, and other "invisibles" (mostly resulting from past imports of capital) normally place Canada in an overall deficit on current account. Thus Canada remains a net importer of American capital, whether in the form of long-term investment or short-term credit. An increasingly high proportion of Canadian trade, currently about 76 per cent, is with the United States, of which a very large portion is "intra-firm" trade, in other words, between parent and subsidiary, not at arms-length. It has been estimated that about 20 per cent of Canadian employment may depend on exports to the U.S. All these factors underline Canada's peripheral position within the North American economy, and emphasize that the negotiation that took place was between unequals.

No one has drawn out the implications of this situation more cogently than did Simon Reisman in April 1985, before he became Canada's chief trade negotiator. Speaking at an Ontario Economic Council conference, Reisman declared: "Whether Canadians like it or not, the harsh truth is that the only real option available to us today is to try to reach a bilateral free-trade arrangement with the United States to cover all or virtually all the goods and services we produce."[26] He went on to declare his confidence that, despite our "great vulnerability," we could hold our own in negotiations with the United States, though we would also have to be cognizant of the risks involved. Adjustment

---

26 Simon S. Reisman: "Trade Policy Options in Perspective," in *Canadian Trade at a Crossroads: Options for New International Agreements*, edited by David W. Conklin and Thomas J. Courchene (Toronto: Ontario Economic Council, 1985), pp. 389-90.

costs would have to be minimized by the terms of the agreement itself, and it would be necessary, through the agreement, to obtain "easier and assured access to the U.S. market." However, Reisman noted that the economic benefits from free trade would be "asymmetrical"—they would be greater for Canada than for the U.S.—because "U.S. industries already have their mass market, and the potential gains from new investment and improved productivity are certain to be less impressive for the United States than for Canada."[27] He suggested that because of these facts, one risk lies in the possibility that a future U.S. government might abrogate an agreement that it came to view as disadvantageous. He said:

> There is no easy or complete answer to the risks for Canada arising from the possibility of abrogation of a free-trade agreement or from significant breaches in its terms as political convenience requires from time to time. There would, of course, be risks for the United States as well, since our record in matters of trade restrictions is not without blemish. The truth of the matter, however, is that if the United States became dissatisfied with such an arrangement it could walk away without suffering irreparable damage. For Canada, the consequences of such an eventuality would be very serious indeed....

Could an agreement be designed to ensure adequate permanence and stability to the arrangement? In theory, yes. As a practical matter, probably not unless its substance, as distinct from its formal provisions, contained elements that made the continuation and non-impairment of the agreement as vital to the United States as it would obviously be to Canada.

Reisman's proposed solution on that occasion was to include the export of water in the deal. The clauses on water would provide for the construction of a "Grand Canal" from James Bay to Lake Huron in order to supply the upper Great Lakes with enough water to irrigate both the Canadian plains and the American midwest.[28] There is nothing to suggest that this scheme, or anything like it, is now in the cards, public controversy notwithstanding;[29] but Reisman's reasoning is nonetheless valid. An agreement that was strictly limited to reducing trade barriers would have very limited appeal south of the border; from the beginning, the Americans made it clear that their objectives lay mainly in the

---

27 Reisman, "Trade Policy Options," pp. 393, 396.
28 Reisman, "Trade Policy Options," pp. 397-400.
29 Some opponents of the FTA say the Americans could claim the right to establish firms in Canada that would export water to American consumers. However, the water rights are owned by the provinces (along with crown lands and minerals), and there is nothing in the agreement affecting the disposition of such rights. In addition, restrictions on the export of natural water are permissible under the GATT, and there is nothing in the FTA to override this.

fields of investment, trade in services, and access to Canadian energy supplies. These matters are indeed covered by the FTA; they are the elements that make the continuation and non-impairment of the agreement attractive to the Americans, if not as vital to them as it is to us.

The essence of the FTA is that, besides eliminating tariffs over a ten-year period, it offers Canada easier and more secure access to the American market while in return offering the United States significant gains in the three areas of primary concern to it—liberalization of trade in services, protection for American investments in Canada, and access to energy supplies. This does not necessarily mean that Canada has sacrificed its interests in these areas, or that the Americans are uninterested in the reduction of Canadian trade barriers; but it is an acknowledgement that each of the two countries had its own agenda going into the talks, and that the agreement reflects this. Canada wanted to escape the threat of trade harassment through the application of U.S. countervailing duties, anti-dumping duties, and safeguard provisions;[30] if it could get adequate guarantees of access to the American market, firms could be expected to locate in Canada when they could produce more cheaply here than in the U.S., even if the main market lay south of the border. The ideal means of obtaining "guaranteed" or "assured" access would be to exempt Canada from the application of American trade remedy laws, and instead to apply a new set of rules bilaterally agreed upon. Any disputes arising out of the application of those rules would be adjudicated by a jointly established mechanism, the decisions of which would supersede those of the national courts.

Throughout the course of the negotiations the Canadian team was apparently encouraged to expect that these features would be included in any agreement that might be made. However, to many observers of the American political scene this outcome did not appear credible, as there seemed no real possibility that Congress would agree to cut itself out of the future formulation of trade

---

30 *Countervailing duties* may be imposed in order to neutralize the effects of a supposed subsidy on imported goods; an example is the threatened American duty of Canadian exports of softwood lumber, averted by the federal government's imposition of an export tax in December 1985. *Anti-dumping duties* may be imposed to counteract actions by exporters who "dump" excess supplies on world markets at prices below the cost of production or below the price charged domestically. Both are responses to trade practices considered by the importing country to be unfair. *Safeguard provisions* authorize the restriction of foreign imports in circumstances where foreign suppliers sharply increase their share of the domestic market; such restrictions must be temporary, and ease the process of adjustment, not offer long-term protection. Unfair trading practices by foreign competitors are not necessarily alleged in these cases.

law as it might apply to Canada. On the Canadian side, the inclusion of a new subsidies code would have required a non-reversible commitment by the federal and provincial governments to adhere to the new rules—a politically and constitutionally dubious prospect. Thus there were, on both sides of the border, strong and even compelling reasons for the failure of the attempt to negotiate new rules on "fair trade." The FTA does provide for a binding dispute resolution mechanism, but it will be applying the national law of the two countries. The two countries have committed themselves to attempt to devise a new, joint set of rules over a five to seven year period, but it remains difficult to see how Congress could be persuaded to go along with any negotiated result that would further restrict its capacity to legislate regarding trade remedies (fair trade laws). Moreover, the Canadian federal government would have to be able to offer credible assurances that the new rules would be observed by provincial governments as well as by itself, implying that in the meantime Ottawa would have to gain the power to supervise and control most features of provincial economic policy. (For a consideration of the issues relevant to such a development, see chapter 5 in this volume.)

Provisions of the FTA responding to American objectives include the following: Canadian controls on U.S. investment will be eased (but not eliminated); new investment controls will be prohibited except in very specific circumstances; Canadian policy will not discriminate against foreign-owned or foreign-controlled firms; trade in services and agricultural goods are brought partially within the agreement; and Canada is committed to sharing its energy resources with the United States.[31] In summary, this is an agreement that goes far beyond

---

31 Most export restrictions on energy supplies are prohibited. According to advocates of the agreement, its energy provisions mainly confirm commitments already made under the GATT or the International Energy Agreement. On this and other matters, see Richard G. Lipsey and Robert C. York: *Evaluating the Free Trade Deal: A Guided Tour through the Canada-U.S. Agreement* (Toronto: C.D. Howe Research Institute, 1988). This book contains a moderately detailed exposition of the content of the FTA, together with a sympathetic commentary on an article-by-article basis.

the establishment of a free trade area as that term is conventionally under-stood.[32] It does not establish a customs union, although one may question whether, in practice, Canada will be able to establish tariff and non-tariff bar-riers against third parties that diverge widely from those established by the United States. More significantly, the agreement encompasses certain elements of a common market, providing in most circumstances for the free movement of capital, and in much more limited circumstances (through temporary busi-ness travel access) for the movement of labour.

The main point to be made about the FTA is that a literal or legalistic read-ing of its terms, while essential to understanding the extent of commitments made under it, cannot uncover what is arguably its most significant feature.[33] The agreement carries the two countries a substantial distance toward closer economic integration. This is not a static condition from which one may sub-sequently choose to depart if it seems advantageous to do so. It is a dynamic process that can be halted or reversed only at considerable cost to the smaller party, and at slighter cost to the bigger one. Anyone who doubts this need only ask why, in 1985, Simon Reisman described the attempt to negotiate a free trade agreement as "the only real option available to us today;" why later that year the report of the Macdonald Commission on the economy said very much the same thing; and why very shortly afterward the Prime Minister announced that Canada would indeed seek the opening of negotiations. Economic integration had at that time proceeded to a point where signs of increasing protectionism in the United States forced Canada to choose between a renewed effort to diver-sify its trade (necessarily, at considerable cost to itself) and an attempt to bind itself still more tightly to its main, indeed dominant, trading partner. There are plenty of frayed edges in the agreement that has now been negotiated, ensuring that the same choice will repeatedly face Canada in the years ahead. Each time the "only real option" will appear still more sharply etched.

Debate on the FTA is about the strategic choices open to a politically sovereign country in the economic orbit of another. By negotiating the FTA,

---

32 A free trade area eliminates tariffs and non-tariff barriers to trade in goods and (depending on the scope of the agreement) services among member states. A customs union provides for the establishment of a free trade area and, in addition, a common set of trade policies towards third parties. A common market is a customs union that also provides for the free movement of capital and labour.

33 Thus the study by Lipsey and York, *Evaluating the Free Trade Deal,* while certainly informative about this particular agreement, seems to miss what is most important about the decision to implement or to reject it. The authors are entirely inattentive to power relationships, whether among firms or among states, and they pay no attention to the dynamics of an evolving situation.

Canada has chosen to bind itself still more closely to its powerful neighbour on the calculation that integration will increase prosperity. This is clearly the main argument put forward by its proponents. In addition, some proponents argue that a more prosperous country is better able to preserve its social and cultural distinctiveness; others either do not care about such matters, or believe that economic integration has no bearing on culture or social values. The counter-proposition is that opting for the FTA represents a dangerous miscalculation both as regards its economic effects and in relation to social and cultural matters.

Let's take first the question of economic effects. The rationale for the agreement is that intensified continental economic integration will contribute mightily to the rationalization of Canadian industry. That should translate into more efficient use of resources, greater productivity, and stronger competitiveness; rationalization of industry is the only way that high levels of employment can be achieved simultaneously with high standards of living. It is argued that countries that have opted for the preservation of jobs in traditional industries— Britain, for example, has done this through much of its postwar history—have sacrificed living standards and, in the end, lost the jobs too. Of course proponents of the agreement acknowledge that there will be costs associated with the process of adjustment entailed by the FTA, but they argue that costs will be slight relative to benefits, and that costs will be temporary whereas benefits will be permanent. In rejoinder, opponents insist that the costs of adjustment have been underestimated, and will be long-lasting; employment effects may be negative. Unfortunately there seems to be no way authoritatively to resolve such disagreements. The benefits (or losses) are not readily quantifiable, and perhaps are not quantifiable at all, because they necessarily depend on dynamic factors such as future investment decisions (which in turn reflect entrepreneurs' confidence in their ability to sell into the U.S. market).

It was stated earlier that part of the attraction of the FTA is that it is virtually a bill of rights for those in industries that have suffered in the past from nationalist policies. Nonetheless, even among its proponents there are many who apparently want and expect Canadian governments, federal and provincial, to exercise control over economic development, particularly when interventionism is directed toward the development of disadvantaged regions. The question therefore arises: with this agreement, has Canada preserved its control over major instruments of economic policy?

Opponents of the agreement tend to suppose that if it is rejected, Canada will be able to exercise a substantial degree of control over the future evolution of the economy through a combination of regulatory policies, entrepreneurial activities of public corporations, and industrial incentives, whether for regional development or other purposes. Paradoxically, some of the agreement's supporters also seem to believe this; and they add that the situation will not be altered by its passage. They point out that the FTA explicitly does not prohibit nationalization, nor apply to taxation measures and subsidies, as long as such actions do not discriminate among investors on the basis of nationality. Accordingly, advocates of the FTA have sometimes drawn the dubious inference that regional development and other policies to influence industrial structure are protected under the agreement. It would be more accurate to say that the agreement is neutral in relation to such policies, which will continue to be subject to American trade remedy laws (especially countervailing duties) unless and until a supplementary bilateral agreement—as earlier alluded to—amends or supplants them. In other words, the FTA makes no obvious change in the *status quo* as regards regional development and other industrial assistance policies.[34] It thus appears that certain individuals in both camps, pro and con, exaggerate the significance of the agreement, in the sense that in opposite ways they apparently see it as crucially determining the extent to which the federal and provincial governments will be able, in future, to intervene in the economy to shape industrial development. Opponents tend to say the FTA will mean the end of regional development; supporters tend to say it protects such policies. Both are probably wrong.

Similar exaggeration of the significance of the FTA is evident when one turns to questions of social policy. Supporters point out that the agreement touches neither income security laws nor social services, and they insist that Canadian policies in these areas are therefore immune to challenge. However, many opponents evidently fear that under the FTA Canadian social values will come under attack, and that Canada will lose its ability to make its own choices in the social policy field. In my view, nervousness about this may indeed be justified, but not so much from the terms of the agreement as from the continuing integration of the two economies. It would appear, as a general rule, that as integration between two states proceeds, a logic of policy harmonization (meaning the gradual elimination of difference) tends to come into play if one of them is much bigger than the other. In the case at hand, the threat of countervail may steer Canadian governments—both federal and provincial—away from policies that American producers object to on the grounds that such policies confer un-

---

34 Cf. Lipsey and York: *Evaluating the Free Trade Deal*, p. 88: "Straightforward province-building by granting special privileges and subsidies will be subject to fair trade laws as before. But the Agreement does not hamper such actions unless they are focused on Canadian firms." I have found no references by Lipsey and York to federal regional development policies; but this comment, though ostensibly about *provincial* policies alone, applies with equal force to federal ones.

fair advantage on Canadian producers. (This is most credible in the case of industrial assistance policies; but we have seen it applied to the management of crown forest reserves and the question of stumpage dues; moreover, certain American interests have occasionally complained about Canadian unemployment insurance as it applies to fishermen, and about public medical insurance as it applies to workers in industries where, in the U.S., medical insurance can be a major cost item.) Thus, in sectors where Canada is an effective competitor, American producers may insist that Canada avoid all forms of policy offering advantage to its industry. Whether or not they are successful will depend on the content of American trade law and its application, which ultimately will be determined under the agreement by the bilateral dispute settlement mechanism. The other aspect of the logic of policy harmonization is that *Canadian* employers may complain about taxation and/or regulation—including safety and environmental controls—that they see as burdening them relative to their foreign (mainly U.S.) competitors. As I have remarked in a different context, it remains to be seen how powerful the logic of policy harmonization will turn out to be in the Canada-U.S. case; perhaps the most ominous thing about it is that it can be compelling even in the absence of any formal trade agreement.[35]

Here, I believe, we are at the nub of the issue. The trade agreement is intended to promote the further integration of the two national markets, a process which is already far advanced. Opponents shy away from this prospect, in some cases because they wish to see moderate or extensive political control of the economy, and in other cases because—though committed to the extension of markets as a means of achieving greater efficiency and competitiveness—they prefer multilateralism over bilateralism. They argue that in bilateral negotiations between parties of grossly unequal size, the smaller cannot possibly hold its own with the larger. In the case at hand, they reject the FTA on the grounds that Canada failed to achieve its main objective, guaranteed or assured access to the U.S. market on the basis of a single, mutually agreed code of fair trading practices. They complain that Canada gave away all the United States is interested in, leaving us without bargaining chips in the round of talks that really matter to us, the negotiation of a common subsidies code over the next five to seven years, as mandated in the agreement.

Animating the free trade debate is a set of issues that will long survive the question of its implementation or rejection. If the FTA is rejected, Canada will still have to adapt to and live with American protectionism, and that will mean forming economic and social policy with an eye not only to domestic preferen-

35 *Federal State, National Economy* (Toronto: University of Toronto Press, 1987), p. 170.

ces but to international constraints. If the implementing legislation is passed, it will be succeeded on both sides of the border by an endless chain of administrative decision, regulation, and further legislation, much of which will engender controversy about consistency with (or infringement of) the terms of the agreement itself. Passage of the implementing legislation will not finally resolve the complex issues bound up in Canada's economic relationship with the United States and the rest of the world, and nor obviously will rejection; but the fate of the FTA will certainly alter how that relationship (or those relationships) evolve over time. Unfortunately it is not clear—or not to me—whether its effects will augment or diminish Canadian independence.

The case for believing that the FTA will severely limit Canadian independence has already been surveyed: beyond the specious arguments are two serious ones, (a) that economic integration (which will be accelerated by the FTA) curbs the *de facto* powers of a small state, and (b) that in this particular agreement Canada has given away its most effective bargaining chips, which therefore will be unavailable to us in the next round of negotiations. These are serious criticisms, to which there may be no conclusive answer. However, there is a rebuttal, which should be considered on its merits. It goes like this:

a)   Canada has been shown to be vulnerable to American protectionism, particularly in the matter of countervailing duties. Like it or not, we were forced to choose between losing ground in American markets— with nowhere else to go—and doing what we could to retain and perhaps expand continental trade links.

b)   We were bargaining from a relatively weak position, and in the circumstances, we could not have obtained stronger guarantees of access than we did. We have to judge whether future American behaviour toward Canadian imports will be more predictable under the agreement than in its absence. The dispute settlement mechanism will have advantages for us, even if it will be applying American law.

c)   In addition, future changes in U.S. trade law that Canada challenges under the agreement will be referred to a joint commission for review and possible conciliation *within the principles set out in the FTA*. The benefits of this provision are not conclusive, but they have potential for stabilizing and improving Canada-U.S. trade relations over the years, even if the negotiations toward a joint subsidies code result in failure. The activities of the commission will work to Canada's advantage to the extent that major economic interests in the United States acquire a stake in close and unruffled commercial relations between the two countries.

d)   While, therefore, the FTA falls short of what was aimed for, it does improve access now, and may initiate a process that yields further improvements in the future. If we reject the FTA, that process will not get started for many years (a point on which, however, political judgments differ sharply).

This, I believe, is a measured set of arguments for the trade agreement, seen as a strategic response to a difficult situation. The most uncompromising opponents of U.S. free trade reject the agreement because they see continental economic integration as destructive of the social values that distinguish Canada from the United States. For this group, the line of argument just outlined is probably irrelevant; they oppose the FTA on grounds that are impervious to economic reasoning. They are opposed in principle. The counterpart of this group on the "pro" side consists of those who are unreservedly committed to the market as the favoured mechanism for economic decision-making, and have a corresponding distaste for political involvement in economic affairs. Either they do not care about social consequences or, more likely, believe the market society is just as advantageous to virtually everyone. Of course, this group is the easiest target for the FTA's opponents-in-principle to attack. However, between these extremes are those who want to gain the freest possible access to international markets (necessarily including the American one), but also want to see that, in Canada at least, government has the capacity to intervene fairly extensively in the market to shape economic development. This middle group may well be the largest; in any case, it is for them that the trade agreement is a strategic choice, possibly a difficult one. They have the problem of forecasting possible and probable outcomes of a yes-or-no decision on the FTA, including its social and cultural effects, and its effect on the future economic roles of (respectively) the federal and provincial governments. It is for them, also, that the question of possible interplay between the FTA and the Meech Lake Accord is pertinent.

CONCLUSION

The debate over the free trade agreement is about Canada's ability to control its economic, social, and cultural destiny, and about the role that political and market mechanisms respectively will play in shaping its future. The Meech Lake Accord is about Quebec's ability to develop in ways consistent with its own cultural preferences or values; more generally, it is about the acceptable degree of interprovincial variability in citizenship rights (language use, individual freedoms, and social entitlements). In the case of both Meech and the FTA, opposition comes from Canadian nationalists and—perhaps this about the same group—those who look to the federal government as the agent and protector of Canadian social values.

The basis of the apparent or supposed threat to national values differs in the two cases. With Meech, the nationalists' concern has to do with internal differentiation or fragmentation; with the FTA, their unease is about continental homogenization. This observation may seem to emphasize the separateness of the two issues, but in fact it emphasizes how closely they are linked. The reason is, simply, that the more vulnerable our income support and economic development programmes appear to be, the stronger the instinctual response to pull together to defend them. Interprovincial differences can, in these circumstances, be seen as a source of weakness, requiring reinforcement of federal power. Those who regard the Meech Lake Accord as dangerously decentralizing, must be all the more concerned if they regard the FTA as homogenizing in its effects.

This reasoning underscores again the importance of being clear (or as clear as circumstances allow) about the probable effects of the two agreements. It is just as important to recognize the consequences of failure in either or both cases. If the FTA is rejected—and it will come to decision first—Canada will face the problem of restructuring its economic policy in a situation where internal divisions are severe, and American sympathy for our situation will be at a low ebb. The interprovincial tensions that the defeat of the agreement would engender would also, in themselves, be a major problem. Resentment would be intense, probably more so in the west than in any other part of Canada. Quebec too (both the governing Liberal Party and the Parti Québécois) is committed to free trade; and this fact has at least two important consequences. First, with the defeat of the FTA, one could predict a strengthening of the alliance between Quebec and other provincial governments against Ontario. (The consequences of such an alliance are, however, hard to foresee, since those provinces would already have suffered defeat on the major issue on which they could agree.) Second, the stakes in the Meech Lake debate would predictably be heightened, because if Meech also were to fail in implementation, Quebec would have two major sources of grievance; it would have suffered defeat on both of the issues that, ostensibly, are really important to it. In that situation, the apparently calm waters of federal-provincial and interregional relations would surely be whipped up into a storm.

II

Canada-U.S. Free Trade

TWO

Issues of Constitutional Jurisdiction

Anonymous[1]

Le texte de l'entente sur le libre-échange canado-américain, et particulièrement l'article 103 concernant la mise en oeuvre du traité, contiennent en germes de nombreuses sources de conflit entre le fédéral et les provinces.

La plus importante de celle-ci a trait à l'incertitude concernant la capacité juridique du gouvernement fédéral de mettre en oeuvre tous les aspects du traité (dont certains relèvent exclusivement du ressort des provinces). En effet, pour avoir force de loi au Canada, un traité international doit faire l'objet de mesures législatives, et ces mesures doivent être adoptées au niveau de gouvernement approprié. Sans cela, les lois ordinaires prévaudront sur les dispositions du traité.

Afin de pallier à ce problème de mise en oeuvre, le gouvernement fédéral favorisa une approche souple (projet de loi C-130) modifiant immédiatement les lois fédérales existantes, de façon à répondre aux obligations du traité; et remettant l'adaptation des lois provinciales, à l'exception du domaine des vins et spiritueux, au moment où les événements l'exigeront.

Toutefois, rien n'empêche les provinces ou les groupes d'intérêt de porter devant les tribunaux, afin d'en vérifier la constitutionnalité, les mesures de mise en oeuvre élaborées par Ottawa. Si cela ce produit, l'enjeu sera de taille pour les deux niveaux de gouvernement, puisque le partage des pouvoirs en matière d'application des traités et de réglementation du commerce en sera affecté. En dernière analyse, il est plus que probable que le traité sur le libre-échange et son application renforcent les pouvoirs du gouvernement fédéral dans ses relations avec les provinces.

---

1   The author of this chapter holds a position that does not permit him/her to publicly express opinions on the subjects discussed here.

Article 103: Extent of Obligations

The Parties to this Agreement shall ensure that all necessary measures are taken in order to give effect to its provisions, including their observance, except as otherwise provided in this Agreement, by state, provincial and local governments.[2]

INTRODUCTION

Enfolded in the Canada-United States Free Trade Agreement (FTA), and especially into the 37 words of Article 103, are manifold present and future federal-provincial issues and disputes, both political and legal. Some of them have emerged during negotiation of the Agreement and afterwards; others have been glimpsed; the rest are, as yet, remote and hypothetical.[3]

The stakes in these disputes are big. Proponents and opponents of the FTA are agreed on the complex of factors that are involved: dismantling/maintenance of some form of national policy; trust/distrust of the U.S.; curtailment/maintenance of the Canadian welfare state; restraints on the central government versus a larger role in the economic life of Canada for the central government; and rationalization of industry leading to increased competitiveness versus short- or long-term job losses and dislocations. Proponents express confidence in Canada's ability to compete internationally; opponents express fears about our competitiveness. Proponents argue the necessity of forming new domestic and international arrangements to compete in the changing world trade atmosphere, while opponents express their fears of surrender of sovereignty and perhaps, ultimately, political union with or absorption by the U.S.

2   From the legal text of the Canada-United States Free Trade Agreement as tabled in the House of Commons on 11 December 1987 (the FTA). The text was signed on behalf of both countries on 2 January 1988. It put into the formal language of an international agreement the set of principles contained in the *Elements of the Agreement,* 4 October 1987.

3   During the time this was being written in mid-June, 1988, debate had not yet commenced in the House of Commons on Bill C-130 (the *Canada-United States Free Trade Agreement Implementation Act*), while in the United States, the drafting of implementing legislation was bogged down, with the result that no bill had yet been formally presented to the Congress. In addition, the House of Commons had under consideration a motion to extend its sittings into the summer in order to deal with Bill C-130 and other matters on the federal legislative agenda. The Opposition had promised to be unco-operative and there had been indications of impending difficulty in securing the approval of the Senate. Of necessity, then, some of what will be said here will be overtaken by events.

In short, the FTA was negotiated to provide a basis for a new national economic order. If the agreement comes into force as intended on 1 January 1989 and remains in force for long, the capacity of federal and provincial governments to shape economic development will be affected—though in what degree, is not yet clear. The potentially large impact of the agreement, and the likelihood of continued or even sharpened dissent from its terms in certain provinces or regions, is what gives significance to a set of legal questions about the authority of the federal government to take "all necessary measures" to implement it. Moreover, one should remember here that the federal government will not be the sole deciding agent regarding the form of implementation required: the FTA provides for joint dispute resolution mechanisms, which may determine what Canada has to do to fulfill its Article 103 obligations, both legislatively and otherwise. On what constitutional basis, then, will or can the federal government act, and *how effectively* can it act?

TREATY-MAKING AND IMPLEMENTATION IN CANADA

Constitutional law has played an important role in shaping the Agreement, and will continue to play a vital role in its implementation. The Constitution of Canada contains no express grant of treaty-making authority. That authority does, however, reside in the federal executive, which acts under Crown prerogative. The ability of the federal government to enter into treaties and agreements which bind Canada in the international legal sense is quite clear. Neither the Parliament of Canada nor the legislatures or governments of the provinces have any necessary legal role with respect to entering into international legal obligations. This is unlike the situation which obtains in some countries where formal ratification of treaties by legislative bodies is required.[4]

The implementation of Canada's international obligations is in law a matter distinct from the legal authority to enter into the agreement in the first place. A treaty does not automatically become the law of Canada by its mere existence. (By contrast, in the United States, some kinds of treaties, once ratified by the Senate, have legal effect and even override ordinary Acts of Congress and of the state legislatures.) In Canada, if a treaty or agreement is to be given the force of law or if it requires some change in the domestic law of Canada, legislation is necessary and that legislation must be passed at the appropriate level, federal

---

4   See P. Hogg, *Constitutional Law of Canada*, Second Edition (Toronto: Carswell, 1985), 240-244.

or provincial. Without such legislation, the ordinary law of Canada, which does not include the treaty, prevails over any treaty obligation.[5] At most, Canada's international legal obligations may be used as an aid in the interpretation of Canadian legislation, but they do not control the law. In international law, on the other hand, it is no excuse to say that the domestic law of a nation conflicts with the international legal obligation.

The next question is whether Parliament or the legislatures, or both, have the authority to pass any particular legislation required to implement international obligations. Until Canada gained full independence as an international legal person (somewhere between 1926 and 1931) Parliament did have full authority under section 132 of the *Constitution Act, 1867* to implement treaties by legislation as long as those treaties were Empire treaties. That power is now spent and has no application to new international legal obligations entered into by Canada in its own right.

The *Labour Conventions* case of 1937[6] decided that Parliament can validly legislate to implement Canada's treaty obligations only in respect of matters which are ordinarily subject to federal legislative authority. If changes in the law are required with respect to matters under provincial legislative authority, it must be for provincial legislatures to enact the legislation. The *Labour Conventions* case has been criticized by academic commentators and, indeed, in subsequent cases there have been indications that, given the right circumstances, the doctrine of that case could be confined or even overruled.[7] If the *Labour Conventions* doctrine is ultimately upheld, however, there remains the issue whether existing federal powers over the regulation of trade and commerce under subsection 91(2) of the *Constitution Act, 1867* or the general powers of Parliament under the Peace, Order and Good Government clause (the opening words of section 91) could be expanded to include many if not all elements of legislation implementing a trade treaty.

---

5 *Francis v. The Queen*, [1956] S.C.R. 618; *Capital Cities Communications Inc. v. CRTC*, [1978] 2 S.C.R.

6 *Attorney General for Canada v. Attorney General for Ontario*, [1937] A.C. 326 (P.C.).

7 *Johannesson v. West St. Paul*, [1952] 1 S.C.R. 292; *Francis v. the Queen, supra,* note 4; *Re Offshore Mineral Rights*, [1967] S.C.R. 792; *MacDonald v. Vapor Canada Ltd.*, [1977] 2 S.C.R. 134; *Schneider v. the Queen* [1982] 2 S.C.R. 112; and see M. Milani, "The Canadian Treaty Power" *Saskatchewan Law Review* 44 (1980-81), 205-207, and 208-210; Hogg, *Constitutional Law of Canada*, 251-254; J. Whyte, "Federal Powers Over the Economy" *Canadian Business Law Journal* 13 (1987), 287-92.

The legal uncertainty and risks attendant on those issues had considerable effect on the federal-provincial consultative process during negotiation of the FTA and will continue to influence implementation. While the Canada-U.S. negotiations on the FTA were going on, there were extensive federal-provincial consultations at the official and political levels. Apart from the substance of the proposals being advanced, one of the difficulties encountered throughout was the implementation issue, particularly since the Americans had made it clear on a number of occasions that they wanted assurances that the provinces would be bound to implement whatever agreement emerged. The process was made even more difficult by the rather ambitious nature of some of the models for an agreement being promoted by the Canadian negotiators. Some of those models may, indeed, have required constitutional change in Canada to implement them. The substantive content of the various models had potential to affect, depending on the ultimate terms of the Agreement, matters of both exclusive federal competence and exclusive provincial competence. In addition, even in areas of exclusive federal jurisdiction, provinces could well be affected by implementation measures to be taken at the federal level and, although provinces would have no legal claim to involvement in that process, they do have some claim to consultation simply as a matter of good federal-provincial relations. Because there is no current method by which provincial governments could bind themselves and their legislatures as to the content of future laws, except as regards procedural requirements as to manner and form, there could be no actual "formula" of binding legal effect for implementation unless the Constitution itself were amended in the meantime to secure such a formula.

The process of consultation aimed, but failed, to achieve consensus. What was sought was a commitment by all governments that if some groupings agreed on certain sets of issues, and other groupings agreed on others, all would "sign onto" the FTA. Thus, some provinces attempted to advance an informal approval mechanism with respect to the entry into the Agreement and its subsequent implementation in law. The mechanism would have taken into account a number of factors, including, in respect of any particular issue, the relative importance of the issue to the provinces and regions, the number for and against, the populations concerned, the regional nature of the country, the extent to which any particular issue affected provincial jurisdiction, the strength of any objections and possible trade-offs. However, consensus on an approval mechanism proved elusive. The problems inherent in this approach, considerable in themselves, were compounded by partisan politics in Canada and the intervention of the Ontario election.

Ultimately, the *Elements of the Agreement* were concluded at the eleventh hour on 4 October 1987. The legal text followed, but not without additional negotiations. In Canada the political die was cast with the Peterson government in Ontario strongly opposed, the Ghiz government in Prince Edward Island less vehemently opposed, and the soon-to-be-defeated Pawley government in Manitoba also opposed. Several provinces had voiced their concerns over the *Elements*, and some of those concerns were taken into account in the formulation of the final text. Nevertheless, the implementation problem remains.

FEDERAL IMPLEMENTING LEGISLATION

Most of the legislative changes required to implement the FTA involve areas of exclusive federal jurisdiction: trade remedy laws; procedures and review of decisions; import and export standards; tariffs and customs duties and procedures, including rules of origin; federal excise and other forms of taxation; import and export regulation; foreign investment rules; certain rules pertaining to federally regulated works, undertakings, services and businesses such as banking and broadcasting; federal government procurement; immigration rules respecting temporary entry for business persons, etc.

Chapter 8 of the FTA dealing with wine and distilled spirits is to have immediate effect on provincial actions; other chapters, including those on energy, services, and investment (Chapters 9, 14, and 16, respectively) could well have implications for future provincial measures. The potential impact of the energy provisions on the provinces is likely rather limited given the boundaries of provincial jurisdiction with respect to export from Canada.[8] With respect to services and investment, extensive "grandfathering" provisions in Articles 1402.5 and 1607, respectively, save most measures in effect at the time of entry into force of the FTA.[9]

As a result, the first and immediate provincial implementation issue concerns wine and spirits. The problem is a highly visible one in the sense that it has been a long-standing trade irritant to which a separate chapter of the FTA is devoted. In addition, Ontario is seen to be one of the major offenders in dis-

---

8   See W. Moull, "Section 92A of the Constitution Act, 1867", *Canadian Bar Review* 61(1983), 722-27.

9   Article 103 of the FTA, reproduced at the beginning of this chapter, states the general rule on observance of the provisions of the FTA by provincial governments, "except as otherwise provided" in the FTA. Specific provisions on the contrary are found in Article 602.2 on technical standards; Annex 1304.3, applying procurement provisions only to specified federal entities; Articles 1701.2 and 1703, financial services generally, except for investment obligations. Special mention in the FTA is made with respect to provincial matters not only in Article 103, but also in Articles 502, provincial measures re national treatment; Articles 802 and 804, on wine and spirits; Article 1402 on services; and Articles 1602 and 1611, on investment.

criminatory treatment of imported wines and has made it clear that it has no intention of mending its ways.

When preparing draft implementing legislation, the federal government considered a number of options, and eventually floated three possible approaches to the provincial implementation issue. The first approach, the strongest of the three, would have declared virtually the whole of the FTA to have the force of law in Canada and would have declared such law to be binding on the Crown in right of Canada and any province. This option would have given the FTA general overriding effect. Any person who performs duties under any law of Canada or a province would have been prohibited from doing anything inconsistent with the federal implementing legislation, the regulations made under it, or the FTA. The Governor in Council (i.e., the federal cabinet) would have been given power to make specific regulations to implement the wine and distilled spirits provisions, but those regulations would come into force in any province only after consultation by the Minister with the province. Finally, this option would have prohibited private persons from suing to enforce any right under the Act without the consent of the federal Attorney General.

The second option also would have bound the federal and provincial Crown to the legislation and contained the same prohibition of private causes of action. The FTA itself would not, however, have been given the force of law; the Agreement would have been merely approved and provisions in federal law would declare that it had paramount effect over inconsistent federal laws and practices. Paramount effect over inconsistent provincial practices and laws would have been provided for, but only in those cases specified by order of the Governor in Council. Again, there would have been a consultation requirement before any such order was made. The particular provisions of the first option with respect to the wine and spirits issue would also have been contained in this version.

The third option would have in most respects bound only the Crown in right of Canada, i.e., the federal government. It would also have contained the prohibition against private suits and would have expressed approval of the FTA. Inconsistent federal practices would be subordinate to the Agreement and the Act. On the provincial implementation side there would be the same provisions regarding wine and spirits, and those would bind relevant provincial governments if and when regulations were made. Finally, under this option there would be an express declaration that nothing in the legislation limited the right of Parliament to enact future legislation to implement any provision of the FTA or fulfill any of the obligations of Canada under it.

The first option would have been an extremely aggressive one from the point of view of provincial jurisdiction. This aggressive action would have taken place virtually immediately, except for the specialized wine and spirits issue.

The second option would have been almost as aggressive in the general sense, but would have put off until some future time the actual triggering of the intrusion into provincial areas. The third would have been confined in its scope in provincial areas to the particular wine and spirits issue, but, at the same time, would contain the express warning that Parliament reserves the right to enact additional measures in future.

Consultations were held with a number of provinces and in those consultations provinces were shown the drafts of the key elements of the three options. It is rumoured that more than one pro-FTA provincial government warned the federal government that if it were to be too aggressive in the implementing legislation, it risked losing provincial support and would encounter a much greater possibility of litigation challenging the constitutional validity of the federal measure. On the other hand, the federal government thought it necessary to have in place a method of dealing with the immediate wine and spirits problem and to show the Americans that the provinces could be brought into line. Within the federal government itself, it is rumoured that there were hawks and doves on the question of which option to choose: it is said that the Department of Justice would have preferred one of the more aggressive options and that the Federal-Provincial Relations Office was in favour of the third option.

In the end, the federal government chose the third option for Bill C-130. That option offered a number of advantages:

- it gives an indication to the Americans that recalcitrant provinces will be brought into line
- at the same time, it does the minimum necessary to address provincial non-compliance at the present time and will do so only when needed
- it offers virtually no present target for an attack in the courts when enacted; only when regulations are made will there be an opportunity for private citizens to attack its validity; in turn this may be important from the point of view of U.S. concerns because a constitutional challenge now to the validity of federal implementing legislation would highlight doubts entertained there
- it contains a clear warning actually written into the legislation of possible future measures by Parliament to implement the FTA.

Other aspects of Bill C-130 are worthy of comment. 1) Section 3 expressly declares that the purpose of the Act is to implement the FTA. This picks up on a comment by Chief Justice Laskin in *MacDonald v. Vapor Canada Ltd.*[10] to the effect that, assuming Parliament has jurisdiction to pass legislation im-

10 *Supra*, note 6, at pp. 171-172.

plementing a treaty or international convention in relation to matters covered by the treaty or which would be otherwise lie within the provincial domain, the exercise of federal power must be manifested in the implementing legislation and not left to inference. 2) Section 5 of Bill C-130 prohibits private causes of action without the consent of the Attorney General of Canada to enforce rights arising from the general implementation provisions of Part I. This may be successful in precluding ordinary actions at law based on the federal statute, but could not stop a person from challenging the law on constitutional grounds. Clearly, allowing either Parliament or the legislatures to preclude judicial constitutional review of legislation would itself undermine the Constitution of Canada, and in the present case, the division of powers.[11] 3) Section 6 of the Bill, which contains the statement that nothing in the Act limits in any manner the right of Parliament to enact legislation to implement any provision of the FTA or fulfill any of the obligations of the Government of Canada under the FTA, has little legal effect. The purpose of this section is clearly one of a legislated warning. 4) Section 7 of the Bill which declares that the FTA is "hereby approved" is probably superfluous. As mentioned above, Parliament has no necessary legal role in the making or "ratification" of such an agreement.

The by far greater portion of Bill C-130 is devoted to making necessary changes to existing federal legislation. Apart from the wine and spirits provisions, then, Bill C-130 should be rather unobjectionable from the point of view of the provinces. The federal government has clearly taken a soft approach. It is one which, as mentioned above, offers many immediate advantages. Its disadvantage lies in the possibility that future federal implementing legislation will be needed in other areas of provincial intransigence. There was, of course, an even softer approach that could have been considered, and that is to deal only with matters of federal legislative concern and leave aside the matter of wine and spirits to be dealt with like any other dispute arising between Canada and the U.S. under the FTA. One suspects, however, that one of the major objectives of the implementation package would not have been achieved by that route, namely, an indication to the Americans that the Government of Canada was prepared to embark on the sorts of "necessary measures" contemplated by Article 103 of the FTA. Bill C-130 sends the same message to the provinces.

---

11 See B. Strayer, *The Canadian Constitution and the Courts*, Third Edition (Toronto: Butterworths, 1988), Chapter 3.

LITIGATING THE IMPLEMENTATION ISSUE

As mentioned above, the present form of Bill C-130 makes it rather difficult for private parties or interest groups to attack its constitutional validity when it is enacted. Until regulations are made under the wine and spirits provisions of section 9, there is little to attack. If and when those regulations are made and come into force in a province, however, there is a real possibility of a challenge by private parties or interest groups. In recent years, the rules as to "standing"[12] in constitutional litigation have been relaxed considerably for private parties, and in the right circumstances should not constitute a bar to an action for a declaration of constitutional invalidity.[13] Rules on standing and hypothetical issues problems[14] are of far less concern to a province than to a private litigant, if it wishes to attack the validity of an actual or proposed federal measure. In each of the provinces there is legislation empowering the government to refer constitutional questions to provincial courts of appeal—whose decisions may subsequently be appealed as a matter of right to the Supreme Court of Canada. There have been instances in the past where such questions have been referred even before the legislation has been enacted by Parliament and also cases where regulations have been invented for the purposes of framing the questions to be put to the court.[15]

It is quite likely that there will eventually be litigation over the wine and spirits provisions of Bill C-130, or future federal implementation measures. Litigation may be commenced either by a provincial government or a private party or interest group. A reference commenced by a province now would, of

---

12 Rules as to standing are rules determining who can properly claim to have a stake in the outcome proposed litigation sufficient to be authorized to bring a case before the courts.

13 Strayer, *The Canadian Constitution and the Courts*, Ch. 6.

14 In general, courts will not consider suits on hypothetical issues, or on *potentially* adverse effects of legislation. Usually, a person must demonstrate that actual injury has occurred or will occur and claim redress. If the suit is successful, the relevant law or regulation may be declared constitutionally invalid.

15 Strayer, *The Canadian Constitution and the Courts*, pp. 170-174; *Re Exported Natural Gas*, [1982] 1 S.C.R. 1004 is an example of a provincial reference commenced prior to the enactment of a federal measure; *Attorney General of Manitoba v. Manitoba Egg and Poultry Assoc.*, [1971] S.C.R. 689 is an example of a provincial reference based on a set of circumstances created by the referring order-in-council.

course, highlight the doubts entertained in the U.S. about the ability of Canada to "deliver" the provinces and would put the federal government in the position of having to resolve the matter quickly. In order to do that, the federal government could put the matter directly to the Supreme Court of Canada by a reference under section 55 of the *Supreme Court Act.*[16] A similar technique was used in 1976 when doubts arose as to the validity of the *Anti-Inflation Act.*[17]

If and when these matters do come before the courts, the stakes will be very high for both the federal government and the provinces. Expansion of the federal trade and commerce power or an overruling of the *Labour Conventions* case,[18] or both, could constitute rather large areas of jurisdiction for Parliament from which it has been previously excluded by relatively narrow interpretations of the federal trade and commerce power (subsection 92(2) of the *Constitution Act, 1867*) and of the general federal power to legislate for "the Peace, Order, and Good Government of Canada" (the POGG power, contained in the opening words of section 91). A unified treaty-making and treaty-implementation power without qualification has virtually unlimited scope to intrude on areas of provincial jurisdiction with paramount federal laws. Given those considerations, it will be most interesting to see, if and when a challenge arises and reaches the Supreme Court of Canada, which of the provinces intervene and what position they take before that Court on any intervention.

Although the federal government's "line" on implementation questions seems to be that Parliament need rely on no more than its power over the regulation of trade and commerce, it would be quite surprising if counsel for the Attorney General of Canada does not advance an argument that the *Labour Conventions* doctrine should be overruled and that a unified federal treaty-making and implementation power be put in its place. In this regard, it is likely that counsel would attempt to park this power under the POGG clause. In

16 R.S.C. 1970, Chap. S-29.
17 *Re Anti-Inflation Act,* [1976] 2 S.C.R. 373.
18 As cited in note 5.

both the regulation of trade and commerce and POGG, there have been recent
indications of expansionary tendencies in the Supreme Court of Canada,[19] and
it is very likely that the federal government would enter upon the litigation in
the most vigorous way possible. Consequently, the pronouncements that all the
federal government is relying on is the trade and commerce power should be
taken with a grain of salt. Support for the theory that the federal government
seeks to expand the treaty implementation power can be found, as mentioned
above, in the express declaration contained in Bill C-130 that its purpose is to
implement the FTA. If one examines the whole of the FTA, one comes to the
conclusion that even though it is an agreement respecting trade between the two
countries, not everything it contains pertains only to the regulation of trade. As
mentioned at the outset of this chapter, the FTA was negotiated to provide a
basis for a new national economic order. The provisions dealing with the retail
sale in Canada of wine and spirits and the chapters on services and investment
illustrate the pervasive reach of the FTA. The relevant clauses pertain in many
respects not to trade between the two nations in goods and services but rather
to the regulation in Canada and the U.S. of the provision of goods and services
and the mobility of capital. In other words, the FTA and legislation implementing it may be in part the regulation of international trade and commerce, but at
many points come down to the regulation of individual trades and businesses
to remove international commercial irritants.

The federal government will also, no doubt, argue that the wine and spirits
provisions of Bill C-130 were required in order to secure the FTA itself with
respect to the ratification and legislative machinery in the U.S.; in that way, it
will attempt to argue that the wine and spirits provisions, for example, are necessarily incidental to the main purpose of the rest of the legislation, which pertains to the regulation of international trade and commerce and to the general
regulation of trade. To some extent, that argument is really another way of arguing for a unified treaty-making and implementation power. The federal

---

19 On the regulation of trade and commerce, see the reasons of Dickson J. (as he then
was) in *Attorney General of Canada v. C.N. Transportation*, [1983] 2 S.C.R. 206
and see Whyte, "Federal Powers," 272-287. Issues pertaining to the "second branch"
of s. 91(2), i.e., general trade regulation, are now under consideration in the Supreme
Court of Canada after argument of the appeals this spring (1988) in *General Motors
of Canada Limited v. City National Leasing Limited and Quebec Ready Mix Inc., v.
Rocois Construction Inc.* Those cases may also resolve conflicting authorities on
whether a test for use of federal ancillary powers is a "necessarily incidental" test
or a "rational connection" test. For the latest swing of the pendulum towards an
expanded federal POGG power, see *R. v. Crown Zellerbach Canada Ltd.* (1988), 84
N.R. 1 (S.C.C.).

government also would rely on a very broad test of what is necessarily incidental or rationally connected to the rest of the implementing legislation. This makes it clear that the litigation battle, if and when engaged, will be an epic one, and one in which the jurisdictional and political stakes will be very high.

OTHER NECESSARY MEASURES

Article 103, the Extent of Obligations Article quoted at the beginning of this chapter, is considerably stronger than the equivalent provisions contained in the General Agreement on Tariffs and Trade (GATT), as negotiated in 1946-8. Article XXIV, paragraph 12 of the GATT states:

> Each contracting party shall take such reasonable measures as may be available to it to ensure observance of the provisions of this Agreement by the regional and local governments and authorities within its territory.

The FTA provision clearly imposes much stronger obligations on the contracting parties (the two federal governments) with respect to the measures that must be taken to ensure observance by provincial and local governments. The GATT provision merely requires such reasonable measures as may be available to Canada whereas the FTA provision insists on all necessary measures. In fact, it appears that Article 103 of the FTA contains language very similar to that which was rejected for the GATT in 1946 and 1947. There had been attempts by non-federal states to strengthen the draft GATT provision to require member states to take "all necessary measures" to ensure observance by regional and local governments. These attempts were abandoned because of the objections of a number of federal states. For example, in its report to the Canadian Government at the time, the Canadian delegation had stated that the proposals to require member states to take "all necessary measures" were unacceptable to

Canada for "obvious reasons." The delegation noted that even though a measure may be available constitutionally, it may not be reasonable and that under the GATT formulation there is no obligation on the part of a state to take any measure which the state itself considers unreasonable.[20]

It is an interesting and open question as to what the dispute resolution mechanisms of the FTA will require the Government of Canada to do to fulfill its Article 103 obligations. The sections of Bill C-130 dealing with wine and spirits illustrate the legislative route to fulfillment of obligations. There seems to be in Article 103 no requirement that such legislation not be very heavy-handed. Legislative measures could include new legislation, amendments to existing legislation or repeal of existing legislation. As noted, the courts will eventually establish what subjects are open to implementation through federal legislation. However, where the legislative route is not available to Parliament for constitutional reasons, conceivably other forms of federal action may be required. It is very much an open question what other steps might be mandated by the "all necessary measures" clause. For example, would the federal government be required to:

- alter or retract federal powers delegated to provincial boards, etc;
- withhold federal monies;
- dust off and use the still legally vital federal powers of disallowance and reservation;
- commence litigation to challenge possibly invalid provincial measures;
- impose new conditions on federal grants which were formerly unconditional or alter conditions imposed on conditional grants;
- employ various forms of moral or political persuasion;
- use any and all federal powers in whatever way may frustrate the provincial objectionable measure?

20 Canada's argument before the GATT Panel on Import, Distribution and Sale of Alcoholic Drinks by Canadian Provincial Marketing Agencies is set forth extensively in the Report of the Panel dated 12 October 1987 at paras. 3.68 to 3.70. That Panel did not, in its decision, give any real guidance on what would be "reasonable measures." It seemed to agree with Canada's submission that the offending contracting party would be the judge as to whether a specific measure could be taken, but it went on to say that the offending party would also be required to demonstrate to all the GATT Contracting Parties that it had taken all reasonable measures available to it. It would then be for the Contracting Parties to decide if Canada had met its obligations under Article XXIV:12 (para. 4.34 of the Report). The question of what must be done under Article XXIV:12 was left open, although the Panel did find that the Article had not been complied with at the time of its Report (para. 4.35).

Whereas many of those sorts of things would likely not be considered to be "reasonable measures" available to the Government of Canada for the purposes of the GATT, they may well be necessary measures at the disposal of the federal government for the purposes of Article 103 of the FTA. Obviously, there is within these areas large potential for federal-provincial disagreement and friction, whether the necessary measures are taken by the federal government on its own initiative (in order to pre-empt provincial actions or omissions, thought to be contrary to the FTA) or whether the dispute settlement mechanisms established under the FTA oblige the federal government to act. (The penalty for inaction would be American sanctions authorized under the FTA.) Many provincial governments may well, with greater or lesser degrees of enthusiasm, bring their statutes, regulations and practices into conformity with the FTA—either before or after the dispute mechanism is engaged—but there will, no doubt, be many instances where provincial governments will encounter the effects of Article 103. In this connection it is useful to recall that provincial governments now in favour of the FTA may be replaced by others that are hostile to it, just as anti-FTA governments may be replaced by pro-FTA ones. The present line-up of the provinces, pro and con, may well be temporary.

OTHER ISSUES

The FTA contains many provisions which require Canada as a party to act in certain ways or consult with the U.S. on specified matters. Because what will be done under many of these provisions will affect provinces both directly and indirectly, in economic and non-economic areas alike, some provinces have been insisting on formal and clear understandings about provincial involvement in those processes. Their involvement may go considerably beyond mere consultation, either before or after particular disputes arise. In addition, there are longer range concerns about the provincial role in the five to seven year period during which the parties have agreed to examine their respective trade remedy regimes. Again, provinces have clear interests in that area because it is often provincial action which is seen to, for example, unfairly subsidize Canadian products. There is also the not unrelated matter of the current GATT Uruguay round of multilateral trade negotiations.

Provinces are calling for a formal and permanent arrangement, going beyond mere consultation, to deal with issues arising from the FTA. Some want to see new institutions created for this purpose. Whether the federal government will agree to anything more than a vague undertaking to consult remains to be seen. It is likely that the federal government will be reluctant to give any more precise an undertaking, because of the jealous way in which the conduct of Canada's external relations has been guarded in the past, especially by the Department of External Affairs. Some have suggested that there be a permanent federal-provincial commission, perhaps as some adjunct to the annual First Ministers' Conference on the Economy, to deal with these issues. Whatever happens in this area, it is clear that if acute federal-provincial friction is to be avoided, a good deal of consultation, co-operation and provincial input will be needed. Informal discussions on a bilateral basis, between individual provinces and the federal government, will not be enough.

The FTA, because of its far-reaching effects on governmental action, will cause both orders of government to continually review their laws, regulations, policies, etc. for compliance with its terms. It will require them to participate in whatever mechanisms are established for consultation or co-operation, to comply with its extensive reporting requirements, and to deal with matters of dislocations within Canada resulting from its implementation. On this last-mentioned issue, there is also potential for friction between provinces and regions and the federal government over the amount and allocation of dislocation assistance.

As well, there remains the matter of non-tariff barriers to trade within Canada. The FTA and its affording "national treatment" to many American goods and services only serve to point up the fact that there still remain within this nation non-tariff barriers which discriminate in some provinces against the goods and services of other provinces. A re-examination of our own economic union is both desirable and inevitable.

CONCLUSION

The controversy currently surrounding the FTA and its implementation and the inevitable controversies to come engage many aspects of the long-standing debates in Canada on national economic policies and constitutional balance. The FTA has not—or not yet—provided a basis for a new national economic order that has the support of the federal government and of all provinces and regions.

It is not likely that it will provide that basis in the near future. The issues are just too large and complex; there is too much uncertainty about the federal government's implementation power; there is too high a potential for federal-provincial friction and disputes. If one adds to that the fact that many people see the FTA as amending the Canadian social contract, one concludes that the FTA is much more than a simple commercial arrangement which will quickly and easily be accepted as a legitimate part of our national life.

Will the FTA and its implementation lead to a stronger federal government?

The answer is probably "no", in the context of the FTA's restrictions on the freedom of governmental action, including that of the federal government. The federal government will be obliged by the FTA and its enforcement machinery to abide by the "disciplines" of the agreement and those require it to take certain action and refrain from other actions.

The answer to the question becomes probably "yes" when the context becomes that of Canada's domestic intergovernmental arrangements. One of the federal government's duties under the FTA will be to monitor and enforce compliance with it by provincial governments. In this sense, then, the FTA and its implementation could well lead to a stronger federal government vis à vis the provinces. This could come about in one or both of two ways. 1) There is the possibility of new or expanded federal jurisdiction in relation to treaty implementation in areas otherwise within provincial jurisdiction, through an expansion of POGG or of the power over the regulation of trade and commerce. Those jurisdictional gains would come about through court decisions favourable to the federal government on the implementation and enforcement issues. 2) The federal government could become stronger through more frequent and practiced use of the power that it now has in law but exercises rarely or in limited ways. Such use of its existing powers could well be made necessary by the FTA, especially through Article 103. Thus the practical and conventional relationship between Ottawa and the provinces could well be altered in ways that would greatly strengthen the federal government. Even without changes in federal constitutional powers (in law), usage could consecrate behaviour that hitherto has been considered intolerable.

THREE

The Free Trade Initiative and Regional Strategies

Sheilagh M. Dunn

La décision de chaque province de supporter ou de s'opposer à l'Accord sur le libre-échange comporta d'importantes considérations d'ordre stratégique et intergouvernemental. Ce chapitre analyse le calcul stratégique que chaque province effectua pour déterminer sa position sur le libre-échange et l'impact que celle-ci est susceptible d'avoir sur leurs relations intergouvernementales.

Ainsi, la position que prit l'Ontario face au traité de libre-échange fera en sorte qu'elle demeurera isolée et sur la défensive dans ses relations intergouvernementales. Si le libre-échange n'apporte pas les résultats économiques escomptés dans les provinces de l'ouest, celles-ci exigeront plus d'indépendance et de contrôle sur leur avenir. Le Québec, quant à lui, maintiendra son approche pragmatique et intensifiera sa coopération avec les provinces de l'ouest. Enfin, les provinces maritimes continueront de raffiner leurs relations intergouvernementales et rechercheront d'avantage des alliances ponctuelles avec des provinces plus populeuses.

INTRODUCTION

The focus of this chapter is the regional implications—both cleavages and alliances—that developed as the ten provinces formulated and acted upon their individual decisions to support or oppose the federal government's free trade initiative. Just as businesses assessed the threats and opportunities posed by free trade, so did the ten provincial governments. The decision to support or oppose the federal government's free trade initiative was a major strategic one for each province, with important implications for its approach to intergovernmental relations.

In this chapter, the strategic factors and choices underlying the decision-making process that faced the provincial governments will be examined. Without claiming that any government explicitly followed such a formal process, this analysis will attempt to use the approach of contemporary strategic planning and decision-making to elucidate the various factors—and the weight applied to them—that could have influenced each government's decision. A major focus will be an assessment of the extent to which the impact on intergovernmental relations was a major criterion affecting a province's decision to oppose or support the free trade initiative, or whether the intergovernmental implications were regarded more as a possible, but manageable, risk arising from that decision.

FREE TRADE AND STRATEGIC DECISION-MAKING

As is common now in analyzing reactions to the free trade initiative, James Fleck and Joseph D'Cruz, in their article "The CEO's Guide to Strategy under Free Trade"[1] point out that responses by Canadian corporations to free trade follow a consistent pattern. Canada-U.S. free trade can be regarded as a threat to the *status quo*, or as a source of opportunity. The authors suggest that businesses typically will move from the former position to the latter, particularly as they face the fact that "the most significant changes in their external environments go far beyond the North American economic system."[2]

The same basic premise can be said to hold for provincial governments. On one hand, a province, as would a business, can see free trade as a chance for provincial entrepreneurs to compete, to take the offensive, and to force the provincial economy to restructure in the light of new products, technologies and competition. On the other hand, free trade can be seen by a provincial government as undermining the natural advantages, factors and policies that have in the past allowed Canadian industry to develop, thus provoking a defensive, protectionist stance. What explains the approach each province has taken? The concept of strategic planning may help to sort out why some provinces would throw their hats into the arena of competition while others would resist the allure of the promised benefits of competition. The approaches offered by the literature on strategic decision-making can be useful in interpreting the importance of various factors in a provincial government's decision to support or oppose Ottawa's free trade initiative.

George Steiner, the acknowledged leader in the strategic planning field, suggests that this approach deals with "anything that is highly important to the success of the [company], including coping with the environmental forces,

---

1   James D. Fleck and Joseph R. D'Cruz, "The CEO's Guide to Strategy Under Free Trade", *Business Quarterly* (Spring 1988), 43-47.

2   *Ibid.*, 43.

capitalizing on advantages, repulsing threats, and identifying new opportunities."[3]

The strategic planning process generally follows several steps which are of interest to our analysis. They are:

- the environmental scan or analysis in which current and anticipated external factors and conditions are identified and assessed;
- the internal audit of strengths and weaknesses;
- the formulation of a strategy or decision;
- the implementation of that strategy or decision.[4]

This chapter will attempt to identify for each province those factors which fed into strategic decisions on the free trade initiative.

THE WEST

In the late 1970s and early 1980s, the four western provinces, under the aegis of the annual Western Premiers' Conference, were a formidable force in federal-provincial relations. Their annual meetings served as strategy sessions to fight the federal government; several positions then became the basis for a provincial common front on fiscal arrangements and the constitution.

By the mid-1980s, however, the western provinces had become divided, not united on national issues. Under the NDP, Manitoba gradually and irrevocably distanced itself from the 1985 unanimous communiqué of western premiers that endorsed free trade. As well, until mid-1988, Manitoba alone was wrestling prominently with the issue of official languages. The four provinces also diverged on responses to the *Canada Health Act* and the Crow's Nest Pass freight rate issue which highlighted economic differences among the four western provinces.

The issue of free trade united the three westernmost provinces with a fervour that had not been evident for some years. The basis of that unity was a commonly-held and strongly entrenched belief that free trade was virtually the final answer to unlocking the West's economic potential and unleashing it from years of subservience to a tariff structure that favoured manufacturing based in central Canada and which had undervalued the West's trading advantages. Thus, a traditional West versus central Canada cleavage was rejuvenated, but it became

---

3   Quoted in John B. Olsen and Douglas C. Eadie, *The Game Plan: Governance With Foresight* (Washington, D.C.: Council of State Planning Agencies, 1982), p. 15.
4   *Ibid.*, p. 19.

harsher, more specific and more focussed as it transformed into animosity toward Ontario when that province opposed the free trade initiative.

SASKATCHEWAN

At the time the free trade initiative surfaced, Saskatchewan was arguably the province most vulnerable to current and anticipated external factors and conditions governing trade. Oil, gas, uranium, potash and wheat—natural resources in which Saskatchewan trades heavily—had been subjected to low world prices, international subsidy competition and other protectionist actions such as dumping charges. In scanning the prospect for the future, a report prepared by Premier Devine's policy and planning secretariat predicted low land prices, considerable out-migration, low commodity prices and weak personal incomes until 1995. No mega-projects were planned that could stimulate the provincial economy. Thus the Saskatchewan government could conclude only that vulnerability to international forces would persist unless and until dramatic structural changes took place in bilateral and international trading patterns.

In terms of internal strengths and weaknesses, bilateral free trade would play to Saskatchewan's trading strength in natural resources, particularly uranium and potash which is sold largely to the U.S. It would also offer a golden opportunity to stabilize the cyclical agricultural industry and help promote diversification into biotechnology and telecommunications. Given such a survey of the economic environment facing the province and an assessment of how bilateral free trade could solidify Saskatchewan's strengths and bolster its long-term economic vitality, it was not surprising that Premier Devine and his government chose to support the federal government on the bilateral free trade initiative.

The level of that support was pitched high—for free trade in principle on ideological grounds, and for the proposed deal itself. The decision was implemented in a hard sell campaign across the province and across Canada, prominently featuring Premier Devine who claimed "the more people know about the deal, the better they will like it."

The intergovernmental implications of Saskatchewan's decision to support free trade can be seen in terms of opportunities to be taken advantage of rather than risks to be managed. The free trade initiative offered Premier Devine another opportunity to show his consistent, uncritical support of the federal government, commonly seen as the *quid pro quo* for two years of federal agricultural deficiency payments, the first of which was announced shortly before the October 1986 Saskatchewan election.

Devine adopted a strong anti-central Canada approach to selling free trade, at times castigating Ontario for blindly holding to the *status quo* and at other times, entreating Ontario to embrace, what he claimed were, the virtually guaranteed benefits of free trade. This approach became more pronounced as the NDP became more popular in the polls under new leader Roy Romanow.

Strong support of free trade also gave Devine an opportunity to cultivate Quebec Premier Bourassa; the two accepted invitations to speak on the subject in each other's provinces. As long as he stays in power, Devine may attempt to extend this common interest with Quebec into other federal-provincial issues, considering Quebec a likely prospect for co-operation in the area of advanced technology projects, an area where Saskatchewan is attempting to diversify its economy.

The Saskatchewan premier's anti-Ontario rhetoric—and the ideas behind it—will likely not disappear from Saskatchewan's intergovernmental relations strategy. Free trade is only one example of where Devine can charge Ontario with "holding Saskatchewan back"; future discussions on federal procurement policies, changes in regional development policies and interprovincial trade barriers will offer Saskatchewan the opportunity to suggest to Ontario that it "slow down a bit" and allow the West to benefit from policies which are more regionally sensitive after years of Saskatchewan's being short-changed by a protectionist policy that benefitted Ontario.

ALBERTA

Alberta and Saskatchewan, along with Quebec have been the strongest provincial supporters of the federal government's free trade initiative. These two western provinces shared many of the same economic and ideological motivations supporting this strategy. Premier Getty of Alberta, however, was less obviously beholden to Prime Minister Mulroney for federal assistance at crucial times and less inclined personally to adopt the high-profile, salesmanlike approach of his colleague in Saskatchewan.

Free trade fitted well with the established economic development approach in Alberta. Alberta's experience with the roller coaster effect of international commodity prices on natural resource-based provincial economies is clear to all Canadians. When prices were up, the provincial economy boomed; when prices were down, it fell into recession. Provincial policy planners, therefore, attempted to mitigate this boom and bust tendency by promoting economic diversification over the long term, particularly in the areas of tertiary processing of petroleum products and biotechnology.

Ironically, running counter to such a strategy, free trade offered Alberta the opportunity to trade largely on its strength in natural resources, most notably energy in the short and long run. The immediate gratification offered by a more secure access for those products when international markets were increasingly threatened by competition, protectionism and uncertain pricing, seemed to be of greater allure than the less certain impact free trade could have in promoting economic diversification. In this respect, Alberta and Saskatchewan were motivated in supporting the free trade initiative by a similar factor—the timing of the deal would provide an immediate respite to problems plaguing their natural resource industries, even though it would not eliminate the boom and bust cycle afflicting these industries.

Thus, in assessing the factors that explain Alberta's decision to support Ottawa's pursuit of a free trade deal with the United States, we can conclude that the timing of the deal—to begin in 1989—was most attractive to this province which had just recovered from the recession of the early 1980s. Other factors, however, can also explain why Premier Getty was so deeply committed to the initiative.

First, in terms of scope of commitment, Getty and the Alberta government were ideologically convinced of the merit of reducing barriers. This extended to strongly advocating that GATT negotiations be speeded up to ease the international subsidy war over agricultural products. As well, Alberta was pushing hard for an end to interprovincial trade barriers in federal-provincial discussions. Bilateral free trade conformed nicely with Alberta's already displayed, widespread commitment to reducing trade barriers.

Second, political factors could also explain the depth of Alberta's commitment to the free trade deal. Alberta respondents in public opinion polls showed some of the highest levels of support for the deal and confidence that it would benefit the provincial and national economies. Accordingly, Premier Getty's strong stance in favour of free trade, illustrated by his performance at the 1987 First Ministers' Conference, won him considerable support in public opinion polls within his province. His attempts to place the burden of proof on Ontario, for example, at the 1988 Premiers' Conference, also fitted well with trends in public opinion in the province. This more aggressive approach to intergovernmental relations, based largely on the trade issue, was intended to counter the perception that Getty was not as strong a defender of Alberta's interests as his predecessor, Peter Lougheed, and to detract attention and criticism from Getty's less personal involvement in the management of the government.

It seems apparent that internal economic and political factors explain best Alberta's decision to support the free trade initiative. Intergovernmental considerations do not appear to have been a major motivating factor. The Alberta government was supportive of most policy thrusts of the federal government and its criticism of federal assistance to the region concentrated on the extent and distribution rather than the purpose or value of such assistance. In terms of the western provinces, Premier Getty seemed inclined to take his cue from Premier Devine, who had taken on the role of orchestrating the western position on trade. At times, Getty's pointed but polite criticisms of Ontario's position on the trade deal could be seen in tandem with Devine's more colourful but equally pointed appraisal of Ontario's "misguided" stance.

While Ontario had been making attempts to patch up relations with Alberta that had been severely strained over constitutional and energy issues during Premier Davis' reign in Ontario, Alberta did not appear to consider the politically deleterious effects its position and approach to trade might have on any improved relationship with Ontario. In other words, Alberta was not rebuffing Ontario's advances in other areas, such as through the Western Coal Task Force, but did not consider itself constrained by co-operation with Ontario on these and other initiatives from supporting the Canada-U.S. free trade proposal.

Alberta also found itself in the same corner as Quebec on the trade issue. This convergence of interest could be expanded to other policy areas, though so far Saskatchewan rather than Alberta seems to have been most inclined to use a common position on trade as the springboard for more co-operation with Quebec.

If the free trade deal goes through, Alberta may find itself relying as heavily as in the past, if not more heavily, on trade in energy and other natural resource products. Its attempts to diversify the provincial economy may be weakened if provincial producers are caught up in a flurry of trading activity satisfying demands from the south. If this should be the case, free trade will not, in the long run, satisfy many of Alberta's long-standing grievances about the maldistribution of economic—and political—power within Canada. If free trade does not promote economic diversification, and hence a greater sense of more independence in Alberta, its campaign to rectify a perceived maldistribution of political power—especially through Senate reform—could intensify. In either case, it seems likely that the relative political strength of provinces will remain a core issue with Alberta.

BRITISH COLUMBIA

While the British Columbia government, under Premier Vander Zalm, did decide to support the free trade initiative of the federal government, free trade was not the centrepiece of that province's internal or intergovernmental policy strategies. Rather, B.C., more so than any other province during this period, seemed diverted by internal organizational matters, as well as by a more generalized concern about B.C.'s place in Confederation. To this extent, intergovernmental relations—or more precisely, the relations that would flow from an improved stature for British Columbia in the federation—were the central focus of B.C.'s policy efforts. Free trade fitted neatly in this pattern but was by no means the sole driving force.

Support for free trade flowed from the ideology of the Social Credit government whereby individual initiative was valued and government interference with market forces deplored. As well, free trade offered British Columbia the prospect of more markets and more secure access for its natural resource exports which were suffering from low international prices, increased competition and uncertain demands. The province had seen the need for economic diversification and was promoting this through increased trade with the Pacific Rim and by trying to attract more foreign investment through the designation of Vancouver as an international banking centre.

While supporting the federal initiative on free trade, Vander Zalm and the British Columbia government took pains to distinguish themselves from other provinces and to decrease their dependence on Ottawa. Internally, this took the form of internal decentralization within the province, a "new kind of philosophy and a new kind of approach" that would bring government "closer to the people".[5] In dividing the province into eight development regions, the government claimed that more autonomy and freedom would be available for communities to shape the quality of life and shape goals and priorities to local needs.

Intergovernmentally, the same concepts of "fairness" and equality of treatment or "regional equity" assumed centre stage in British Columbia's policy strategy. Fairness was to be expressed through giving less populated regions a greater voice in decision-making: internally through development regions, and intergovernmentally through the advocacy of fairer distribution of federal procurement contracts and more equal distribution of Senate seats. The claim for equality of treatment in the intergovernmental realm took the form of the promotion of B.C. as a region distinct from the other three western provinces.

British Columbia's relations with other governments on the trade issue were thus influenced by its internal and intergovernmental organization strategy. While in agreement on the trade issue with Alberta and Saskatchewan in supporting the free trade initiative and in explicitly criticizing Ontario's position, the B.C. government did not place the same emphasis on the issue nor did it commit itself so deeply to the trade initiative. The broad ideological commitment to the merits of reducing trade barriers shared by all three provinces did not become the policy *sine qua non* for B.C. that it appeared to be for the other two. British Columbia had other intergovernmental priorities to pursue.

As the fate of the free trade initiative develops, British Columbia is likely to pursue its independent course. The prospective gains from bilateral free trade may be perceived as less dramatic and less immediate than for its neighbours.

5   Premier William N. Vander Zalm, "Address to the 75th Annual Union of British Columbia Municipalities Convention", Vancouver, 24 September 1987, p. 2.

Desire for gains from an increased emphasis on trade with the Pacific Rim may match the hopes of gain from more open trade with the U.S. More political independence—or at least, less dependence on the centre—will also remain a priority in the advocacy of "fairness" and "equality" in intergovernmental policies.

MANITOBA

To other provinces which supported free trade, Manitoba's position under the NDP seemed as ill-advised as that of Ontario, and for many of the same reasons. Manitoba's economy is more diversified than other western provinces, its recovery from the 1980s recession took place earlier than the other western provinces where economic growth was stimulated by government-led megaprojects. Public opinion in Manitoba was also more strongly pro-business than the position of its government would indicate. The NDP government itself had chosen to focus on health and social policy issues, rather than economic priorities which put Manitoba even more at a distance, in policy terms, from other western provinces.

However, it does not appear that the NDP government of Manitoba based its decision to oppose the free trade initiative primarily on an assessment of current and imminent economic forces and conditions. In contrast to Ontario, where a review of available economic opportunities, and the prospective costs and benefits of bilateral free trade indicated risky prospects, Manitoba's decision stemmed, for the most part, from political ideology. In concert with the federal stance of the NDP, Manitoba rejected bilateral free trade as another step down the road to an integrated, homogeneous North American society, culture and economy where the "humanizing" impact of government involvement would be lost.

While the decision to oppose the deal was thus motivated, the formulation and implementation of the strategy to support this decision was, to a considerable degree, impelled by the state of Manitoba's relations with Ottawa. The federal decision not to award the CF-18 maintenance contract to a Manitoba firm became the nucleus around which Manitoba's opposition to a number of federal policies crystallized. The province had already assumed a leadership role in resisting federal reductions in the Established Programs Financing, the offloading of other federal programmes and Ottawa's attempts to reduce government involvement in some areas of social policy. As well, the Manitoba government had misgivings about the Meech Lake Accord on the Constitution.

To this list, then, was added free trade. Manitoba's attacks on Ottawa intensified, partly because of Premier Pawley's assessment that the federal government was treating the province and its position on certain policies in a cavalier fashion, and partly because the NDP was threatened politically by its Conservative opposition within the province. This defensive position led to an aggressive response by the Pawley government, doing what, in intergovernmental circles, seemed blasphemous—linking its passage of the Meech Lake resolution to satisfying its concerns about the free trade agreement.

This strategy did not survive, however, as Premier Pawley resigned at the same time as calling an election, and the Conservatives won the largest number of seats in the ensuing election. The new government, under Premier Filmon, has become the fourth western government and eighth province to support the bilateral free trade agreement. In the process, free trade has become a less pronounced issue on Manitoba's intergovernmental agenda, overshadowed by the threat of the combined force of the Liberal and NDP opposition to defeat the Meech Lake resolution. If the trade deal comes to fruition, the minority government in Manitoba may be too preoccupied with other issues at least in the short turn, to prepare for, evaluate and act upon the effects of bilateral free trade.

ONTARIO

At the time the federal government's free trade initiative was announced, Ontario's Premier David Peterson had already proven that he was willing and able to challenge the federal government. An example was his dispute with Prime Minister Mulroney over the latter's promise to restore harmonious federal-provincial relations while cutting 1.5 billion dollars from the financing of major established provincial health and social programmes. It was also clear that Ontario had recovered from the recession of the early 1980s and was enjoying economic stability and prosperity, at a time when most provinces were trying to hold onto a slim margin of economic growth or were perched on the edge of recovery but still facing a cyclical economy. Though operating with a legislative minority, Premier Peterson's first government had established policy priorities that they hoped would propel the province "into the 21st century" as a centre of "world class" excellence. As the economic boom in Ontario continued unabated from 1985 into 1988, this prosperity, and the emphasis upon excellence in education and a world-class health and social system as policy priorities, emphasized a growing gap between Ontario and the other provinces (including Quebec, although to a lesser extent). In addition, the confidence and independence that the economic situation lent to the Ontario government's policy drive, came to be contrasted with the complexity, frustration and slow pace that appeared to afflict Ottawa's policy agenda. Ontario, then, was approaching a position of isolation in federal-provincial relations—its challenges and problems in sharp contrast from those of most other provinces. Its vision for the future and ability to achieve that vision challenged the federal government which still faced fundamental unresolved linguistic and regional conflicts before being able to move dramatically on new and emerging priorities.

After many months of federal-provincial consultations and the provincial election of September 1987 which produced a majority for his party, Premier Peterson made Ontario's position on the free trade initiative known: Ontario was not opposed to free trade in principle but was opposed to this particular deal because it gave away too much and did not secure enough. Thus, Ontario's opposition was pitched at a significantly lower level of intensity compared to the unqualified nature of the support given by many provincial governments. What led Ontario to that decision and to what extent were present and future intergovernmental relations a major decision criterion?

The Ontario government, in assessing economic developments, technological changes and the nature of the competition facing Ontario producers and manufacturers, found that conditions were relatively favourable—without any Canada-U.S. free trade agreement. The province had a substantial base in the technology and financial services field, and showed expansion in the area of services generally. Economic trends showed a shift away from labour and capital-intensive manufacturing into tertiary services based, to a considerable extent, on the production and dissemination of information and its technology. While some industrial restructuring was required, Ontario chose to emphasize training and retraining of the labour force to meet these new market demands.

The nature of the competition in the manufacturing areas where Ontario had long predominated, however, was becoming fiercer. Cars, for example, were now being manufactured in South America and Southeast Asia where low wage rates provided a major competitive advantage. Ontario, though, judged that it could more aggressively pursue markets for its manufacturing products in the Pacific Rim, and elsewhere to lessen its reliance on the North American market, and offset through expanded markets for other products the potential loss of established markets to competitors.

In short, then, for Ontario, external economic developments and technological changes did not threaten the province with instability; the potential changes and likely impact were already evident or were being absorbed by policy changes. However, free trade could upset that stability and create new problems for which policy solutions would have to be found. While many analyses of the impact of free trade showed a net benefit for Ontario, there were also indications that Ontario would suffer the largest consequential losses and the biggest adjustment challenge. Consequently, in scanning the environment for sources of possible instability, Ontario concluded that free trade was riskier than the *status quo*.

To what extent did Ontario's existing intergovernmental strategy affect its position on free trade? Ontario had, with Premier Peterson's active involvement, promoted and obtained a closer and more co-operative relationship with Quebec. While it was recognized that the two provinces would always be competitors for large, new manufacturing deals, for example in the automobile and aerospace industries, it was also felt that other ties that bound the two provinces would survive, despite differences of opinion over free trade. As well, Premier Peterson had made several attempts to smooth relations with western provinces, particularly Alberta, which had previously suffered from differences over energy pricing. In its relations with the federal government, Ontario has always been a force to contend with because of the 95 seats at stake in the federal Parliament. Ontario could have assumed therefore that no federal government could afford to ignore that province's position on a major policy issue such as free trade. Furthermore, Premier Peterson was in a more independent position from which to challenge the Prime Minister than a number of other premiers, being less beholden for federal favours and to party loyalties.

Nevertheless, in actually formulating and implementing a strategy based on the decision to oppose the Canada-U.S. free trade initiative, Ontario appeared to tie its own hands and restrict its ability to manoeuvre and potentially defeat the deal. It did so by seeming to give as much weight to a desire not to upset relations with other provinces as to its desire to defeat the deal. Indeed, it is unclear whether Ontario ever really came to grips with which was to be its overriding objective. During the course of the debate, Premier Peterson travelled to Alberta, listening to a strongly pro-free trade Albertan perspective while sharing his misgivings about the deal. Considerable pains were taken, not only by Ontario, but by virtually all participants, to ensure that the 1987 First Ministers' Conference, held in Toronto, did not turn into a battle among opposing provinces. Ontario's "constitutional audit"—or legal analysis of the impact of the bilateral trade deal on provincial jurisdiction—tried to avoid talking exclusively about Ontario's jurisdiction and spoke instead about how the trade deal would "dramatically and systematically reduce the ability of all provincial governments to shape and implement social and economic policy."

As the debate developed, Ontario's initiatives to maintain good relations with all the provinces appeared to take a back seat to efforts to protect and defend the province against the traditional negative image of an exploitative central Canada, an image which intensified as the debate progressed. Ontario's decision first to challenge the free trade deal on the issue of ownership of health centres rather than on the issue of protection for the wine industry was apparently the result of strong concerns that the latter route would only reinforce an image of Ontario as a selfish, self-centred, "spoiler" province.

It seems that Ontario never really had much control over its free trade strategy, clouded as it was in uncertainty over the true objectives of that strategy. Furthermore, the "brokering" strategy—trying to maintain good relations with other provinces despite a wide divergence of opinion over a major issue—dissolved in the face of a need to defend itself against strong, repeated charges that Ontario was not only blind to the interests of other provinces, but to its own best interests as well. The "provincial rights" tactic advanced in the constitutional audit, gained grudging recognition from Alberta and Quebec, but appears likely to end up appearing as self-interested as the previous provincial rights campaigns in the late 1930s and 1940s.

QUEBEC

The free trade initiative came at a very opportune time for the government of Premier Robert Bourassa. His government had carefully sought to distinguish itself from, what it deemed, the PQ government's insularity, by stressing a new openness to modernization and external influences. Conditions were ripe for the province to adapt to and take advantage of external opportunities; a bilateral Canada-U.S. free trade agreement fitted nicely into this economic strategy.

In assessing the likely impact of external conditions and trends on the Quebec economy, many of the same positive factors that applied to Ontario applied to Quebec. The province had a base in high technology and financial services, two areas in which movement was strong and expansion possible. Moreover, a considerable shift in public attitudes had taken place which buttressed a new orientation to modernization. It was apparent that Quebecers were no longer as interested in political issues such as independence and were more interested in exercising newfound entrepreneurial instincts and risk-taking. Quebec's status as a well developed industrial economy, relative to many other francophone countries, gave it another entrée and competitive advantage in a growing market in those countries for technical goods and services and information technology and support.

Thus, even without free trade, Quebec's trading prospects appeared bright. However, in analysing its strengths and weaknesses, Quebec may have concluded that despite its new strengths, it could not develop new markets with the same degree of stability, security and access and in such a short timeframe as a Canada-U.S. free trade agreement might provide. As well, Quebec shared with the West a deeply ingrained sense that the current structure of tariffs had, for too long, favoured Ontario industry. In reality of course, Quebec had in the past also benefitted from national tariff policy. However, as Quebec's "soft" sectors such as textile and clothes, footwear and furniture become less prominent, it could afford a more openly anti-protectionist policy. Bilateral free trade offered that province the opportunity to "make it on its own."

Consideration for intergovernmental relations was an important aspect of Quebec's strategy to support the free trade deal. While the Quebec government felt privately that Ontario was blind to its own best interests, it refrained from the kinds of attacks—albeit polite and even humorous—that Alberta and Saskatchewan were inclined to levy against Ontario. On the other hand, Quebec and Ontario were in competition to attract the national space agency, private high technology research and development and production contracts, not to mention new auto plants. Consequently, Quebec expressed its support of the free trade deal in a way intended to avoid antagonizing Ontario, although the two provinces recognized that they were fundamentally competitors.

Quebec also downplayed points of contention with Ottawa at least in public, in order to show its support for free trade. Premier Bourassa's high profile appearance with Prime Minister Mulroney at a luncheon in Montreal was a signal about the depth of Quebec's commitment to the free trade initiative. While Ottawa and Quebec remained at odds on a number of other issues, notably the regulation of financial services, the province chose to "pull its punches", at least temporarily.

Quebec's advocacy of free trade also led to a deepening relationship with the western provinces where support was high for the free trade initiative. In particular, Premier Bourassa and Premier Devine of Saskatchewan traded speaking engagements. This new intergovernmental relationship was more likely the product of accident than of design on Quebec's part. Premier Devine actively cultivated pro-free trade spokesmen across the country as he travelled on his self-proclaimed "mission" to sell the benefits of free trade. It is interesting to note that Saskatchewan was one of the first provinces to pass the resolution in support of the Meech Lake Accord, Quebec's foremost intergovernmental priority.

If the Canada-U.S. free trade agreement is implemented, Quebec will consider itself extremely well-placed to take advantage of new opportunities. It will pride itself on having had the foresight to lower the provincial deficit, increase the number of employed employables, and reform the tax system and lower taxes in order to create the environment in which entrepreneurially-minded Quebecers can flourish. This impetus and momentum may carry the province a long way if the benefits of free trade are realized. The province may assume the aura of a "winner" and attract even more industry and residents.

What implications would this situation pose for intergovernmental relations? On one hand, Quebec could adopt an altruistic strategy, developing contacts and projects with many of the other provinces and acting as a leader in interprovincial relations. On the other hand, Quebec could continue its present, more businesslike approach to intergovernmental relations wherein cordial relations are maintained with other provinces without sacrificing Quebec's best interests. It is this latter scenario that is likely to prevail over the next five years. If the Canada-U.S. free trade agreement is not implemented, Quebec will likely be at the forefront of provinces pressing Ottawa to resolve outstanding economic problems and satisfy provincial priorities. Most provinces are likely to feel the need to gain more control over their economic situations and to press for that control immediately, unwilling to hope any longer that outside forces and conditions would be favourable to their interests. Should this state of affairs develop, Ottawa may be inclined to deal quickly with Quebec's demands, both for obvious political reasons and because, if current trends persist, the province would appear to have a better chance to "make it on its own", compared to the eastern and western provincial economies with their more deeply entrenched structural weaknesses.

THE ATLANTIC PROVINCES

In comparison to the western provinces, the Atlantic region did not appear to have as coherent a regional position on free trade. The three Maritime provinces, Nova Scotia, New Brunswick and Prince Edward Island, have a long history of co-operating on administrative, technical matters, but co-operation has rarely reached the level of devising common tactics and strategies on important federal-provincial issues. Furthermore, Newfoundland holds itself aloof from any regional characterization on the grounds that its needs and interests are unique.

The strategies employed by each of the four Atlantic provinces in relation to the Canada-U.S. free trade agreement will, in the long run, effectively push these provinces even further away from co-operation on a regional scale. Instead the trend is likely to be towards more aggressively linking issues and seeking allies from Alberta, Quebec and Ontario, and other provinces, on an issue-by-issue basis.

For the three Atlantic provinces that eventually gave their support to the free trade agreement—Newfoundland, Nova Scotia and New Brunswick—that support may have been seen more as a means towards ends other than free trade. The standard economic analysis foresaw benefits for each of the Atlantic provinces from a free trade agreement. However, the perception of the adjustment costs in Nova Scotia in particular and more widely a genuine concern over how regional development policy and programmes fared in the Agreement, led to an ambiguity in many quarters, perhaps reflected in the more hesitant support from Newfoundland, New Brunswick and Nova Scotia. (This compares with the almost immediate support from B.C., Alberta, Saskatchewan and

Quebec.) Indeed, free trade did not appear to promise enough to warrant the "leap of faith" seemingly required. In strategic terms, though, if these provinces could use their support for Ottawa's help in realizing other economic development priorities, their provincial economies could be strengthened, regardless of the effect of free trade. While these three provinces supported the goal of securing and improving access for goods to the U.S., they were equally as concerned about securing immediate federal assistance on existing issues. They were unwilling to embrace the potentially limited benefits of free trade without pinning down more certain and timely benefits through other means. Consequently, support for free trade became a bargaining chip in other, ongoing bilateral issues with the federal government.

These provinces concluded that the external conditions and their likely impact were too inconclusive to guide a decision on the merits of free trade alone. They proceeded to the level of assessing the strengths and weaknesses of their positions: their strength was Ottawa's need for as much provincial support as possible; their weaknesses were the many unresolved policy and programme decisions that required federal financial assistance.

For Newfoundland, free trade in energy as provided by the FTA was without meaning unless major potential hydro and oil resources were to develop enough to be traded southward. Virtually on the eve of the 1987 First Ministers' Conference at which Premier Peckford formally announced his government's support for the trade deal, Newfoundland obtained federal assurances that Ottawa would attempt to arbitrate the long-standing dispute over the Churchill Falls contract with Quebec. Furthermore, in July 1988 the federal government was instrumental in providing guarantees and assistance for the launching of the Hibernia oil field development.

For Nova Scotia, support for the free trade agreement was tied to assurances from Ottawa that regional development programmes would be protected from being defined as an unfair subsidy under the Canada-U.S. Free Trade Agreement and that adjustment assistance would be forthcoming. While Nova Scotia had made a number of policy gestures toward embracing the economic exigencies of the 21st century—emphasizing training and education, and research and development—and economic conditions had improved, the provincial government was still reluctant to let go of existing regional development measures. Federal procurement, in particular, had become a policy tool favoured by Nova Scotia for regional development.

New Brunswick for its part, under Premier Frank McKenna, also proposed a long term provincial policy focus on education, training and high technology, but its preference for the certainty and immediacy of funding from the Atlantic Canada Opportunities Agency and federal frigate contracts had an influence upon the strategy which it adopted in supporting the federal initiative for bilateral free trade with the U.S. As with Newfoundland, New Brunswick was a major resource exporter, and as such, strongly supported the objectives of the trade negotiations. Indeed, New Brunswick's strategy on free trade—withholding its decision for some time, so that the federal government began to court assiduously its support, eventually leading to the possibility of *quid pro quos*, could be a strategy that other Atlantic provinces will adopt in the future.

It is a truism that the Atlantic provinces are quite dependent on the federal government for ongoing transfers and financial assistance for one-time projects. It comes as no surprise, therefore, that, for the three provinces who supported the initiative, their relationship with Ottawa lay at the heart of the free trade calculus. It is interesting, however, to note that only Nova Scotia adopted a "quiet diplomacy" approach to balancing its support against federal assurances. New Brunswick under Premier McKenna and Newfoundland under Premier Peckford were quite assertive in calculating and presenting the tradeoffs for support. This strategy appeared to work as these two provinces were awarded substantial federal assistance while Nova Scotia settled for assurances that regional development grants would be protected. We can question, then, the traditional wisdom that the extent of financial dependency shackles the ability of provinces to manoeuvre vis-à-vis the federal government.

Prince Edward Island is a case in point. It depends on the federal government for over 50 per cent of its revenues but it chose to oppose the free trade initiative. The benefits of free trade in the fisheries sector were, to some extent, balanced by concern over potential losses in the agricultural sector. P.E.I. Premier Ghiz pitched his opposition, at least initially, at a very symbolic level, decrying the pact's potential diluting effect upon the sense of Canadianism. However, as the debate progressed, it became clear that the island government lacked the intergovernmental strength to work against the deal at anything other than a symbolic level. The P.E.I. government declined to commit itself to participating in a potential constitutional challenge. The Premier announced in December 1987 that the province would remain opposed, but would no longer actively fight the trade agreement. In strategic terms, in comparison to Ontario, P.E.I.'s opposition was shorter-lived and not as intense. It did not extend, for example, to a constitutional audit. These factors may have saved P.E.I. from alienating the federal government, enabling P.E.I. to press its case for "equality of opportunity" and regional balance, and for solutions to its sectoral issues, without having done undue damage to its bargaining position.

IMPLICATIONS FOR FUTURE INTERGOVERNMENTAL RELATIONS

Regardless of whether the Canada-U.S. free trade agreement is implemented and regardless of the overall benefits to Canada, many provinces will continue to act upon the themes that they developed during the intergovernmental debates on the free trade agreement.

First, the western provinces, and Newfoundland more recently, have long pushed for "more control" over their economic destiny. These provinces have supported free trade as a means of further developing their resource-based economies, and reducing the cost of Canadian protectionism.

For most provinces outside of Ontario, the free trade agreement may inevitably loosen the bonds of east-west economic integration. This may increase the amount of control which economic actors in these provinces have over their own destiny, and may in turn tempt them to move more aggressively beyond their traditional strengths in trade into more diversification.

This could lead to increased competition among provinces to attract investment, with a consequential increase in "beggar thy neighbour" policies. If this situation ensues, ties among provinces and governments will be weakened, with each trying to outdo the others in the extent to which it can "stand on its own". As economic independence grows, so too may governments try to exercise their clout through unique social policy experiments designed to fit local conditions. At the same time, polls may show that identification with and loyalty to individual provinces will intensify.

Whether free trade will actually produce the desired economic independence and diversification which many provinces have sought for years, remains to be seen. Whether it does or not, the prospect for intergovernmental relations is cheerless, albeit challenging. On one hand, as suggested above, many provinces may lose sight of, or just lose entirely, common needs and interests, in the face of north-south ties and competition for bilateral trade. On the other hand, if free trade fails to be the "final solution" for unleashing the economic potential of the West, greater political and economic independence from the federal government may be sought by the western provinces to enable them to solve their own problems. Senate reform, if it were to give the West equal status with Ontario and Quebec, would continue to be a priority, but could only provide an opportunity to bombard the federal government with demands to grant the West even greater freedom of action.

Second, as a result of the free trade debate, we can expect Ontario to continue to be isolated and on the defensive in intergovernmental relations over the next five years. Ontario's attempts to act as an "honest broker" and appear well-intentioned have not succeeded. Its arguments that regional disparities must be solved by helping provinces to "run faster", rather than by forcing Ontario to slow down, have been criticized as merely cloaking its self-interest in rhetorical flourishes. This strategy is unlikely to prevail in the near future in the face of charges that Ontario's stance in the free trade debate illustrated once and for all that the province is protectionist, fearful of competition and unwilling to see other regions prosper. Ontario is likely, therefore, to be forced into a defensive posture to respond to these charges. Any attempts to speak on behalf of all the provinces, say, for example, on federal transfers, will be coldly received by most other provinces.

Ontario may therefore find it has nothing to lose by resorting to a strong, "Ontario-first" strategy, particularly in dealings with the federal government. The result would be a calculating, "bargaining chip" approach to intergovernmental relations where issues and political clout are more directly and explicitly linked. The Ontario-Quebec relationship, built up slowly and carefully into a wide-ranging number of areas of co-operation might also be similarly affected. In short, Ontario could turn from the "statesmanlike" approach that has traditionally characterized the Ontario governments, to a very cool and calculating approach to intergovernmental relations whereby the province would explicitly trade on its political and economic clout in a hostile environment.

Such a strategy could be counterproductive. The approach of intergovernmental altruism that Ontario has followed under Premier Peterson may be morally laudable. Strategically, however, it makes little use of Ontario's strengths and caters to its weaknesses—primarily its "fat cat" image—in intergovernmental relations. Ontario may find the time has come to reassess its intergovernmental relations strategy.

Third, Quebec's approach to federal-provincial relations is unlikely to change as a result of the free trade debate. It is pursuing a clear-cut, comprehensive economic strategy in which free trade plays a supporting part, but a part that is dispensable if the deal falls through. Indeed, Quebec's current disposition to intergovernmental relations is a muted version of the scenario sketched out above for Ontario—a kind of boardroom politics applied to federal-provincial relations.

In the short run, Quebec may find itself enveloped in co-operative projects with Alberta and Saskatchewan, the two provinces that have shared most Quebec's advocacy of the free trade deal. In the long run, however, it is unlikely that Quebec will tie itself to any intense long-standing relationship with another province as such ties could potentially constrain the province's overall intergovernmental strategy.

Finally, for the Atlantic provinces, their strategy toward intergovernmental relations will continue to centre on their relationship with Ottawa. What is likely to be different, however, is the more pronounced use of some of the tactics apparent throughout the course of the free trade debate. More linkage of issues will be made and more soliciting of allies outside the region will be conducted.

While, at the moment, all the provinces agree that national programmes must be more regionally sensitive—particularly in the area of regional development—the trend is more likely to be towards settlement of provincial grievances on a bilateral basis with Ottawa. "National sensitivity to regional differences" will remain a popular cry at First Ministers' Conferences, but in practical terms is unlikely to advance as far as the resolution of bilateral issues.

The overall prospect for intergovernmental relations—interprovincial and federal-provincial—over the next few years is one of weakening ties among provinces while the federal government will be faced with an ever more complex matrix of short-term demands to settle. Provinces will increasingly make linkages between issues and grievances, and will escalate the urgency of resolving these problems. It remains to be seen whether this will be a passing phase after which provinces will return back to co-operation from competition, or whether free trade—the prospect, if not the reality—has offered them the chance to become symbolically independent and depend less on the federation for nourishment and guidance.

FOUR

The Federal-Provincial Consultation Process

Douglas M. Brown[1]

Les négociations canado-américaines sur le libre-échange donnèrent lieu à un degré élevé de consultations et de négociations entre les gouvernements fédéral et provinciaux. Ce chapitre a pour objet d'analyser le mécanisme de consultations fédérales-provinciales qui fut mis en place à cet occasion, et qui servira sans doute de prototype pour de futures négociations.

Dès le départ, le gouvernement fédéral affermit sa position de maître d'oeuvre des négociations bilatérales en créant, sans le concours des provinces, une nouvelle institution chargée des négociations et relevant exclusivement d'Ottawa: il s'agit du Bureau des négociations commerciales. L'apport des provinces à la stratégie fédérale se fit au sein du Comité permanent sur les négociations commerciales réunissant des hauts fonctionnaires des deux ordres de gouvernement, et par des rencontres régulières au niveau des premiers ministres et des ministres concernés.

Malgré tout, ces mécanismes ne permirent pas de maintenir un consensus durable entre les provinces et le fédéral, de sorte que certaines provinces prirent une position hostile vis-à-vis un éventuel accord de libre-échange, ce qui créa un climat de suspicion entre les différents intervenants provinciaux et fédéraux. Finalement, l'Accord politique conclu à la dernière heure entre les deux administrations, suite à une suspension des négociations officielles, le fut sans aucune consultation avec les provinces.

Il ne fait aucun doute que dans le futur les provinces voudront être de plus en plus associées aux négociations commerciales internationales. Ainsi, dans le but de maintenir une position canadienne cohérente de nouveaux mécanismes devront être développés pour intégrer les provinces au processus de négociations.

---

1   At point of writing, the author was employed with the Government of Newfoundland. The record of events and views expressed in this paper are personal observations and do not necessarily represent the views of the Government of Newfoundland

INTRODUCTION:

The Canada-United States Free Trade Agreement was negotiated in a remarkably short period of time: just two years from the start in September 1985 to the finish in December 1987. These negotiations were also remarkable for the unprecedented degree of federal-provincial consultation, compared to any previous trade policy initiative in Canadian history.

In recent months, public attention has focussed on the opposition of a few provinces to the Free Trade Agreement, and to the progress of the implementing legislation through the Parliament of Canada and the U.S. Congress. The debate surrounding these events has obscured the long process of negotiation. The intent of this paper is to review the genesis and development of these negotiations from the perspective of the complex consultative relationship between the two orders of government in Canada. However, this paper does not provide a detailed account of the interests and positions of individual provinces in the trade negotiations. Nor does it discuss the issue of ratification or implementation of the Agreement, except where these issues impinged directly on the evolving process of consultation.

While the implementation of the agreement will depend upon the outcome of the next federal election, the process of federal-provincial consultation at the negotiation stage has created a precedent that will have continuing consequences for the conduct of trade policy in Canada. It can be argued that without this intergovernmental process Canada would not have achieved the Agreement at all. If this is believed to be so, it will encourage future federal governments to involve the provinces in any subsequent trade negotiations. For this, the 1985-87 process stands as a model to be adapted to new agendas and new circumstances.

THE INITIAL PHASE: THE MEANING OF "FULL PROVINCIAL PARTICIPATION"

The first formal hint of major Canada-U.S. trade negotiations came with the "Shamrock Summit" of U.S. President Ronald Reagan and Prime Minister Brian Mulroney, at Quebec in March 1985. At those meetings, it was agreed that the U.S. Trade Representative, Clayton Yeutter and Canada's Minister of State for International trade, Honourable James Kelleher, would after six months present a progress report on "ways to reduce and eliminate impediments to cross-border trade." On 26 September 1985, both trade ministers reported to their respective leaders recommending the negotiation of a comprehensive trade liberalization agreement. The President and the Prime Minister spoke on the telephone, and Prime Minister Mulroney announced the Canadian Government's decision in the House of Commons on the same day.

The decision to launch comprehensive trade "liberalization" negotiations was a momentous step for Canada. Nonetheless, an impressive consensus around that option had formed by the fall of 1985. Almost all Canadian provincial governments supported the Macdonald Commission's[2] major recommendation to pursue the policy of a comprehensive free trade agreement.

There was a frank exchange on the prospects for free trade at the Annual Premiers' Conference in St. John's, Newfoundland in August 1985. Ontario's newly elected Premier, David Peterson, found himself in a distinct minority in questioning the need for free trade. There was no communiqué on the issue, reflecting a lack of formal unanimity, but not even the Province of Ontario was openly opposed to the idea.

In his letter to the Prime Minister on 26 September 1985, Honourable James Kelleher wrote: "I am satisfied that there is a strong provincial consensus in favour of bilateral negotiations with the United States".[3] The Prime Minister, who the previous day had spoken to each of the Premiers by telephone, also told the House of Commons of the provincial support.

> Canadians will also be aware of the very strong representations on trade which have been made by their provincial Premiers over the past several months. I have taken care and shall continue to take care, to consult my fellow First Ministers as the process unfolds... We have already agreed to establish a special mechanism with the provinces, to assure their continuing involvement throughout the process.[4]

There was considerable confusion regarding what sort of "special mechanism" was meant by the Prime Minister. Apart from making the decision to launch the negotiations, it is clear now that neither the Canadian nor U.S. side was then adequately prepared to begin to talk in any detail.

Canada had the advantage of having the three-volume Macdonald Commission Report which, among many detailed recommendations, gave its views on the most practical means of bringing the provinces along.

The Report had reviewed the nature of federal-provincial consultation for previous trade negotiations. In the Tokyo Round of Multilateral Trade Negotiations, the federal government established a special mechanism for federal-provincial consultation. This mechanism brought senior federal and provincial officials (and occasionally Ministers) together to review provincial interests,

2   Royal Commission on the Economic Union and Development Prospects for Canada
3   Report by Honourable J. Kelleher to the Right Honourable B. Mulroney, Tabled in the House of Commons, 26 September 1985.
4   Statement by Prime Minister B. Mulroney on Canada-U.S.A. Trade Negotiations, House of Commons, 26 September 1985.

and receive advice. At the same time, there was no question that the federal government was in charge and with the negotiations proceeding in Geneva, only the most determined provinces raised an effort to be as close as possible for the occasional briefings. In the final analysis, however, the Tokyo Round commitments did not involve provinces in a significant way, apart from the Statement of Intent on Liquor Board Practice of 1979. (This may be an unfortunate precedent, given the continuing GATT dispute with the European Community on Canadian provincial compliance.)

The Macdonald Commission recognized that provincial powers would clearly be involved in a comprehensive bilateral trade agreement with the United States. Provincial subsidies, procurement practices, liquor board policies, agricultural marketing boards and regulations of services were only the most prominent areas of provincial jurisdiction which the comprehensive trade negotiations were expected to cover.[5] The Macdonald Report therefore recommended "sustained and continuous consultation by federal and provincial Ministers." Before negotiations begin, the Commission recommended "close consultations about provincial, as well as federal, objectives and the binding commitments to achieve them." During the negotiations, provincial representatives should be "on hand", to counsel the federal delegation, which would in turn keep the provinces informed and obtain their advice throughout the bargaining process.[6] Thus there was considerable advice and some degree of consensus that in bilateral trade negotiations with the U.S., provinces should be integrally involved. How this should take place, and to what extent, was another matter.

The issue landed squarely in the lap of the Annual First Ministers' Conference (FMC) at Halifax, 28-29 November 1985. The federal government, perhaps hoping to avoid too much definition, too early, promoted the idea of a rather vague statement on the issue. A brief communiqué on the trade negotiations went as follows:

---

5   For an excellent discussion of the necessity, in economic policy and constitutional terms, of involving provinces in international trade negotiations, see R. Simeon, "Federalism and Free Trade" in P. Leslie (ed), *Canada: The State of the Federation, 1986* (Kingston, Ontario: Institute of Intergovernmental Relations, 1986).

6   *Report of the Royal Commission on the Economic Union and Development Prospects for Canada.* Vol. I, Part II, pp. 368-73; Vol. III, Part VI, pp. 151-56. (September 1986).

PREPARING FOR TRADE NEGOTIATIONS

The Ministers agreed to the principle of full provincial participation in the forthcoming trade negotiations between Canada and the United States, and in the GATT.

The Canada-U.S. negotiations are now in their preparatory phase. During that phase, the Ministers agreed to give effect, within the next 90 days, to the principle of full provincial participation through, among other things:

— establishing a common basis of facts and analysis;
— each province and the federal government setting out their objectives for the negotiations;
— establishing an agreed view of the obstacles to the achievement of these objectives that may exist in the United States.

The Ministers agreed further that this preparatory work should include the determination of how best to give effect to the principle of full provincial participation in subsequent phases of the negotiations; and that the work might be accomplished, among other ways, through holding further meetings at the level of Ministers or First Ministers if necessary.[7]

Difficulty arose from the vague meaning of "full provincial participation." Both Premiers Getty of Alberta and Peterson of Ontario were quoted in the press soon after the FMC as saying that it meant that the Canadian negotiators would take their instruction from the First Ministers. In Getty's words, "The negotiating team becomes our team." At the same time, the federal Secretary of State for External Affairs, Rt. Honourable Joe Clark, was quoted to the effect that the provinces would certainly not be "at the table."

There followed six months of intensive jockeying for position. (The commitment to agreement within 90 days was ignored.) The actual negotiations with the United States did not get underway until June 1986, but there were in the meantime some exploratory talks and a great deal of discussion in Canada about the "mandate" or negotiating objectives of the Chief Negotiator.

The appointment by Prime Minister Mulroney of Simon Reisman as Chief Negotiator and Ambassador for Canada, just prior to the November 1985 FMC, was an issue in itself. The most sanguine of political observers argued that if the Chief Negotiator was to represent all 11 governments, that person ought to be chosen by consensus. Reisman's appointment created some consternation given his apparent reputation for aggressive relations with provincial governments in the past. This, and the steady build-up of a federal negotiating team in

7   Statement of the Annual Conference of First Ministers, "Preparing for the Trade Negotiations", Document #800-21/071, Halifax, 28-29 November 1985.

Ottawa, formalized in early 1986 as the Trade Negotiations Office (TNO) with Reisman at its head, were unsettling signs to the provinces of a federal government determined to get on with the job. The TNO was a new creature, both to the federal bureaucracy and the provinces. It took a while before federal-provincial relationships adjusted to the new agency. It was thus of concern to the provinces that the TNO was getting established without having first settled, to the provinces' satisfaction, their role in the process, and without any formalized provincial political input to the Chief Negotiator's mandate.

The provinces' position jelled by March, in a letter from Premier Donald Getty of Alberta[8] to Prime Minister Mulroney. The letter outlined the consensus among the provinces of what "full provincial participation" should mean:

1. The overall negotiating mandate should be established by the 11 First Ministers.
2. There should be one Chief Negotiator for Canada, representing all 11 governments.
3. First Ministers or their Designated Ministers should meet regularly at the call of the chair or at the request of any province.
4. Provincial representatives should be full members of the Canadian negotiating team with a full reporting relationship to their governments.
5. Provincial representatives should participate fully in Canadian preparations and strategy for the negotiations.
6. Provincial representatives should have the option of being "in the room" at negotiating sessions and to speak if requested by the chair.
7. There should be a full sharing of information on impact analyses, sectoral analyses, results of industry consultations, etc.
8. All information should be kept secret with provincial representatives party to the confidence.

Some of these positions ran counter to the actual operating assumptions of the federal negotiating team. In essence, these were, by early 1986, that the federal government had full constitutional authority to act, except in areas of provincial jurisdiction. Only in those areas was consultation strictly required. The federal team was also operating on the basis that direction would come only from Ottawa, and that the negotiating team would be composed entirely of federal officials.

At the same time Simon Reisman had, since January 1986, been chairing monthly meetings of a senior committee of federal and provincial officials,

---

8   Getty, in his capacity as host of the 1986 premiers' conference, also acted as spokesman for the provinces that year.

called the Continuing Committee on Trade Negotiations (CCTN). This forum became, in these early months, the locus for the forging of a more practical *modus vivendi* among officials on the consultative process, while provinces were officially awaiting settlement of the outstanding issues by ministers. There was considerable initial wariness on both sides, until at least May and June. At that point, the substance of the CCTN discussions began to reflect a genuine interest by the federal government to bring the provinces into their confidence, in particular with respect to the detailed objectives for the negotiations.

The issue of the extent of provincial participation in the negotiations reached formal resolution at an evening meeting of First Ministers in Ottawa on 2 June 1986. The Prime Minister had written the premiers with his views on the process on 29 May 1986. With some adjustments, these views prevailed on 2 June. While the First Ministers did not release a communiqué, the basic consensus can be summarized as follows:

1. The First Ministers would meet once every three months for the duration of the negotiations, to review their progress. The first such meeting was set for 17 September 1986.
2. Designated Ministers would meet as required, chaired by the new federal Minister for International Trade, Pat Carney.
3. There would be only one Chief Negotiator for Canada, Simon Reisman, who would be fully responsible to the federal cabinet for the conduct of the negotiations. The Trade Negotiations Office (TNO) would be completely under the Chief Negotiator's supervision. There would be no provincial representatives in the TNO or in negotiating sessions with the United States.
4. The Chief Negotiator's mandate would be established by the federal government, in consultation with the First Ministers and the Designated Ministers.
5. There would be close ongoing consultation through the CCTN with Simon Reisman as Chairman. The CCTN, which had met once a month since January 1986, would continue to meet as often as required. Its function would be to provide liaison and advice.
6. The federal government would formally seek the views of all provinces prior to endorsing any agreement. There was no agreement on the issue of the role of provinces in the ratification or implementation of the agreement.

This result may be viewed as a typically Canadian, workable compromise. The federal government achieved the control it felt was essential over the Chief Negotiator and his team. The provinces obtained their minimal requirements for consultation. The provinces would not be "in the room," but would have an input to the Canadian strategy and conduct of the negotiations.

The effectiveness of these mechanisms would hinge crucially on the political will of First Ministers, particularly the premiers, to allow the federal government room to do the job. This in turn was dependent on the degree of trust and confidence which was achievable between federal and provincial Ministers and officials on the overall conduct of the negotiations. Many premiers were in a co-operative mood by June 1986. Canadian public opinion was behind the negotiations. Also, the Chief Negotiator had in mid-May reviewed at length the proposed mandate or negotiating objectives with provincial representatives in the CCTN. Reisman thereby obtained their confidence and agreement on the basic features of the mandate. This helped to pave the way for the 2 June First Ministers' meeting. Whether the continuing mechanisms would work out as well remained to be seen, but after months of often open wrangling, the issue of full provincial participation appeared to be settled amicably.

THE MIDDLE PHASE: JUNE 1986-AUGUST 1987: THE PARALLEL NEGOTIATIONS

By the summer of 1986, a comprehensive and complex set of federal-provincial consultations on the Bilateral Trade Negotiations was in place. This parallel set of negotiations often eclipsed, in the public's view, the actual bilateral negotiations led for Canada by Simon Reisman and, for the U.S. team, by Ambassador Peter Murphy.

The Canada-U.S. negotiations proceeded on the basis of roughly once-monthly "plenary meetings" between Reisman, Murphy and their respective teams of officials. At one stage about midway through the negotiations there were, in addition to the plenary meetings, eight working parties and two information task forces established to report to the plenary. The "heads of delegations" (Reisman and Murphy) would also meet to talk more privately about thorny issues.

The U.S. side was organized along interdepartmental lines, with frequent internal disputes over negotiating objectives and positions. Peter Murphy could be more forthcoming in the private heads of delegation sessions. The Canadian TNO team was, by contrast, better organized, more cohesive, and even better financed than their U.S. counterparts. Reisman and his able Assistant Chief Negotiators were fully in charge of a large group of federal officials, handpicked from across various federal departments, with only one boss and only one agenda.

Another major difference between the U.S. and Canadian side was that Canadians had clear negotiating authority from the beginning. Without dwelling on the details, the U.S. negotiators had to proceed on partial authority from Congress in the early stages; they almost did not obtain the crucial "fast track" negotiating authority from the Senate halfway through; and in the final states, they had to mount a continuous liaison and lobby effort to achieve bipartisan Congressional support.

In Canada, the real obstacles to a smoothly functioning negotiating stance came, both in potential and in actual circumstances, from the provinces. Peter Murphy made a point throughout the negotiations of focussing on the often public disagreement in Canada about the negotiations, and about the seeming inability of the federal government to deliver provincial approval.

In turn, Reisman, and the Prime Minister took frequent opportunities to impress upon the provinces the need to maintain a common front. That this front was sustained so well and so long may seem remarkable in retrospect. This was in no small measure due to the fairly effective operation of the federal-provincial process agreed upon in June 1986.

This process was, as noted above, capped by quarterly meetings of the First Ministers. The First Ministers met to discuss trade issues eight times after June 1986, until the last special meeting on 17 December 1987. Not counting the two Annual First Ministers' Conferences in 1986 and 1987 where trade issues played a prominent role, the First Ministers held special meetings on the bilateral negotiations on six other occasions.

These special meetings typically lasted only two or three hours—not long enough for detailed discussion of every negotiating issue, but certainly long enough, and frequently enough, for major sensitive issues to be aired. Until 7 October 1987, the Prime Minister was able to maintain a consensus of support behind the negotiations. On most occasions Simon Reisman briefed the Premiers directly on the progress of the negotiations; with few exceptions, the meetings consisted of the 11 politicians alone, plus Mr. Reisman, as the other officials waited outside. This format contributed no doubt to the Prime Minister's ability to maintain a political consensus, without getting overly bogged down in detail.

The second step in the intergovernmental process was meant to be regular meetings of "Designated Ministers." The term was coined to indicate those regular cabinet ministers appointed especially by their governments to handle the trade negotiations issue. Most of these provincial ministers chaired special cabinet committees on the trade negotiations. In many cases, however, the designated minister did not coincide with the minister normally assigned to "trade development" issues. The latter, most often ministers of industry or economic development, had been meeting about twice yearly since 1982, as the Federal-Provincial Ministers of Trade, with their federal counterpart, the Minister of International Trade (Ed Lumley, Gerald Reagan, James Kelleher, and Pat Carney in succession).

These ministers continued to meet while the bilateral trade negotiations were underway: in October 1985, February 1986, June 1986, January 1987 and May 1987. For the most part, however, the BTNs were only one item in a long agenda which covered major bilateral trade irritants with the U.S., EEC, Japan and others, the multilateral trade negotiations, and trade development and promotion policies and programmes.

As such, the designated ministers met only once: on 10 September 1986, one week prior to the First Ministers' meeting on 17 September. There were attempts in certain quarters to have more frequent meetings, but they came to naught. Perhaps the frequency of First Ministers' meetings obviated the necessity for another layer of political meetings. In any case, by tacit consent the process collapsed to two levels of consultation: the First Ministers and the CCTN.

The CCTN thus became the focus for the detailed exchange of views and information as the negotiations proceeded. It met as such on at least 18 occasions from January 1986 to December 1987. Chaired by Reisman, the committee consisted of "Provincial Trade Representatives" for each province, with observers from the Yukon and Northwest Territories. Also in attendance were several TNO officials, federal officials from a number of other departments (e.g. Finance, Federal-Provincial Relations Office, DRIE, Consumer and Corporate Affairs, Agriculture, etc.), as well as two or three additional officials from each province. While this made for large numbers and created obvious security problems, the actual discussion took place among the 11 main principals.

The provincial trade representatives were drawn from two different types of officials. Ontario, Quebec, Saskatchewan, Alberta and Nova Scotia appointed full-time trade representatives solely responsible for the negotiations, drawn from expertise in international trade negotiations or special experience in economic or industrial relations in their province. The remaining provinces chose to have as their representatives senior officials from within the existing structure, such as development or trade departments, executive council or intergovernmental affairs offices.

The choice of representative does not seem to have made any major difference to the effectiveness of provincial participation. An initial drawback for some provinces was clearly the lack of depth and experience in trade issues and negotiations. The larger provinces had well established bureaucracies for trade development and policy matters. Smaller provinces by contrast were forced to embark on a much steeper learning curve, but at the same time may have been able to focus more clearly on relatively fewer and more distinct provincial objectives. In any case, as is common in federal-provincial committees of this sort, one larger province may speak either implicitly or explicitly for others. On many issues, if Ontario, Quebec and Alberta took differing views, most other provinces simply echoed the position of one or other of the lead provinces.

The CCTN's agenda frequently began with an update on the progress in the bilateral negotiations (as well as the multilateral trade negotiations also underway during this period). The remainder of the one-day meetings normally focussed on two or three major topics. Frequently Reisman and TNO officials would review in the CCTN the Canadian objectives on a negotiating issue (e.g. agriculture, subsidies, services, tariffs etc.) prior to its discussion, within the month, with the Americans.

Federal officials maintain that the CCTN would often hear the first explanation and elaboration of the Canadian negotiating position, even before the federal cabinet. And this discussion was at a level of detail and confidentiality which surpassed any other consultation within the federal system, or with industry. This contributed significantly to a feeling among provinces that they were part of the broader enterprise. It enabled provinces to give immediate feedback on the sensitivity of particular positions to their jurisdictions, but also allowed Reisman to go forward to the subsequent negotiation session with the U.S. on the basis of strong Canadian consensus, where achievable.

The proceedings of the CCTN were not overly formal. After an initial attempt at maintaining a record of proceedings, this was abandoned. There were no other formal procedures or votes. Provincial representatives were given reams of background documents, sectoral analyses, discussion papers and so on; and many provinces reciprocated, passing their own documents to the federal government. However, federal officials were extremely reluctant to distribute hard copies of actual negotiating texts or proposals. More often, important proposals were reviewed by slide presentations, with provincial officials taking their own notes.

This process was dependent to a crucial degree on a frank and confidential exchange of information and views from both sides. This climate did not always prevail. Towards the end as some of the provincial governments became more and more uncertain about their support of the outcome, their representatives at the CCTN were much less forthcoming. This was especially so with respect to committing their views on sensitive negotiating positions. The federal negotiators began to feel exposed as a result, and the occasional leak of information, whether from within the Committee or not, strained relations all around.

The CCTN was not a decision-making body. At its best, it was an effective mechanism for the exchange of views and information. At its worst, the information flow was one-sided: lengthy federal presentations with little room for discussion. Nonetheless, the Committee functioned very well as a means of keeping all provinces fully briefed on the progress and outcome of the negotia-

tions. A vital part of this function included conference call debriefings but, by
and large, the provincial representatives were able to have a fairly clear and
detailed understanding of the progress of the actual negotiations.

There were of course many debates within the CCTN on issues central to the
negotiations: agriculture, breweries, the autopact, cultural programmes,
government procurement, regional development, investment, subsidies, dispute
settlement and so on. A full treatment of the conflicting provincial views on
these topics is outside the scope of this paper. It is fair to say, however, that the
exchange of information was in most instances sufficiently detailed to have a
reasonable debate. This contributed to the effectiveness of the forum, and went
a long way towards sustaining an integral Canadian position. Without a full understanding of the complex issues involved, the provinces could not have had
the same confidence in the Canadian position. Without that confidence, Canada
would not have been able to enter the final stages of the negotiation with the
support of a majority of the provinces.

THE FINAL PHASE: SEPTEMBER 1987-DECEMBER 1987: THE POWER PLAY

From June 1987 onwards, the Canadian negotiating position began to run out
of steam. Except in a few sensitive areas such as investment and alcoholic
beverages, of greater importance to the U.S., Canada had been the "demandeur"
in the negotiations. It had sought, in Reisman's phrase, "a big deal," comprehensive liberalization across all areas of trade. It became increasingly obvious in
the summer of 1987 that time was running out, with the Canadians having
proposed sweeping, dramatic change and the U.S. side unable to respond in
kind. On the key Canadian demands in the areas of trade remedy process and
dispute settlement, the U.S. were dragging their heels. The "deal" began to
shrink, and was close to falling apart entirely before the apparent 1 October
deadline to the negotiations, imposed by U.S. legislation.

In this context, the federal-provincial process was also wearing thin. The
federal team had briefed provinces at the end of June and early July on their
best guess at the outline of an agreement, only to have the U.S. dither week
after week on the essential elements. Political support began to wilt and
Canadian nerve, at least in some quarters, also seemed to be failing.

On 10 September 1987 the Ontario Liberal government of David Peterson
was returned with a majority. Throughout September, Peterson cast public
doubt on the negotiations and raised concerns, especially about U.S. proposals
on the autopact. Both he and Premier Pawley of Manitoba were quoted in the
press as not being willing to give "approval in principle" to an agreement prior
to holding public consultations. The federal negotiators began, it would appear,

to take this as a signal that full provincial consensus would almost certainly not be forthcoming. It can be assumed that scenarios for an agreement which minimized direct encroachment for provincial jurisdiction were reviewed with increased emphasis from this stage onwards.

By the time of a 13 September CCTN meeting, followed by a First Ministers' Meeting the next day, the provinces were warned that, unless the U.S. side were more forthcoming on the key issues of trade remedy and dispute settlement, the negotiations would end without agreement. This in fact seemed to be the case when on 24 September 1987, Reisman announced the termination of negotiations.

At this point the formalized process of negotiations stalled and a more ad hoc, clearly political process took its place. The Canadian negotiating team, while still involving Reisman and the TNO, was now led by Finance Minister Wilson, Trade Minister Carney and the Prime Minister's Chief of Staff Derek Burney, who met in several marathon sessions with U.S. Secretary of the Treasury James Baker, and U.S. Trade Representative Clayton Yeutter from 25 September to 3 October 1987.

The result of this last minute "brinkmanship" negotiations was the *Elements of the Agreement* released 4 October. This 31-page document left much to be assumed and many questions to be answered, but was a deal nonetheless. Throughout this last push, provincial governments were not consulted in any formal way, and neither the First Ministers nor the CCTN met.

The *Elements of the Agreement* contained many features which could not have been completely foreseen by the provinces. Chief among these was the lack of agreement on trade remedy process, except within the context (as important as it was) of a new binding dispute settlement mechanism. Other aspects of the Agreement were surprising for their absence: intellectual property and beer, to name two.

Most other features of the Agreement were not a surprise. The provisions with respect to the Auto Pact, cultural programmes, investment and energy were, in their basics, known to the provinces as a likely outcome well before the final push. It is still a matter of debate in some provinces whether the full import of the proposed measures was appreciated, let alone debated. Nonetheless much of the subsequent debate must honestly revolve around the ideological thrust of these provisions, more so than the actual details.

Perhaps the more complete surprise to provinces was the realization that, when taken in its entirety, the *Elements of the Agreement* impinged directly and immediately on so little in provincial jurisdiction. The exact extent of the intrusion is of course a matter of keen legal debate. It is clearly in the federal government's interests to portray the Agreement as "99 per cent in federal jurisdiction", to downplay the opposition in certain provinces. Whatever the outcome of this debate, however, it is clear that the Agreement is much less involving of provincial jurisdiction than first conceived. The postponement of the subsidies issue for a second phase obviated immediate provincial impact, as did the prospective nature of the provisions on services and investment.

This may beg the question as to whether provincial support was, at this stage, needed at all. This view may be taken from a strictly jurisdictional perspective. Given certain legal advice and a will to fight court battles, that view may have its supporters. However, in the immediate political context of October 1987, the Government of Canada clearly needed the political support of at least a majority of provinces. This was especially so given a widespread public perception that the Agreement was somewhat less than ideal.

How many provinces were needed to support the Agreement is also a matter for debate. With Ontario's support unlikely, the most common view was to seek provincial consensus along the lines of the general amending formula of the *Constitution Act of 1982:* the Parliament of Canada, plus seven of ten provinces with, in total, over 50 per cent of the population. This is not to suggest that this formula was to be formally applied in this instance, but it assumed a kind of rule of thumb for measuring sufficient provincial support.

Whatever the case, by the time the premiers met on the afternoon of 6 October with Prime Minister Mulroney, they and their officials had only a few hours at most to review the Agreement in detail. The CCTN had met the day before. Within a day or two of this meeting the premiers of British Columbia, Alberta, Saskatchewan, Quebec and New Brunswick (Hatfield) announced their support of the Agreement. The premiers of Ontario, Manitoba and Prince Edward Island announced their opposition, while the premiers of Newfoundland and Nova Scotia indicated a need to review the text more carefully.

The latter two provinces, as well as the new Government of New Brunswick elected on 17 October under Premier Frank McKenna, eventually came down in support of the Agreement. This followed detailed discussions of various aspects of the Agreement and, in the case of Nova Scotia, a set of public hearings. Premier Peckford announced his support for the Agreement at the Annual First Ministers' Conference in Toronto, 26-27 November 1987. At that Conference, a frank if muted debate on the Agreement took place on Premier Peterson's home turf.

Throughout the period from 6 October to the release of the final legal text of the Agreement on 11 December 1987, there were no formal federal-provincial sessions, apart from a conference call on the progress of legal drafting in early November. Provincial governments were not privy to legal drafts and did not see any of the final text until its public release in December.

Yet while there was no formal process, a substantial amount of informal consultation occurred on the finer details of the text. Not a few minor compromises and concessions were made by both the U.S. and Canadian sides in this period of text refinement, although it is fair to say that no major changes took place. In terms of provincial input, those provinces supportive of the Agreement, or tending towards support, were clearly at an advantage at this stage. It is obvious that communication lines were more open to these provinces than those which were opposed from the outset.

The final review of the full legal text of the Agreement took place by the CCTN and a First Ministers meeting on 16 and 17 December 1987. At this point, seven of ten provincial governments declared their support. This left Ontario and Manitoba opposed as well as Prince Edward Island, whose Premier Joseph Ghiz nonetheless stated that he would no longer "actively" oppose the majority view.

This last phase of the process of negotiations was clearly frustrating for genuine federal-provincial consultations. Had negotiations with the Americans gone as planned, and the U.S. side not forced the last-minute brinkmanship, the more laborious federal-provincial process could have continued without interruption. A more realistic view may be that, in the final power play, protecting the Canadian position could not allow for the niceties of federal-provincial diplomacy.

As the largest and very influential province, Ontario's role was key. Throughout the summer of 1987 and into the fall, Ontario's position became highly politicized, making its participation and commitment to the negotiation process suspect. Once Ontario support was finally withdrawn, formal federal-provincial consultation became very difficult. The crucial elements of trust and confidence disappeared, along with the sense of common purpose.

CONCLUSIONS

An assessment of the success or failure of the extensive federal-provincial consultations on the free trade negotiations depends on where one sits. From the author's perspective, sitting in a province that shared the overall Canadian objectives and ultimately supported the result, the process will be perceived more positively than perhaps in other provinces. Participants from those provinces opposed to the Agreement, particularly Ontario, seem to be somewhat embittered by the experience. The Trade Negotiations Office similarly may feel that the effort of maintaining the federal-provincial relationship may not in the final analysis have been worth it.

Such subjective assessments are not in the long term likely to prevail. Most outside observers would probably be little surprised that the process ended the way it did, given the almost complete lack of formal institutionalized decision-making. Consultation after all is just that. Those who expect more are certain to be disappointed. There is as yet no binding, legal mechanism in Canada for federal and provincial governments to reach agreement on such matters as international trade agreements.

The actual FTA signed on 2 January 1988 by Prime Minister Mulroney and President Reagan did not intrude into provincial jurisdiction nearly as far as initially expected. That the negotiators in the final analysis withdrew from greater involvement in matters of provincial jurisdiction may be to Canada's overall loss. In any case, as the Agreement is implemented there will be ample scope for jurisdictional conflict in Canada. That is a fairly safe prediction, but not one that necessarily brings comfort to those with an interest in Canada's international economic relations.

At the point of writing (July 1988) the federal and provincial governments have resumed discussions on trade issues—this time over the Multilateral Trade Negotiations (the "Uruguay Round"). The process being followed at the non-political level appears to be modelled on the CCTN experience. Much of the heat and interest has dissipated, however, as the MTN issues are more diffuse, more long-term and perhaps, less challenging of established interests.

In these negotiations the provincial governments can be expected to demand to be a part of the Canadian team at least to the same degree as in the Bilateral Trade Negotiations. Every single provincial government has in the past three years become sensitized and informed about the importance of trade policy issues to the economic well-being of their province. This interest will manifest itself in a continued demand to be involved. The more diffuse and distant negotiations in Geneva will be more difficult to follow. Yet the development and successful promotion of a Canadian negotiating position will continue to require as a key ingredient, mechanisms to keep provinces informed, receive their advice and, to the extent possible, achieve consensus.

To expect more of the process will require institutional reform. Constitutional amendment or constitutional jurisprudence which departs from current precedent is not out of the question. Certainly a major court challenge on the constitutional validity of federal implementing legislation is a possibility. Perhaps a less confrontational route would be more formalized intergovernmental agreements to bind provincial governments to a negotiated agreement in areas of provincial jurisdiction.[9]

---

9   For recent suggestions along this line see Murray Smith, "Closing a Trade Deal: The Provinces' Role", C.D. Howe Institute *Commentary*, No. 11, August 1986.

None of this detracts from the ultimate, unwritten rules of Canadian politics. A federal government which feels it has public support for a course of action will risk the wrath of provinces, and, within the confines of its legal advice, the judgement of the courts. That the current federal government is pursuing implementation of the FTA over the objections of a minority of provinces is not something new in Canadian history. While this result could have been predicted, it does not take away from the significant achievement of federal-provincial consultation during the negotiations.

III

The Meech Lake Accord

FIVE

Much Ado About Meech

David A. Milne

Les conséquences juridiques et politiques de l'Accord du lac Meech ont été interprétées d'une multitude de façons par les spécialistes, de même que par ceux qui prirent part à son achèvement. Ces divergences reposent davantage sur l'idéologie de chacun face au fédéralisme canadien, que sur les implications techniques et légales de l'Accord. A cet égard, l'analyse de l'article reconnaissant le Québec comme une société distincte est celle où les considérations idéologiques jouèrent le plus. Au centre de ce débat se trouve le vieil antagonisme entre la vision d'une nation canadienne bilingue (enchâssée dans la Constitution en 1982) et celle reconnaissant le Québec comme une société distincte du Canada anglais. Avec l'Accord du lac Meech les deux visions se trouveront donc présentes dans la Constitution canadienne. De ce fait, elles seront en compétition et le Canada, suivant celle qui prédominera, en sera profondément changé.

Un autre aspect qui fut pris à partie est le caractère anti-démocratique du processus qui mena à l'Accord et la dynamique qu'il institue pour les prochaines modifications constitutionnelles. Dorénavant, les modifications constitutionnelles seront l'apanage des premiers ministres sans qu'aucun mécanisme intermédiaire ne permette la participation du public.

Dans l'ensemble, l'Accord ne déséquilibre pas les rapports fédéraux-provinciaux au profit de l'un ou de l'autre ordre de gouvernement, bien que son impact sur d'autres aspects du fédéralisme canadien laisse songeur.

What the sound and fury over the first ministers' deal-making at Meech Lake may or may not signify is indeed the question. Certainly the public clamour during the ratification phase of the country's new amendment process stands in marked contrast to the long earlier series of quiet and secretive negotiations between governments. While ministers and officials publicly gloated over their success in coming to an agreement at the bargaining table, the sense of satisfaction dimmed when faced with carrying that agreement through a whole series of legislative hurdles in the face of noisy public opinion. The issue then was how to prevent an unruly public from upsetting their delicate handiwork. For its part, the Canadian public has not looked kindly on elite bargaining as the Canadian route to constitutional change, particularly since it offends their sense of democratic process. Not only does it appear to undermine their idea of the constitution as a "peoples' document", but also their sense of the constitution as a fundamental restraint upon government itself. Evidence of that disquiet came up again and again in public statements and hearings throughout the country, but perhaps was put nowhere more extravagantly than by the imagery of Deborah Coyne in her submission to the Joint Committee:

> [At Meech Lake] 11 men sat around a table trading legislative, judicial, and executive powers as if engaged in a gentlemanly game of poker, with little regard for the concerns of individual Canadians, who will ultimately feel the impact and bear the burden of their moves.[1]

Nor was the stark contrast restricted to questions of process: even with the substance of the agreement there was on the one hand, a quiet and measured contentment with Meech Lake from government officials and supporting academics and constitutional specialists, while on the other, dire predictions from equally qualified people that Meech Lake would, in one stroke as it were, undo the nation. In short, capturing the substance of Meech Lake would be no less political an undertaking than would be the making of judgments about process. So often, for example, mere ideologies of federalism really lay behind debates on the meaning and value of the provisions in the Meech Lake Accord. Once again, competing ideas of Canada re-emerged in the debate, reminding the country of the classic Liberal and Tory divisions of the late 1970s and early 1980s. Continuity was also evident in the ongoing preoccupations with Quebec nationalism, and with how best to give expression to that nationalism in the constitution.

There was even a re-enactment of the old battle between charter advocates and provincialists over the Meech Lake agreement, a war of words that strangely echoed the rhetoric of the first years of the decade. The charter had obviously not lost any of its popular—indeed larger-than-life—appeal to Canadians as the "peoples'" charter. It continued to work as a challenge to provincialism and parliamentary government, although in Quebec it rowed against powerful nationalist countercurrents. There was also more than a hint of the old political alignment between social groups and the federal government in the Meech Lake debate, as interest groups prepared to do battle over what they saw as a weakening of Ottawa's power to develop national social policy.

---

1   Ms. Deborah Coyne, submission to the Joint Committee on the 1987 Constitutional Accord, August 27, 1987.

In effect, events seemed to underline the wisdom of the old adage: "plus ça change, plus c'est la même chose." The actual constitutional text did not help shed light on these matters. Although specialists were quick to pronounce on the likely meaning of the different sections to the Meech Lake agreement, they did not speak with anything like a single authoritative voice. Moreover, many of the experts had already been so deeply implicated in the politics of constitutional negotiation as the hired guns of one governmental party or another, that their intellectual neutrality remained in some doubt. About the only sure ground on which constitutional experts could agree was that, in the last instance, the Supreme Court would decide, and that in the meantime it was impossible to predict what interpretations of the Meech Lake agreement might finally be settled upon. This outcome did not reassure worried critics, although it seemed to satisfy a remarkable number of Accord supporters.

If the legal implications of the agreement remained so often unclear, it was even worse with the different political readings which were being taken of the Meech Lake agreement. Politicians themselves started this confusion, as they fanned out to explain the agreement to their constituents in entirely different terms. Judging from their diverse and often conflicting public statements, first ministers, who had collectively signed the same constitutional document, had no shared sense of the meaning and purpose of some of its provisions. This was particularly so with the statements of politicians in Quebec, and those elsewhere in the country. Whether the issue concerned the meaning of the distinct society clause, the question of the charter of rights and freedoms, or the spending power, the answers given to Canadians in different regions of the country were often incompatible. Since the constitutional significance of Meech Lake depended as much on the understandings of politicians and publics as on the courts, this confusion from the architects of the deal was not a helpful sign.

However, this outcome in itself may not be surprising in a complicated constitutional negotiation. There is always ambiguity over the meaning of provisions even under the best of circumstances, and uncertainty over what has been wrought may be the common fate of all constitutional architects, including founding fathers. The effect of these conditions here has been to politicize the debate around Meech Lake more sharply than would otherwise be the case. With ambiguous wording and conflicting statements by politicians, the battle over ideology can feed on the imprecisions of the text, so often dragging out "worst case scenarios" in support of prior political positions. This is the charged ground upon which the student of Meech Lake must warily walk.

QUEBEC NATIONALISM AND THE FUTURE OF THE FEDERATION

Perhaps no parts of the Meech Lake text revealed these elements more sharply than the provisions for recognition of Quebec as a distinct society. While first ministers had managed to agree on these clauses with relatively little difficulty at their negotiating sessions, they drew by far the most critical fire from an alarmed public. The whole section set off a series of questions probing the first principles of the Canadian state. What did it mean to recognize Quebec as a distinct society and give its provincial government a role to "preserve and promote the distinct identity of Quebec"? What did it mean to balance this provision with another recognizing the distribution of French and English-speaking Canadians grouped in majority and minority linguistic communities throughout Canada? How satisfactory was the agreement's commitment merely "to preserve" the linguistic minorities? What had become of bilingualism and the idea of one Canada? How did the new clause affect the rest of the constitution and in particular, the charter of rights and freedoms?

It was not long, in fact, before the apparently technical answers to these questions revealed a sharp political and ideological gulf not only between Accord supporters and critics, but also between supporters inside or outside Quebec. Invariably, supporters in English-speaking Canada treated the issue of recognizing Quebec as a distinct society primarily as an exercise in symbolism, while Accord defenders in Quebec saw this new interpretative clause contributing significantly to the powers of the province. There were constitutional specialists ready to back each of these views, often providing governments with the kind of reassuring counsel needed to support their preferred political positions. While supporters of the accord pointed to clause 2 (1) to show that bilingualism was not being deserted in this granting of special status to Quebec, opponents argued that the clause left linguistic minorities more vulnerable. In fact, unlike the strategy of bilingualism, they argued that this version of Québécois nationalism led logically to the rationalization of two unilingual societies in Canada. It was a dualism which fostered separation, legitimized unilingual policies, and fractured the application of the Canadian charter of rights and freedoms.

What are we to make of these arguments? It seems to me that on the face of it, section 2, which attempts principally to accommodate Quebec's wish to be recognized as a distinct society, is clearly an interpretative provision, and not a substantive grant of power. Not only does the opening language of the section make that clear (The Constitution of Canada shall be interpreted in a manner consistent with...), but subsection (4) ensures that nothing in the section "derogates from the powers, rights or privileges of Parliament or the Government of Canada, or the legislatures or governments of the provinces, including any powers, rights or privileges relating to language." It goes too far, however, to argue consequently that "the clause should be seen as an affirmation of sociological facts with little legal significance."[2]

While it is true that the clause will be useful in those "rare" cases "where other constitutional provisions are unclear," that will most likely not be its "only" relevance.[3] As Peter Hogg himself later admitted in his analysis of this section, the distinct society clause can certainly be used in aid of a section 1 defence against the charter.[4] Section 1 permits infringements of the charter where governmental measures are "demonstrably justified in a free and democratic society," and this interpretative clause certainly demonstrably underlines the legitimacy of any Quebec measures which "preserve and promote the distinct identity of Quebec." To add this indirect support to section 1 challenges to the charter is not in itself an insignificant matter.

Moreover, the section lends itself rather handily as a source of strong support for legislative measures exercised under any other ambit of provincial power. The province can now argue in many of these cases that its measures are in relation to a constitutionally recognized objective, namely the promotion of "the distinct society of Quebec," and thus confer much more significance and legitimacy to them. Since the characterizing of legislation as "in relation to" a given constitutional subject matter is at best an artful exercise by the courts, deeply influenced by what the courts take to be the importance and legitimacy of the legislative object, it is certainly not clear how far this clause might be used to broaden the whole base of Quebec powers. It is difficult to predict what the court might say if faced, for example, with legislation promoting Quebec's distinctive financial institutions as against the claims of the federal banking power, or in telecommunications where so much of the field might otherwise have been declared exclusively federal. The province may well find, in effect, additional legislative room, perhaps in a willingness of the court to recognize new areas of concurrency. Certainly, with recognition of its unique constitutional responsibilities, Quebec will be able to argue forcefully for the most expansive reading of its own legislative powers. Indeed, everything in the constitution, including the division of powers and the charter, must be interpreted in the light of the clause.

Even though it would appear that Parliament's powers are protected by subsection (4), the real and effective test will come earlier when the court decides

---

2   Peter W. Hogg, *Meech Lake Constitutional Accord Annotated* (Toronto: Carswell, 1988), p. 12.
3   Ibid.
4   Ibid, p. 16.

how to characterize legislation passed in the name of promoting the distinct identity of Quebec. Will this interpretative principle, prominently placed at the very outset of the *Constitution Act, 1867*, be read as a fundamental part of Confederation, a new directive to treat Quebec legislation passed in its name with unusual expansiveness and generosity? Since this recognition does not arise as an incidental part of a preamble but instead forms the basis of a constitutional section in its own right, it would be odd for the court to treat it as though it were mere rhetoric or symbolism. In other words, the court is likely to assume that the constitutional drafters inserted this prominent section at the outset of our written constitution for a purpose and that it means something rather than nothing. If it is to mean something, it would appear to be a broad directive to the court to read Quebec legislative powers broadly enough for that legislature to carry out its constitutional mandate to promote the distinct identity of Quebec. While the preservation of the anglophone minority may be included within the meaning of the distinct society itself, promoting the distinct identity of Quebec would surely entail further reinforcement of the special French-speaking character of the province probably through measures that might otherwise have fallen afoul of the charter or of a competing federal head of power. In short, a new special status may have been conferred on the province of Quebec, tacitly acknowledging it as "the homeland of the francophone element of Canada's duality."[5]

Now it is, of course, true that the constitution never treated all provinces equally at any time, and that Quebec had a different status from the others even by virtue of section 133 (the use of English and French in the provincial legislature and courts), section 94 (preserving Quebec's civil code), and section 93 (protection of denominational school rights). But these distinctions do not by any means add up to a claim to be treated as a province with a special constitutional status, especially since other provinces can also show incidental constitutional variation. Quebec learned that the constitution, at least prior to Meech Lake, did not recognize such a distinction when it vainly sought recognition of a Quebec veto in a reference aimed against patriation in 1982.[6]

---

5   This was the language which the Bourassa government had wished to insert into the Meech Lake text through a preamble. In the end, Quebec was able to get recognition of the distinct society in a stronger form by way of a constitutional section, but "homeland of the francophone element of Canada's duality" was dropped. As I have suggested here, the idea remains tacit in any case.

6   See *Re. A.G.* of *Quebec v A.G. of Canada* [1982] (2 S.C.R. 793) where the court recognized the fundamental equality of all provinces and granted no single province a conventional right to a veto.

Although the courts have already recognized the right of the province to protect its French character in several landmark cases, these judgments showed that, at least prior to Meech Lake, the province could not easily assert the primacy of that collective goal as against individual rights. Not only was there no entrenched principle to affirm the Quebec government objective, but even the threshold was lower: earlier the court, as in Quebec Chief Justice Deschênes' rejection of French-only commercial signs, had merely to show that the measures were not needed "to preserve" the fundamental French character of the province; now the test would be easier, since measures aimed at "promoting" the distinct identity could not be struck down because the linguistic *status quo* is presumably adequate.[7]

Whatever the courts might decide, it is just as important to understand how legislators will read and interpret the meaning of the distinct society clause. In the debates over Meech Lake in the National Assembly of Quebec, politicians were already interpreting the clause to mean a licence to expand the scope of policies around an already officially unilingual Quebec. That was the considered conclusion of Quebec's Language Advisory Board on 15 June 1988. Such an understanding also lay behind Quebec's vigorous objection to the application of Ottawa's new enhanced law on bilingualism in Bill C-72 in Quebec; Rémillard insisted on 7 June of the same year, in deference to the recognition of Quebec as a distinct society, that Ottawa must secure the agreement of the province before undertaking the promotion of bilingualism there. Even more startling, Canada's Secretary of State, Lucien Bouchard, at first concurred in this reading of the federal role.

The same message might be drawn from events in Saskatchewan and Alberta. On 25 April, the Saskatchewan legislature chose to disregard a legal commitment to bilingualism in the province stemming from an 1886 territorial statute and imposed a largely unilingual regime on the province. There were some compensations to the linguistic minority, and vague assurances that Saskatchewan might eventually become bilingual, but the politics of unilingualism prevailed. Alberta introduced an even more severe measure on 22 June, expunging existing French language rights, in the name of what Premier Getty called Alberta's

---

7 Hence, Lederman and other constitutional specialists are correct to point out that the courts have long recognized the right of Quebec to promote its distinctive francophone character in a variety of legislative measures. But courts have been careful to ensure that such measures are really needed to "preserve" the francophone character of the province and to counterbalance that objective against the infringements placed upon minority or individual rights. Not many measures have passed that exacting test. Meech Lake will certainly lower the threshold required to sustain such measures.

"distinct society." This train of events was precisely what analysts like Bryan Schwartz in his full-length study of Meech Lake had foreseen:

> ...there is real cause for concern that provincial legislatures will read the "Quebec clause" as a directive to pursue dualist, rather than bilingual, language policies. Legislatures outside of Quebec may read s. 2 (1) (a) as inspiring them to preserve the predominantly English-speaking nature of their provinces, rather than encouraging the acquisition of bilingualism. The Quebec legislature may interpret the affirmation of its role as promoter of the "distinct society" as legitimating its efforts to discourage bilingualism among its francophone majority. It may be believed that Quebec is more "special" and more "apart" if most of its people cannot speak the majority language in the other provinces.

As if to underline the prevailing drift of sentiment against bilingualism among Quebec's political elite and therefore its likelihood to take this reading of the new clause, Schwartz goes on:

> The concern just expressed is not fanciful. The fact of the matter is that Bill 101 legally restricts the ability of a francophone in Quebec to attend an English language school. There are no "English immersion" public schools in Quebec. Little time is alloted in Quebec public schools for the teaching of English to francophones. The hostility or indifference of successive Quebec governments to bilingualism among francophones is ironic in view of the fact the governments themselves have had fluently bilingual francophones at the helm. The same leaders who maintained an intense identification with their language heritage seemed to regard unilingualism for others as a necessary bulwark against "assimilation".[8]

It is here where the fiercest political battles around the distinct society enshrined in Meech Lake have been fought. It is appropriate that this francophone nationalism around the Quebec homeland has been once again engaged by former Prime Minister Trudeau with its classic competitor, an alternative form of francophone nationalism taking the form of bilingualism within a single Canadian homeland. This is, of course, an old debate going to the roots of

---

8   Bryan Schwartz, *Fathoming Meech Lake* (Winnipeg: Legal Research Institute of the University of Manitoba, 1987), p. 31.

Quebec political culture of the late nineteenth century, and Trudeau has acknowledged as much when, in his submissions to the Joint Committee and Senate, he publicly acknowledged his indebtedness to the vision of "the great Henri Bourassa."[9] As I have argued elsewhere, it is Bourassa's vision which has been entrenched in the charter of 1982; yet Meech Lake would propose to entrench its ideological opposite in the Canadian constitution only five years later.[10]

There is probably no more profound element in the Meech Lake package of amendments than this contest. It goes far beyond the nuances of constitutional law that have heretofore dominated the debate. In my view, the question is essentially ideological and political: whether Canada will move increasingly toward the Bourassa-Trudeau vision of a single bilingual nation, or step by step, toward two distinct societies, one centred in Quebec and the other elsewhere. What Meech Lake seeks to do is to acknowledge the second option far more openly, while trying to balance that concession with a modest reaffirmation "to preserve" the existence of the minorities of French and English-speaking Canadians within two unilingually dominant societies. That minimal rule surely understates the commitment needed of all provinces to make a policy of bilingualism work, and it is a woefully inadequate statement of the responsibility of Parliament itself. Further, section 2(1), by linking distinct language populations to specific geographical areas not merely as a statement of sociological fact but of constitutional value, directs judges and politicians to respect these "language states".[11] The effects are likely to be comprehensive and on-going.

If these two expressions of French Canadian nationalism find themselves both entrenched in the Canadian constitution, the question arises whether such a constitutional settlement can be an enduring basis of reconciliation. That appears to be the view of the drafters of Meech Lake. Despite the long ideological struggle between these schools of thought in Quebec, perhaps entrenching

---

9 I have taken up that relationship in my book, *Tug of War* (Toronto: Lorimer, 1986), pp. 48-56 and attempted to show its connection to the new Canadian Charter of Rights and Freedoms. It is important for Canadians to come to grips with that Quebec history and with the development of these two branches of French Canadian nationalism. I can think of no better place to start thinking about these ideas than with the work of A.I. Silver, *The French-Canadian Idea of Confederation, 1864-1900* (Toronto: University of Toronto Press, 1982).

10 A sketch of this argument can be found in my short article in *Bridges*, 5, No. 4, May/June, 1988, 5-7.

11 See John Whyte's argument on this point in his "Submission to the Special Joint Committee of the Senate and the House of Commons on the 1987 Constitutional Accord", *Queen's Quarterly*, 94, 4, Winter 1987, 797-798.

both—bilingualism throughout Canada *and* Quebec as a distinct society—is a workable compromise. Not only do the two conceptions of the future of the French-speaking peoples of Canada compete with one another in their prime locus of loyalty, but they would be understood by advocates of both options to be only incompletely entrenched at this time. Therefore, there will be a whole train of extensions which would flow from either paradigm and constitutional changes that would flesh out each conception. It would be naive, therefore, to expect any settled resting place from the partial constitutional efforts of the 1980s. They are the beginnings of a process of change which promise, one way or the other, to change Canada profoundly over the next decades. It will, of course, make a great deal of difference which of the conceptions ends up dominating the Canadian stage.

THE CHARTER, DEMOCRACY, AND MEECH

As the introduction to this essay has suggested, the Meech Lake Accord (as modified five weeks later at the Langevin Block) has been the focus of sustained public criticism from a liberal democratic perspective. On the one hand, there was the closed and secretive process of constitutional change adopted by first ministers themselves in generating the text of these agreements. On the other, there was the inadequate system of public consultation which followed. Not only had first ministers declared that they would not in any case reopen the accord except in case of "egregious" errors, but some did not even provide for public hearings prior to submitting the resolution to their legislatures.[12] For those legislatures that did offer hearings under these conditions, public distaste for the futility of this exercise was so readily apparent that some legislative committees recommended permanent standing committees for public involvement in constitutional issues in future.[13]

After this exposure to the politics of executive federalism, democratic critics looked with even less kindness on the promises in Meech Lake to entrench first ministers' conferences as a permanent and formal element of our constitutional system. Section 8 of the accord provided for a required annual first ministers' conference on "the state of the Canadian economy and such other matters as may be appropriate." Section 13 directed the Prime Minister of Canada to con-

12 The provinces of Saskatchewan and Alberta, for example, did not provide for hearings before quickly passing the resolutions in their legislatures on 23 September and 7 December 1987 respectively.
13 Ontario, for example, called for exactly this remedy in response to what it recognized as public disquiet over the closed and secretive process of constitutional change adopted at Meech Lake.

vene a constitutional conference at least once each year, with a required agenda containing Senate reform, the fisheries, and "such other matters as are agreed upon." Not only would these provisions preclude any return by Ottawa to a unilateral approach to governing Canada, such as that recently employed by Prime Minister Trudeau during the 1980s, but it would also formalize the first ministers' conference as the normal centre for the consideration of constitutional amendments.

This element of the agreement is easy to overlook, especially since Canadians have become increasingly accustomed to the conference route to constitutional change. That was the practice employed for the amendments of 1982, for proposed amendments concerning aboriginal rights, and, of course, for Meech Lake itself. Indeed, section 37 of the *Constitution Act, 1982* set out the requirement for a constitutional conference on aboriginal rights, including the participation of aboriginal peoples, a precedent reinforced a year later in the 1983 constitutional accord on aboriginal rights. That idea was again taken up in the Meech Lake agreement of 1987, but this time the constitutional conferences have no fixed agenda, no time limit, and no other membership but first ministers. Annual constitutional conferences would now be a constitutional requirement for the foreseeable future unless a constitutional amendment were later passed to remove it; unlike all other precedents, there was here no sunset clause, freeing the Prime Minister of the requirement to convene meetings if negotiations within a reasonable time proved unfruitful.

This part of the Meech Lake agreement has come in for much criticism, particularly from Bryan Schwartz in his extensive study of the accord. The critique has focussed on the endless nature of the commitment, the likely trivializing of constitution-making by this incessant linkage to ordinary politics, and the long-run threat posed by regular provincialist assaults on federal power. These are serious concerns, but so too is the entrenchment of the first ministers' conference as the principal and recognized mode of constitution-making in Canada. Apart from the requirement to discuss aboriginal rights through this means for a limited number of years, there was no legal requirement earlier to use this process. Convention alone sustained the practice. Although there was one solo gesture when a resolution was introduced in the legislature of British Columbia in 1982 to add property rights to the charter, this bold experiment to depart from the diplomatic norms of executive federalism has not been notably successful. It is worth underlining that henceforth constitution-making will be dominated by first ministers in concert who will normally in cases of majority governments have sufficient power over the executive and legislative branches of government in Canada to put through their own agreements. Of course, the confidence of first ministers to do exactly that may well have been shaken by the extent of public dissatisfaction over the process used at Meech Lake. If the Meech Lake agreement is in fact approved without change despite widespread public clamour over both substance and process, it will certainly encourage such ambitious acts of executive federalism in future. If, on the other hand, public discontent is strong enough to block ratification until needed changes to the work of the first ministers are made, then increased cautiousness among first ministers may be the longer-term historical outcome. At the moment, there is no certainty about which of these futures awaits us.

In any event, if major constitutional changes are to be made without acknowledging the need for significant public endorsement either through elections, referenda, plebiscites or other means, then considerable difficulties are raised for liberal democracy. It is surely not enough to answer that first ministers are, after all, elected leaders. For permanent constitutional changes of this magnitude there must be a wide public consensus. Nor can it be assumed that any agreement of 11 first ministers is an adequate representation of that wide national consensus, especially if the matters concern the exchange of legislative powers or major transformations in the makeup of Parliament or other national political institutions. Indeed, since the first ministers themselves are self-interested parties in such negotiations, the end result is not likely to add up to a disinterested view of the broader public good; the ordinary citizens' perspectives are easily overlooked.

Moreover, given legislative compliance, it is difficult to see how the constitution can continue to act as a check upon governments, especially if the constitution itself is to be the subject of perpetual bargaining by first ministers. In practice, the only limits are those which cannot be negotiated away or which cannot be collectively sold to the public by a determined concert of first ministers. As Meech Lake has demonstrated, if only a single minister sits at the table to represent the federal interest surrounded by ten protecting the provincial interest, it is easy to see which side of the federal dynamic is under constant threat. If concessions are made to get an agreement, it is exceptionally difficult for the public to redress the imbalance later.

It is, of course, true that this picture may be somewhat overdrawn, since provincial governments themselves often have an interest in protecting federal power and may well do so. Indeed, Meech Lake demonstrates that the provinces of Manitoba and Ontario probably showed more concern for the protection of the federal spending power in the bargaining than did Ottawa itself.[14] Yet the fact remains that there is an imbalance arising from the broader dynamics of executive federalism, a reality which prompted Prime Minister Trudeau to do what he could to resist the snares of so-called co-operative federalism during

---

14 See the comments of Bryan Schwartz in *Fathoming Meech Lake*, pp. 94-195.

the early years of this decade. The consequences of executive federalism, as strongly reinforced in the Accord, are worrisome when judged from a democratic perspective; whether or not they are also dangerous in terms of the federal-provincial balance of power, will be taken up in the next section of this chapter.

There are other provisions in the agreement which should also give democrats pause. The changes to the amending formula which push more subjects into the unanimity column is one such provision; after Meech Lake, the relative weightings of the Canadian population in favour of constitutional changes will be a largely irrelevant factor when every province exercises a veto over changes to national institutions, and the like. The creation of new provinces is another: here the first ministers exercise a final say on whether the northern territories will be absorbed by the existing provinces or granted provincehood in the future. Not only is there no provision for a role for broader public involvement, but Meech Lake does not even require the consent of the people of the affected territories for such changes.

As John Whyte has argued, the new stress on unilingual language states may even undercut the democratic promise of bilingualism by producing "a nation of citizens [most] of whom are not qualified to govern at the national level."

> One of the social costs of an enclave-based language policy is that it's the elites who will realize that power at the national level accrues to those few people who can communicate to the whole nation. The rest of the population will become disentitled to govern. In other words, the strong bilingualist policy of recent decades has, as its overriding political virtue, not just that it produces a hospitable national environment for francophonism, but that it is democratic. One of the potential consequences of the 1987 Constitutional Accord is the diminution of democracy in Canada.[15]

FEDERALISM, PROVINCIALISM, AND THE STATE OF THE BALANCE

It is not surprising that so much of the Meech Lake debate has been centred around philosophies of federalism. On the surface, of course, the debate has seemed to focus on the specific legal and political effects of the new agreement on the balance of power between the provinces and the federal government. However, that apparently technical exercise was shot through with ideological meaning. From the very first, opponents of Meech Lake, whatever the nature of their objections, so often tended to be cast as centralists, unable to live with

---

15 John D. Whyte, op.cit., 799.

the trend toward decentralization in Canadian federalism; supporters, on the other hand, were seen either as outright believers in what Trudeau called "provincial patriotism," or willing accomplices in a plan to transform Canada into a confederacy. So often, too, the question was tied up with attitudes toward Quebec-state nationalism, and in particular with what price, if any, ought to be paid for the exclusion of that province from the 1982 constitutional changes. History, too, it seemed, was to become grist for the ideological mill.

The conventional view of the agreement was, of course, that it would have a sharply decentralizing effect on the federation. It was easy to point at the reasons for this judgment. Had not virtually all of Quebec's conditions been accepted—indeed, in some cases, even more than was asked for? Had not the federal government declined to advance a single negotiating objective for the concessions it was prepared to make to Quebec and the other provinces? Was it not the case that federal institutions were now subject to what Trudeau called "remote control" by the premiers and federal powers circumscribed? Had not all the provinces got aboard the Quebec train and received substantial new powers as a result? This was the critics' portrait of the Meech Lake Accord, often so sharply drawn that it put supporters on the defensive.

Yet this part of the agreement is really not so clearcut, nor are its implications unidirectional. Regarding federal institutions, for example, how does Meech Lake, in one stroke as it were, put them under the control of provincialist forces? The institutions in question, the Senate and the Supreme Court of Canada, are now to have their members appointed by the federal government from among nominees advanced by the provincial governments; in this way, Supreme Court justices and senators will be able to discharge their serious responsibilities to the federation in the full knowledge that both levels of government have had a hand in their appointment. Yet it is said that if provincial governments are given the power of nomination, not only will the required federal approval be rendered useless, but the nominees themselves will become mere instruments of the premiers. We are encouraged to see in provincial nomination, the weakening—if not eventual capture—of the sovereign legislative and judicial powers of the federal order of government.

This is an overblown argument. Virtually every reform proposal respecting federal institutions over the last quarter century has made room for a provincial role in the appointment process of judges and often of senators. In each case these ideas have been advanced in order to make federal institutions stronger and give them a legitimacy that has often been lacking in the past. Given the key role of these institutions in the federation, it has been long recognized that prime ministerial prerogative is not the best means of appointing members or vesting them with legitimacy and authority. Hardly a commentator on the Supreme Court, for example, has failed to mention the need to involve the provinces directly (or indirectly through a reformed Senate) in appointments, especially with the advent of the Charter of Rights and Freedoms in 1982. In the light of this history and of the fact that executive nomination of judges in many other federations normally requires some independent legislative endorsement, it would seem odd to see this sharing of the appointment power as an abdication of sovereignty.

It is equally misleading to suggest that nominees would be abjectly beholden to the government that had nominated them. Such grateful slavishness has not been a noticeable characteristic of justices appointed by Ottawa in the past, nor has it been the experience in other countries. Since both senators and justices are securely ensconced until 75 years of age, it is far more likely that the governments which appointed them will pass into history long before the work of the nominee is done. Moreover, as suggested above, every appointment requires federal as well as provincial approval: why should the nominee feel responsible to the nominating government alone?

It would appear even less plausible that the provinces could successfully impose a provincialist philosophy on either institution by virtue of their new power under Meech Lake. Apart from the required federal approval and the expected independence of the candidate, there are many other factors working against such a simple scenario: the wide range of political hues likely to be represented from nominations by different provincial governments over time, the socialization from participation in a national institution in Ottawa for a long time, the pool of federally appointed appeal court judges from which most court nominees will be drawn, the influence on senators from political party identification at the federal level and on justices from reviews of their work by a national legal community, and so on. Moreover, Ottawa is not obliged to accept any court nominations from provinces other than Quebec, but can pass over any unacceptable nominee by choosing a candidate put up by another province. As for the feared deadlock with Quebec—either over an *indépendantiste* nominee to the supreme court or the possible refusal of the Quebec government to advance a name—if the court in the United States has been able to live with a vacancy for up to five years, there is no reason why governments in Canada could not "sit it out" until political pressures forced the parties to an accommodation. Certainly, Quebec public opinion would not lightly countenance a vacancy in their allotted quota of three justices on the bench for very long.

If the granting of provincial nominating power does not exactly add up to "remote control" of federal institutions, neither is it likely that a post-Meech Senate would cripple Parliament. While commentators have been quick to point out that a provincially-nominated Senate might take its responsibility to defend provincial interests seriously by vetoing regionally discriminatory bills from the Commons, that guardianship role, after all, is precisely the function which it has been long said is needed. It is no answer against Meech Lake to argue that the new Senate will make governing a little more difficult for the government and the Commons; that is an unavoidable byproduct of the decision to protect the federal principle in a second chamber, as so many other federations have learned. That power will surely be exercised carefully. As Australian experience shows, even an elected Senate would be unequal to the House of Commons, where the prime minister and his colleagues sit; an appointed chamber, as envisaged under Meech Lake, would be no match under normal circumstances.

Of course it is possible, as several commentators have pointed out, for the provinces to nominate individuals who have won election in the province for that purpose and thus to confer an electoral mandate upon them. This is the route which the Getty government in Alberta is considering for its own nominees to the Senate. There may be, in fact, irresistible pressures from the public to move to election of Senators from the provinces once Meech Lake is in place; that would find Canada following the route the United States adopted in 1913. Thomas Courchene has argued that this course will be necessary

> to enhance the Senate's political acceptability among Canadians and therefore, enhance its moral authority to take on the very substantial powers it does have under the *Constitution Act, 1867*. Given that the Senate appointments are going to come from provincial lists in any event, Canadians are likely to insist that the election route (with a time limit) is preferable to some combination of federal-provincial patronage.[16]

It is, of course, exactly the latter point which critics have doubted. The lure of patronage would presumably be so strong, argued the Canada West Foundation, that hopes for a reformed and elected Senate have been set back.[17] However,

---

16 Thomas J. Courchene, "Meech Lake and Federalism: Accord or Discord?," Robarts Professor of Canadian Studies, Robarts Centre for Canadian Studies, Working Paper Series 87-F07, York University, November, 1987, 35.
17 David Elton, President of the Canada West Foundation, argued that Senate reform was "squandered" in this way, *Globe and Mail*, 2 August 1987.

the known preferences of several provinces for election, together with pressure from the public, should work against the politics of patronage.[18] Since the provision is intended as an interim measure, in any case, and the subject is the first order of business on the agenda of the required constitutional conferences, the odds for reform have probably improved.

The change in the amending formula contained in the Meech Lake agreement will make at least some parts of the "Triple E" Senate more difficult to achieve—particularly the principle of equality of representation by province.[19] Here the critics are on stronger ground in arguing that post-Meech requirements for unanimity (in place of the current general amending formula of seven provinces representing 50 per cent of the Canadian population) worsen the prospects by requiring the consent of both Quebec and Ontario for such a change. Yet none of this constitutes a serious threat to the federal-provincial balance of power.

The post-Meech limits on the spending power are often cited as the most acute threat to Ottawa's position. Much of the debate on the legal level has been preoccupied with defining the meaning of a shared-cost programme, the extent to which Ottawa can set "objectives", and how much latitude is granted to provinces who opt out with a programme "compatible ... with the national objectives." Critics are worried that the legal language is so loose that it undermines the capacity of Parliament to set up new shared-cost programmes with nationwide standards; on the political level, the incentives for opting out are so generous that, according to Al Johnson, "the bonds of nationhood are weakened."[20] Defenders of Meech Lake, countering the ideology of the nation-builders, see no problem with federal-provincial negotiation rather than unilateralism as the route to future national social policy, nor the regional or

18 Premier McKenna already supported the idea of an elected Senate. Premier Getty had brought the other western premiers into an agreement on a "Triple E" Senate—equal, elected, and effective—in the meeting of the Western premiers on 20 May 1988.

19 A "Triple E" Senate refers to one which is "Elected, Effective, and Equal", in other words, an elected senate, with substantial powers (but not necessarily coextensive with those of the House of Commons), and equal numbers from each province. See the *Strengthening Canada: Reform of Canada's Senate*, Report of the Alberta Select Special Committee on Upper House Reform, March 1985.

20 Professor A. Johnson, Department of Political Science, University of Toronto, testimony before the Joint Committee, 21 August 1987, 11:33.

provincial variations in social policy which may well arise in a post-Meech Canada. As Keith Banting has argued:

> The Accord would probably lead to greater regional differences in new social ser-
> vice programs. It would do so in two ways. First, federal authorities would likely
> seek to minimize the number of provinces choosing to opt out of a new program
> by allowing for considerable regional variation within the program. In effect, the
> Accord would nudge new initiatives towards the model of the Canada Assistance
> Plan, with a general umbrella program containing relatively few precise condi-
> tions at the national level, and the specific form of each province's program being
> negotiated separately and set out in a subsidiary bilateral agreement. Second, some
> provinces [such as Quebec] would opt out anyway.[21]

What has been often been less well recognized is the extent to which the post-Meech fiscal instruments of the federal level of government remain strong. The capacity to make payments to individuals and institutions for whatever purposes would remain unaltered; unemployment insurance and pensions continue to be constitutionally secure; tax expenditures for social purposes remain invitingly open; existing social programmes are grandfathered. Since new shared-cost programmes or initiatives will certainly entail more bargaining and complexities, it may well be that the Meech Lake agreement will encourage the federal government to move much more decisively toward direct payments and social use of the tax system. Banting concluded:

> Canadians would still look to Ottawa for leadership, social reformers among
> federal politicians would still want to respond, and income security programs
> would provide the more flexible instrument through which to reach all citizens in
> all regions directly. As a result, the proposed constitutional change would, if any-
> thing, accentuate the bifurcation of the Canadian welfare state ... with a relative-
> ly centralized system of income security and a relatively decentralized system of
> social services.[22]

In two respects, the Meech Lake agreement reinforces federal power in relation to the spending power. First, it legitimizes for the first time the right of the federal government to establish shared-cost programmes in exclusive areas of provincial jurisdiction, a matter which heretofore has been politically conten-tious, especially in Quebec. At the same time, it removes any legal doubts about the use of this federal power, establishing for the first time a clear constitution-al footing for its exercise. For this reason, many critics of Meech Lake in Quebec remain unhappy with the provision. Second, despite the fact that the

21 See Keith Banting, *The Welfare State and Canadian Federalism*, 2nd edition
     (Kingston and Montreal: McGill- Queen's University Press, 1987), pp. 197-200.
22 Ibid, p. 200.

Quebec government had set as one of its five conditions that seven provinces representing 50 per cent of the Canadian population must approve the initiation of new federal programmes in provincial areas of jurisdiction, this condition was not accepted. There is no restriction on the initiation of new federal shared-cost programmes. This result is certainly much less confining than several alternatives advanced both by the federal and provincial governments over recent decades.

On balance, in my view, the centralist lament is overdone. Although the implications of endless first ministers' conferences on the constitution are disturbing, in this round at least, the federal level of government has not fatally upset the federal-provincial equilibrium. However, the scorecard on linguistic policy and bilingualism, the charter, Northern peoples and democratic rights is hardly inspiring.

SIX

La signification de l'Accord du lac Meech au Canada anglais et au Québec francophone: un tour d'horizon du débat public[1]

Denis Robert

English Canada and Francophone Quebec have offered distinctly opposing views to the Meech Lake Accord.

In English Canada, those who support a more centralized federation have dominated the public debate, and interpreting the Accord as a major concession to the provinces, particularly to Quebec. The debate has revolved largely around two major points: 1) the impact of the Accord on Canadian unity; and 2) the impact of the Accord on individual rights and freedoms.

In Francophone Quebec, the debate has centred upon the twin dynamics of decentralization and provincial autonomy. The central question has been whether or not the Accord can recoup the losses suffered under the repatriation of 1982, thereby allowing Quebec to flourish linguistically and culturally. By and large, the Accord has been considered an irreducible minimum (minimum vital) below which Quebec could not agree to the Constitutional Act, 1982.

Within Quebec the Accord's distinct society clause has been another major point of discussion. The major concerns have been whether the clause should be defined in a highly specific manner that would guarantee the French character of Quebec or whether it should be left suitably vague so that its interpretation by the courts might be as broad as possible. The precedence of the distinct society clause on Canadian duality and on the Charter of Rights and Freedoms has also been included in the debate.

In conclusion, the author argues that the differing interpretations of the Accord in each community can be explained by three principal factors: 1) the different meaning and symbolism of the Charter in English Canada and in Francophone Quebec; 2) the different perception of provincial governments and their role; and 3) the way each community evaluates the consequences of a failure to implement the Accord.

---

1 L'auteur tient à remercier le professeur Jean-Pierre Gaboury pour ses commentaires sur une première version de ce texte.

Si le Québec a encore une fois l'impression qu'il est plus difficile d'entrer dans la Confédération canadienne que de demeurer à l'écart, vous savez fort bien que cela ne pourra mener qu'à une autre forme d'indépendance, cette fois non pas choisie par un parti politique québécois, mais peut-être choisie et imposée au Québec de l'extérieur.

Solange Chaput-Rolland

INTRODUCTION

Les débats publics qui ont eu lieu au Canada anglais et au Québec francophone sur l'Accord du lac Meech évoquent immanquablement l'image des deux solitudes. Bien que différentes tendances aient été exprimées au sein de chacune de ces communautés, il n'en demeure pas moins qu'une certaine dynamique prédomina d'un côté comme de l'autre. Il transcende de ces débats publics une vision diamétralement opposée du fédéralisme canadien et du rôle des gouvernements provinciaux.

Au Canada anglais, ce sont les adeptes du fédéralisme centralisé (en bonne partie défendu par les artisans du rapatriement de 1982, mais également par certains intellectuels regroupés au sein de la Coalition canadienne sur la Constitution) qui donnèrent le ton au débat public. L'Accord fut en effet décrié comme portant atteinte à l'unité et au caractère national du Canada, de même qu'à la protection des droits et libertés assurés par la Charte.

A l'inverse, au Québec francophone, une dynamique unanimement décentralisatrice et autonomiste marqua le débat public. On évalua l'Accord du lac Meech en fonction de la "marge de manoeuvre" que le Québec est susceptible d'en retirer. Dans le contexte actuel, l'Accord apparut comme un minimum vital. Les appréhensions face à un échec de l'Accord ont amené plusieurs observateurs québécois à le soutenir en dépit de son caractère minimal (en comparaison avec les demandes historiques des différents gouvernements du Québec). On craint en effet qu'un second échec constitutionnel ne ravive le sentiment indépendantiste.

Le présent chapitre se propose donc de passer en revue et de regrouper les différents arguments et analyses émis sur l'Accord du lac Meech au Canada anglais et au Québec francophone.[2]

2　Les sources proviennent principalement des articles écrits par différents commentateurs et experts, de même que de documents officiels (témoignages devant les commissions parlementaires d'Ottawa et de Québec, rapports, etc.).

LE DEBAT AU CANADA ANGLAIS: UNE CONCESSION MAJEURE

> Accommodation with Quebec must not be achieved at the cost of grievous damage to the federation's central institutions of government such that Canada could no longer function effectively as a viable nation-state providing a reasonable measure of justice, security and well-being for all its citizens.[3]

C'est en fonction de ce critère qu'on évalua l'Accord du lac Meech au Canada anglais. Un groupe restreint d'analystes et d'experts, avec en tête le gouvernement fédéral, jugèrent l'Accord (malgré ses imperfections) d'un prix acceptable pour l'adhésion du Québec à la *Loi constitutionnelle de 1982*. Certains parmi ceux-ci supportèrent même l'Accord pour ses valeurs intrinsèques et la vision qu'il dégage du fédéralisme canadien.[4]

Cependant, ceux qui s'opposent catégoriquement à l'Accord ou qui en désirent des modifications immédiates se firent entendre avec le plus de vigueur et donnèrent le ton à la discussion publique. Selon ce courant d'opinion l'Accord affecte d'autres aspects fondamentaux du fédéralisme canadien, à tel point que la simple réintégration du Québec dans la Constitution ne saurait le justifier. D'ailleurs pour plusieurs d'entre eux le Québec est bel et bien lié à la Constitution et aborder l'Accord du lac Meech en ces termes nie la représentativité des députés fédéraux du Québec:

> ... j'estime que le Québec n'a pas été mis en dehors de la Constitution, du moins du point de vue du droit. Or, s'il n'était question que de droit, nous serions dans une situation très difficile.
>
> Si je ne me trompe pas, le Premier ministre qui n'a pas voulu que le Québec fasse partie du Canada lors de la dernière ronde de négociations était un Premier ministre voué à la cause séparatiste. J'ai du mal à admettre qu'un Premier ministre qui s'est engagé à faire sortir le Québec de la Confédération soit moralement habilité à déclarer que le Québec ne fait pas partie de la Confédération ou encore n'est pas visé par un document constitutionnel qu'il n'a pas signé. Cela me semble une contradiction absolue.
>
> Si je me souviens bien du vote qui a eu lieu en 1982, la majorité des députés québécois au Parlement ont voté en faveur de la Constitution.... Ne me dites pas

---

3   Russell, Peter H., *Comments on the Supreme Court Proposals*, Texte présenté lors du colloque sur l'Accord du lac Meech à l'Université de Toronto, le 30 octobre 1987, p.1.

4   Courchene, Thomas J., *Meech Lake and Federalism: Accord or Discord?*, Texte présenté lors du colloque sur l'Accord du lac Meech à l'Université de Toronto, le 30 octobre 1987, p.1.

que la majorité des députés québécois au Parlement fédéral ne représentaient pas les intérêts du Québec lorsqu'ils ont voté en faveur de la Constitution...[5]

De ce point de vue, l'Accord du lac Meech est superfétatoire car le Québec fait partie de la Constitution et sa place à l'intérieur de la fédération fut réglée lors du référendum de 1980. Cette opinion, cependant, non seulement fait peu de cas de la sensibilité des Québécois à l'égard de leur exclusion du processus constitutionnel de 1982, et du vote unanime de l'Assemblée nationale sur cette question, mais elle ignore les conséquences néfastes d'un refus constant du Québec de participer à l'évolution constitutionnelle du pays (en fait, le Québec acquerrait ainsi une légitimité vis-à-vis sa population pour perturber la dynamique constitutionnelle canadienne). A cet égard, l'échec des négociations constitutionnelles sur les droits des peuples autochtones démontre de manière éclatante que "l'absence" du Québec a tout de même des conséquences politiques considérables.

Les premières critiques de l'Accord au Canada anglais portèrent sur le processus menant à l'entente de principe du lac Meech, puis à l'accord constitutionnel de l'édifice Langevin, un mois plus tard. La Coalition canadienne sur la Constitution mentionne à ce sujet:

> Constitution and constitutional change are not just affairs of governments and of first ministers. They are NOT about power plays among 11 self-interested politicians sitting around a bargaining table in isolated, hot-house conditions.[6]

On critique le caractère secret des négociations du début à la fin; on estime que les premiers ministres n'avaient aucun mandat pour réaliser ce changement et on souligne que la population ne fut aucunement consultée. A leurs yeux une telle démarche enlève toute légitimité au texte de l'Accord. En fait, on décèle derrière ces récriminations une frustation plus prosaïque d'assister, sans pouvoir intervenir, à un changement constitutionnel majeur modifiant les données de 1982, auxquelles ils s'identifient pour différentes raisons. En fin de compte, c'est l'enjeu et non le processus qui leur fait problème; c'est d'ailleurs pourquoi le processus nocturne de 1981 ne fut guère critiqué par ces mêmes intervenants.

Ce sentiment de frustration illustre toutefois une nouvelle attitude vis-à-vis le processus de changement constitutionnel au sein de la communauté

---

5   Danson, Timothy, *Procès-verbaux et témoignages du Comité mixte spécial du Sénat et de la Chambre des communes sur l'Entente constitutionnelle de 1987*, Ottawa, Imprimeur de la Reine, mercredi 12 août 1987, fascicule no. 6, p.37.

6   Cité *in* Winsor, Hugh, "Any Debate on Constitution Now Just Exercise in Frustration", *Globe and Mail*, 29 June 1987, p.A2.

anglophone. En effet, les négociations constitutionnelles de 1980 à 1982, particulièrement celles qui menèrent à l'enchâssement d'une Charte des droits, entraînèrent la participation de plusieurs groupes alors qu'autrefois les affaires constitutionnelles étaient l'apanage des seuls gouvernements.

De ce fait, la Constitution prit une importance considérable pour certains groupes (femmes, autochtones, minorités ethniques et linguistiques, etc.), car la Charte sanctionne leur statut et leurs droits au sein de la société canadienne. Outre la protection des droits et des libertés individuels, la Charte, par ses effets uniformisateurs et centralisateurs, constitue également un instrument destiné à renforcer l'unité et l'identité canadiennes.

De cette façon, la Charte devint rapidement, au Canada anglais, un symbol sacré devant assurer à la fois l'épanouissement des droits individuels et le développement de l'unité et du caractère national canadiens. Dans ce contexte, l'Accord du lac Meech, en modifiant l'interprétation de la Charte, devint un acte profanateur pour certains groupes d'intérêt et pour les défenseurs d'une vision centralisatrice de la fédération.

Ainsi, le débat public au Canada anglais s'est articulé autour de deux axes majeurs: A) l'Accord et son impact sur l'unité canadienne; et B) l'Accord et son impact sur les droits et libertés individuels.

A) L'ACCORD DU LAC MEECH ET SON IMPACT SUR L'UNITE CANADIENNE

Pour la majorité des commentateurs et des observateurs anglo-canadiens l'Accord du lac Meech, que ce soit dans son économie générale ou en rapport avec chacun de ses articles, constitue une entrave, sinon un frein, à l'unification et au développement de la communauté canadienne.

Une idée générale en deux volets sous-tend cette assertion. D'une part, l'Accord du lac Meech diminue les pouvoirs du gouvernement central dans des domaines jugés cruciaux pour le maintien et le développement du sentiment d'appartenance nationale. D'autre part, il mine les effets intégrateurs de la Charte des droits et libertés. En d'autres termes, l'Accord du lac Meech se trouve à renverser le processus de *nation building* en cours depuis les années 1970, et dont la Charte en constitue l'instrument de changement idéologique et social par excellence.

Pour les tenants de cette thèse, toutes les dispositions de l'Accord du lac Meech, individuellement ou conjointement, concourent à cet effet. Nous analyserons donc l'argumentation développée à partir de chacun des articles de l'Accord.

1) Québec, société distincte

Pour plusieurs, le fait de reconnaître dans la Constitution le Québec comme
étant une société distincte, même "au sein du Canada", renferme *ipso facto* les
germes du séparatisme. Quelques-uns vont même jusqu'à soutenir qu'il s'agit
là d'un non-sens:

> Quebec is not, however as Meech Lake will have the Constitution declare, a "distinct society", even "within Canada". Rather Quebec is an integral (though distinctive) part of Canadian, North American and western society.[7]

Cependant la discussion publique s'est surtout attardée à monter en épingle les
effets corrosifs possibles (et probables selon eux) de cet article sur l'un des objectifs essentiels de la Charte; objectif que le professeur Allan Cairns décrit
ainsi:

> ... the Charter was an attempt to enhance and extend the meaning of being Canadian and thus to strengthen identification with the national community on which Ottawa ultimately depends for support.... The consequence, and a very clear purpose was to set limits to the diversities of treatment by provincial governments, and thus to strengthen Canadian as against provincial identities.[8]

Or, selon une majorité d'intervenants au Canada anglais, l'Accord du lac
Meech, en stipulant que la Constitution (y compris la Charte) devra être interprétée en fonction du caractère distinct (non défini) du Québec—que le gouvernement a le rôle de protéger et de promouvoir—, permettra à ce dernier, à l'aide
de surenchère juridique, d'étendre le plus possible la signification de son
caractère distinct et d'accroître ses pouvoirs législatifs. L'ex-sénateur Eugene
Forsey résume ce point de vue en ces termes:

> The "distinct society" principle could override, for Quebec, everything in the Charter except multiculturalism and the rights of the aborigines.... The "distinct society" principle could also override everything in the Constitution except multiculturalism and the rights of the aborigines. The courts might decide that it gave Quebec power to legislate on broadcasting, copyright, patents, bankruptcy, marriage and divorce. They might decide that the "distinct society" could invade the federal power over trade and commerce, interprovincial and international

---

7   Scott, Stephen A., "Ghost of Maurice Duplessis Haunts Meech Lake", *The Gazette*,
    1 June 1987, p. B2.
8   Cairns, Allan, "Recent Federalist Constitutional Proposals: A Review Essay",
    Canadian Public Policy, vol.V, no.3, (Summer 1979), p. 354.

transport, telephones, works for the general advantage of Canada, the criminal law.[9]

Ce faisant, le Québec évoluera en parallèle, sinon en contradiction, avec le reste du Canada. En permettant ainsi au Québec d'échapper à certains effets "homogénéisateurs" de la Charte, l'Accord du lac Meech concrétise, aux yeux de la majorité des intervenants anglo-canadiens, sinon le principe des deux nations, à coup sûr celui du statut particulier.

De plus, en assignant au Québec un rôle différent (celui de protéger et de promouvoir son caractère distinct) de celui du reste du Canada (de protéger la dualité canadienne), on impose à l'un et à l'autre des objectifs sociétaux différents,[10] et on entrave la promotion du bilinguisme au niveau national[11] (qui constitue l'un des piliers du *nation building*).

Il en découle de cette interprétation de l'article sur la société distincte (qui est d'ailleurs fort différente de celle de plusieurs analystes québécois), que la Charte ne pourra plus jouer pleinement son rôle unificateur et uniformisateur, et que le Québec acquerra de nouveaux pouvoirs et évoluera dans une direction différente de celle du reste du pays. A plus ou moins longue échéance, estime-t-on, l'action et l'influence du gouvernement fédéral au Québec s'amenuiseront au point où le Québec atteindra, *de facto*, le statut de souveraineté-association: "Après cet assaut sur les pouvoirs fédéraux, on pourrait bien arriver à une espèce de souveraineté-association à l'intérieur du pays sans que la province se déclare indépendante! On aura un Etat dans un Etat!"[12] Afin d'éviter pareil aboutissement on propose de définir précisément le concept de société distincte et de stipuler clairement la préséance de la Charte sur cet article.

Le gouvernement fédéral et un nombre restreint de commentateurs anglo-canadiens ont tenté de dissiper ces inquiétudes en avançant les points suivants. Tout d'abord, l'article sur la société distincte ne constitue qu'une règle d'interprétation, et en tant que tel, n'octroie aucun pouvoir nouveau. Au mieux, cet article ne sera utile que dans l'interprétation de cas ambigus ou dans les "zones grises" du partage des pouvoirs.

---

9 Forsey, Eugene, "Meech Lake Accord Does Weaken Federal Powers", *The Ottawa Citizen*, 6 August 1987, p. A9.

10 Smith, Jennifer, *Political Vision and the 1987 Constitutional Accord*, Texte présenté lors du colloque sur l'Accord du lac Meech à l'Université de Toronto, le 30 octobre 1987, p.5.

11 Whyte, John, "Submission to the Special Joint Committee of the Senate and the House of Commons on the 1987 Constitutional Accord", *Queen's Quarterly*, vol. XCIV, no.4, (Winter 1987), pp. 798-799.

12 Johnston, Donald, "Un accord qui risque de transformer le pays", *La Presse*, 22 juillet 1987, p. B3.

De plus, il convient de lire et d'interpréter cet article dans sa facture générale. Il spécifie que le Québec constitue une société distincte à *l'intérieur du Canada*, que la dualité canadienne est une *caractéristique fondamentale* du Canada (que tous les gouvernements ont pour rôle de protéger) et que le paragraphe 2(4), fixant le partage des pouvoirs dans son état actuel, rend l'acquisition de nouvelles compétences fortement hypothétique. Cela étant, son impact sera minime sur la Charte et nul sur le partage des pouvoirs. Enfin, il serait illusoire de croire que le Québec accepterait un concept de société distincte étroitement circonscrit dont tous les effets seraient prévus et encadrés à l'avance.

2) Le pouvoir de dépenser

Au Canada anglais on déplora dans l'ensemble l'article sur le pouvoir de dépenser considérant qu'il entraîne un transfert de pouvoir du fédéral vers les provinces.

Ainsi en allouant aux provinces le pouvoir de se retirer avec une juste compensation financière des nouveaux programmes à frais partagés, et en associant cette compensation à des termes aussi flous que "mesures compatibles" et "objectifs nationaux", on entrave la capacité du gouvernement fédéral d'agir dans des domaines d'intérêt national. Cet article encouragera plutôt les provinces à établir leurs propres programmes, ou encore contraindra le gouvernement fédéral à édulcorer ses objectifs de façon à obtenir la participation des provinces. Par conséquent, on rend plus difficile l'instauration de nouveaux programmes nationaux et on crée de sérieux problèmes de coordination et de transfert des différents programmes provinciaux.

La conséquence d'une telle dynamique affectera l'unité canadienne de deux façons. Premièrement, en transformant l'établissement de nouveaux programmes à frais partagés en un processus laborieux et problématique, le Canada se prive d'un instrument (programmes nationaux) qui joua par le passé un rôle fondamental dans la création d'un sentiment national, et qui assure, encore aujourd'hui, une cohérence à la communauté politique canadienne.[13] Deuxièmement, en incitant les provinces à établir leurs propres programmes sociaux, on accentue la "balkanisation sociale" du pays qui, à plus ou moins longue échéance, minera le sentiment d'appartenance à l'ensemble canadien.

Le gouvernement fédéral et les partisans de l'Accord voient naturellement tout cela différemment. Pour la première fois le pouvoir de dépenser du fédéral est reconnu constitutionnellement (auparavant il constituait un exercice

---

13 Johnson, Al, "Weakened Bonds of Nationhood", *Policy Options Politiques*, vol. IX, no.1, (January 1988).

litigieux), et la portée réelle de cet article est beaucoup plus limitée que ne le laisse entendre ses détracteurs. En effet, cinq conditions devront être respectées pour que l'article 106A, sur le pouvoir de dépenser, puisse s'appliquer:

1. il doit s'agir d'un programme national;
2. il doit s'agir d'un programme à frais partagés;
3. le programme doit être établi après l'entrée en vigueur de cet article;
4. le programme doit intervenir dans un domaine de compétence exclusive des provinces;
5. les provinces ne toucheront la "juste compensation" financière qu'à la condition qu'elles mettent en oeuvre un programme ou une initiative compatible avec les objectifs nationaux.

Cela laisse une marge de manoeuvre considérable au gouvernement fédéral pour intervenir dans l'intérêt national. De plus, lorsque le fédéral désirera intervenir dans un domaine exclusif des provinces il devra préciser ses objectifs et chaque province aura l'occasion de démontrer qu'elle peut atteindre ces objectifs d'une meilleure façon et/ou à moindre coûts.[14] En fait, le gouvernement central préserve son pouvoir d'initier de nouveaux programmes, sauf que ces nouvelles conditions l'obligent à une plus grande coopération préalable avec les provinces. Ce qui, en dernière analyse, constitue une approche respectueuse du principe fédéraliste.

3) La Cour suprême

L'opinion dominante au Canada anglais estime que l'article traitant de la Cour suprême est une abdication d'un pouvoir du gouvernement central au profit des provinces.

En effet, en laissant aux provinces le soin de proposer les candidats à la Cour suprême, le fédéral perd son ascendant sur une institution appelée, via ses jugements sur la Charte, à jouer un rôle clé pour l'harmonisation de la société canadienne. Le professeur Peter Russell illustre cette dynamique en ces termes:

> I think the Charter's nationalizing influence will be felt most through a process scarcely mentioned by its political sponsors—the process of judicial review.... In interpreting the Charter, the Supreme Court of Canada, at the top of the judicial structure, will set uniform national standards—often in policy areas which otherwise would be subject to diverse provincial standards.... Policy directives flowing

14 Leslie, Peter M., "Meech Lake Accord Good for Both Sides", *Financial Post*, 18 May 1987, p.6.

from the Supreme Court decisions on the Charter are transmitted through a single hierarchy of appeals that binds all the courts in the land, and shapes the rights of all Canadians and the powers of all who govern.[15]

On craint justement qu'une Cour suprême constituée de juges provenant de listes provinciales soit partiale, et interprète la Charte d'une façon contraire à son esprit, soit le renforcement du caractère national canadien.

Cependant, comme l'a souligné le gouvernement fédéral et certains autres observateurs, nul ne peut prédire avec exactitude l'orientation idéologique des futurs juges de la Cour suprême, qu'ils soient nommés par le fédéral ou conjointement avec les provinces. En outre, à l'exception du Québec, le fédéral pourra toujours refuser la liste d'une province et se tourner vers une autre liste si, dans le premier cas, aucune candidature ne lui agrée. Ainsi, croit-on, cette émulation incitera les provinces à sélectionner méticuleusement leurs candidats afin d'obtenir la faveur d'Ottawa. Ce point de vue, toutefois, ne fut partagé que par un nombre réduit d'observateurs.

4) Le Sénat

Tout comme l'article sur la Cour suprême, celui sur le Sénat a été perçu majoritairement comme un affaiblissement du gouvernement central et un pervertissement d'une institution nationale, favorisant la fragmentation au lieu de l'unification de la communauté politique canadienne.

On estime en effet qu'un Sénat formé de gens proposés par les premiers ministres provinciaux ne représentera pas la "nation", mais plutôt les intérêts divergents et concurrentiels des provinces. Cela en fera, allègue-t-on, une institution anarchique, où les minorités seront sous-représentées. En outre, un tel Sénat porterait un coup certain au pouvoir législatif de la Chambre des communes. Il n'hésiterait pas, comme le soutient l'ancien premier ministre Pierre Trudeau, à refuser d'entériner toute mesure législative de la Chambre basse qui ne lui plairait pas (ou qui ne plairait pas à certaines provinces). En somme, le Parlement national deviendrait l'otage des gouvernements provinciaux.

A leur avis, ce type de Sénat perdurera, bien que sa réforme soit maintenant à l'ordre du jour constitutionnel. Ce raisonnement s'appuie sur deux considérations. D'une part, les premiers ministres provinciaux auront tôt fait de s'enticher de ce nouveau pouvoir et ne voudront s'en départir par la suite. D'autre part, la règle de l'unanimité s'appliquant désormais à toute réforme du Sénat, il sera loisible à chaque province de bloquer la moindre tentative de le modifier; on

15 Russell, Peter H., *op. cit.*, pp.40-41.

pense en particulier à l'Ontario et au Québec qui n'accepteront pas facilement une perte d'influence au sein de cette institution.

On objecta à cette conception d'un Sénat assujetti aux provinces, que le mode de nomination en cause, selon lequel les provinces soumettent des candidatures et le fédéral sélectionne en dernière instance, implique, *de facto*, une nomination partagée. Les deux niveaux de gouvernement devront y concourir, de sorte que ni l'un ni l'autre ne pourra asservir le Sénat.

5) *L'immigration*

L'article relatif à l'immigration apparaît à plusieurs au Canada anglais comme un autre exemple d'abandon par le féderal d'un pouvoir intimement lié à l'unité canadienne et au développement du caractère national. Le professeur Stephen A. Scott mentionne à ce sujet:

> But Canada will, it seems, lose final power to admit, without provincial permission, a student, refugee or other immigrant to Canada unless it forces the immigrant to come to a province which waives its powers, or to the Yukon or Northwest Territories (so long as they are not provinces). To me, this demeans and degrades the federal government, and even puts in question our national existence as one country. Moreover, by accepting the principle of a province's control of its demographic character, it opens the door to demands, sooner or later, for provincial power to erect barriers to free movement within the federation, and even for independence if that is refused.[16]

Dans le même ordre d'idées, certains, dont l'ancien premier ministre Pierre Trudeau, craignent que le transfert des responsabilités d'intégration culturelle et linguistique du fédéral aux provinces ne résulte en une "balkanisation des langues et des cultures" au Canada. En fait, on redoute que le noyau de valeurs communes sur lequel repose le pays ne soit compromis en laissant à chaque province la formation des nouveaux arrivants.

Enfin, on exprima d'autres craintes d'une nature plus technique. Ainsi, si le Québec ne peut atteindre le nombre d'immigrants qui lui est assigné, on pourrait restreindre le nombre d'immigrants autorisés à s'établir ailleurs au pays. Ou encore, on peut prévoir des politiques racistes, ou à tout le moins basées sur des critères raciaux si on laisse un tel pouvoir entre les mains des provinces.[17] En outre les pressions pour limiter la liberté de circulation s'intensifieront car,

16 Scott, Stephen A., *op. cit.*.
17 Coyne, Deborah, *The Meech Lake Accord: Fundamentally Flawed*, Texte préparé pour la Coalition canadienne sur la Constitution, juin 1987, p.13.

sans cela, toute politique d'immigration des provinces ne reposerait que sur la bonne volonté des immigrants d'y demeurer.

Pour d'autres, par contre, ces craintes sont injustifiées. Tout d'abord, dans les ententes précédentes sur l'immigration entre le fédéral et le Québec, ce dernier n'a jamais réussi à atteindre ses quotas ce qui n'a affecté en rien ceux des autres provinces. Ensuite, le libellé de l'article sur l'immigration stipule clairement que la Charte s'applique à toute entente sur l'immigration, donc que la liberté de circulation est assurée; et que le fédéral est en droit de garantir que les services de réception et d'intégration des immigrants au Québec (ou dans les autres provinces) soient conformes à une vision nationale canadienne:

> The federal government must decide for itself what services are appropriate; to the extent that those services are provided by Quebec, it is obliged to withdraw. But to the extent that Quebec has failed to provide those services, the federal government retains the right to deliver them directly. If the government of Canada considers that immigrants ought to be offered the opportunity to learn English as well as French, and the government of Quebec fails to provide such services— then the federal government should consider itself free to offer its own courses.[18]

6) La formule de modification

La formule de modification constitutionnelle issue de l'Accord du lac Meech modifie deux aspects de la formule de 1982. Tout d'abord, elle étend la règle de l'unanimité pour toute modification s'appliquant à l'article 42 de la *Loi constitutionnelle de 1982* (auparavant seul l'article 41 était sujet à la règle de l'unanimité). De cette façon, avec l'Accord du lac Meech, chaque province obtient un droit de veto en ce qui regarde "la représentation proportionnelle des provinces à la Chambre des communes, les pouvoirs du Sénat et le mode de sélection des sénateurs, la répartition des sénateurs selon les provinces et les conditions de résidence qu'ils doivent remplir, la Cour suprême du Canada (à l'exception de sa composition), le rattachement aux provinces existantes de tout ou partie des territoires et la création de nouvelles provinces". Ensuite, elle garantit aux provinces se retirant d'une modification constitutionnelle transférant des compétences législatives provinciales exclusives au Parlement fédéral, le droit à une "juste compensation" financière (auparavant seuls les domaines de l'éducation et de la culture étaient sujets à compensation).

D'aucuns soutiennent que ces changements à la formule de modification constitutionnelle introduisent un élément de rigidité et une incitation à la

---

18 Schwartz, Bryan, *Fathoming Meech Lake*, Winnipeg, Legal Research Institute of the University of Manitoba, 1987, p.145.

"balkanisation". Leurs craintes portent principalement sur le fait que dorénavant la Constitution et les institutions nationales (surtout la réforme du Sénat), à cause du veto de chaque province, ne pourront se conformer au rythme de l'évolution de la société canadienne. Outre la réforme du Sénat, la création de nouvelles provinces représente également un changement que cette formule rend des plus problématiques. D'autres vont encore plus loin en affirmant qu'une telle formule de modification permettra aux provinces d'utiliser leur droit de veto pour faire du chantage et de la paralysie au plan politique.[19]

De plus, en assurant aux provinces une compensation financière en cas de retrait d'un transfert de leurs pouvoirs vers le fédéral, on gêne le gouvernement central dans l'élaboration de solutions nationales aux défis qui se posent à l'échelle du pays et qui mettent en jeu la compétitivité et l'intégrité du Canada sur la scène internationale. La nouvelle formule incitera donc les provinces à se retirer et à mettre en place leurs propres solutions touchant des problèmes ayant une "dimension nationale". Là encore on assiste à une balkanisation et à un morcellement de la communauté politique canadienne.

Le ministre Lowell Murray a répondu à ces craintes en soutenant que, eu égard au principe reconnu de l'égalité des provinces, la seule façon d'octroyer un droit de veto au Québec (une de ses cinq demandes fondamentales) était de l'accorder à toutes les provinces.[20] En outre, les questions touchées par la nouvelle règle de l'unanimité (réforme du Sénat et création de nouvelles provinces) et celles relatives aux transferts de compétences sont somme toute restreintes, et elles auraient été tout aussi difficiles à résoudre avec la règle du 7/50 qu'avec celle de l'unanimité. Une formule de modification qui respecte l'égalité des provinces et assure une protection efficace aux revendications du Québec, constitue un élement positif pour l'unité du pays.

B) L'ACCORD DU LAC MEECH ET LES DROITS INDIVIDUELS

L'impact de l'Accord du lac Meech sur la Charte des droits et libertés est le second thème qui domina le débat public au Canada anglais. Certains groupes (femmes, groupes multiculturels, minorité anglo-québécoise) s'élevèrent avec véhémence contre certaines dispositions de l'Accord qui, croient-ils, permettra aux gouvernements (particulièrement celui du Québec) d'outrepasser certaines

---

19 Coyne, Deborah, *op. cit.*, p.6.
20 Murray, Lowell, "Le baroud d'honneur de M. Trudeau; la tranquille audace des artisans de paix n'est pas moins nécessaire à un pays que le panache des guerriers", *Le Devoir*, 30 mai 1987, p.A11.

prescriptions de la Charte et de bafouer ainsi leurs droits et libertés constitutionnels, tels qu'exprimés en 1982.

Pour plusieurs parmi ces groupes, l'enchâssement d'une Charte des droits et
libertés dans la Constitution fut l'aboutissement d'une lutte épique pour la
reconnaissance de leurs droits. A la suite de leur victoire de 1982, ces groupes
développèrent un attachement particulier à la Charte qui, en fait, leur procure
plus qu'une simple protection de leurs droits:

> What it [the Charter] did, rather, was to give them an important and potentially
> powerful tool for pursuing their visions of Canadian society, whether through lob-
> bying for change to existing and proposed legislation said to violate the Charter,
> or through litigation.[21]

Or à leurs yeux l'Accord du lac Meech constitue non seulement un retour
inacceptable à une tradition constitutionnelle qu'ils croyaient périmée (à savoir
l'exclusion des groupes d'intérêt du processus de modification
constitutionnelle), mais également un recul par rapport aux droits et libertés
acquis de haute lutte en 1982. Comme chacun de ces groupes a exprimé des
doléances particulières à propos de l'Accord, nous les examinerons séparément.

1) Les groupes de défense des droits de la femme

C'est avec l'introduction de l'article 16, lors des négociations de l'édifice Langevin, que les groupes de défense des droits de la femme virent poindre une
menace au principe de l'égalité des sexes, tel que reconnu et protégé dans la
Charte des droits et libertés.

L'article 16 de l'Accord stipule que la protection de la dualité canadienne et
la promotion du caractère distinct de la société québécoise ne pourront se faire
au détriment des droits reconnus au multiculturalisme et aux peuples autochtones.[22] Ces groupes de défense des droits de la femme estiment donc que
l'absence de référence relative aux femmes dans l'article 16 de l'Accord,
autorisera le Québec à promouvoir son caractère distinct aux dépens de leurs
droits. Par exemple, en mettant sur pied des politiques natalistes affectant le
libre choix de la reproduction, les services de garderie, etc.

---

21 Swinton, Katherine, *Competing Visions of Constitutionalism: of Federalism and
    rights*, Texte présenté lors du colloque sur l'Accord du lac Meech à l'Université de
    Toronto, le 30 octobre 1987, p.5.
22 L'article 16 se lit comme suit: L'article 2 de la *Loi constitutionnelle de 1867* n'a pas
    pour effet de porter atteinte aux articles 25 au 27 de la *Charte canadienne des droits
    et libertés*, à l'article 35 de la *Loi constitutionnelle de 1982* ou au point 24 de l'article
    91 de la *Loi constitutionnelle de 1867*.

Leur raisonnement repose sur la règle de droit selon laquelle ce qui n'est pas nommé est exclu (*expressio unius est exclusio alterius*). Il appert donc que l'interprétation de l'article 16 de l'Accord ne saurait tenir compte de l'égalité des sexes puisqu'il n'y est pas mentionné. Cela aura pour effet de créer une hiérarchie de droits. Les représentantes de ces groupes recommandent ainsi que toutes les dispositions de l'Accord (société distincte et dualité canadienne, programmes à frais partagés, etc.) soient soumises aux articles 15 et 28 (sur l'égalité des sexes) de la Charte, ou encore que la Charte ait préséance dans son intégralité sur l'ensemble de l'Accord du lac Meech.

Il est à noter que les groupes féminins qui ont avancé pareille interprétation de l'article 16 sont des groupes pancanadiens (Conseil consultatif canadien sur la situation de la femme, l'Association nationale de la femme et le droit, Comité canadien d'action sur le statut de la femme, Comité ad hoc des femmes sur la constitution, etc.). Au Québec, en revanche, les groupes de défense des droits de la femme, tels que la Fédération des femmes du Québec ou le Conseil québécois du statut de la femme, bien que partageant plusieurs de leurs préoccupations, ne constatent aucunement que le caractère distinct du Québec, et le rôle du gouvernement québécois de le promouvoir, soit une menace au principe de l'égalité des sexes. D'ailleurs, certains commentateurs québécois s'interrogent sur la pertinence de ces allégations et doutent de leur sincérité. Ainsi, Paul-André Comeau, rédacteur en chef du journal *Le Devoir*, mentionnait dans un éditorial: "En filigrane dans cette démonstration, on devine les vieilles rangaines contre le Québec des années de noirceur."[23] Et Lysiane Gagnon, de renchérir:

> Qu'y a-t-il donc au fond de cette sollicitude non-sollicitée? Serait-ce par hasard une façon détournée et, pour tout dire, aimablement hypocrite, de s'attaquer à la clause du caractère distinct du Québec tout simplement parce qu'on est contre cette reconnaissance-là, qu'on veut un pays homogène mais qu'on n'ose pas le dire carrément?[24]

D'autres experts en droit constitutionnel ont, quant à eux, contesté directement l'usage que font ces groupes féminins de la règle ci-haut mentionnée: *expressio unius est exclusio alterius*. Notamment, le professeur William R. Lederman:

> ... that is a common sense maxim [*expressio unius...*] about how to read language in appropriate contexts.... But the context of Section 16 is not appropriate for the application of the so-called "expressio unius" rule. The proposed Section 16 is

---

23 Comeau, Paul-André, "Hasard et réalisme", *Le Devoir*, 24 août 1987, p.6.
24 Gagnon, Lysiane, "Une sollicitude suspecte", *La Presse*, 18 août 1987, p. B3.

purely declaratory (i.e. repetitive) and nothing more, respecting the other constitutional rules to which it refers (aboriginal rights and multiculturalism). In other
words, Section 16 is superfluous.[25]

Le jugement rendu par la Cour suprême le 25 juin 1987 à propos de la loi 30
sur le financement des écoles séparées de l'Ontario fit également naître de
nouvelles craintes chez ces groupes. Ce jugement indique que l'article 93 de la
Loi constitutionnelle de 1867, étant donné qu'il constitue un "compromis de la
Confédération", a préséance sur la Charte des droits et libertés, car sa mise en
oeuvre l'oblige à contrevenir à certaines des dispositions de la Charte (liberté
de culte et droit à l'égalité et un traitement égal devant la loi).

Ils arguèrent que l'article sur la société distincte et la dualité canadienne, qui
deviendra l'article 2 de la *Loi constitutionnelle de 1867*, pourra éventuellement
être considéré comme étant "un compromis de la Confédération" et en
conséquence les lois en découlant seront imperméables aux effets de la Charte.

Ces craintes et opinions émis par les groupes de défense des droits de la
femme (qui donnèrent le ton aux délibérations du comité mixte spécial du Sénat
et de la Chambre des communes sur l'Entente constitutionnelle de 1987)
forcèrent le gouvernement fédéral et les autres partisans de l'Accord à atténuer
ces critiques. Selon eux, l'article sur la société distincte et la dualité canadienne
ne pourra avoir les effets envisagés par ces groupes, puisque la Charte ne peut
en aucune façon être outrepassée par des règles interprétatives telles que celle
de la dualité canadienne et celle de la société distincte. Et en tant que règles
d'interprétation celles-ci ne confèrent aucun pouvoir législatif nouveau à
quelque gouvernement que ce soit, comme l'explique le professeur Peter Hogg:

> Even if the linguistic dualism and distinct society clauses were grants of power
> (which they are not), they are not grants that are inherently discriminatory or other-
> wise in opposition to any Charter right, and therefore they would have to be ex-
> ercised in compliance with the Charter.[26]

2) Les communautés culturelles

Les groupes représentant les différentes communautés culturelles du Canada
ont également exprimé des craintes concernant une possible réduction de leurs

25 Lederman, William R., "Put Constitutional Accord in Context", *The Financial Post*,
    31 August 1987, p.10.
26 Hogg, Peter W., *Meech Lake Constitutional Accord Annotated*, Toronto, Carswell,
    1988, pp.15-16.

droits et libertés, de même qu'une diminution de leur représentativité au sein de la société canadienne.

Dans un premier temps, leurs critiques portent sur la description qui est faite du Canada. Ils dénoncent en effet que la caractéristique fondamentale du Canada soit définie en termes linguistiques se rattachant seulement au français et à l'anglais. Cela laisse les Canadiens provenant d'un héritage linguistique autre sans aucun statut constitutionnel: "... le bilinguisme n'englobe pas tous les Canadiens."[27] A cet effet, ils recommandent unanimement de reconnaître le caractère multiculturel du Canada comme une caractéristique fondamentale, au même titre que la dualité linguistique.

Ils considèrent en outre que le libellé de l'article sur la société distincte et la dualité canadienne établit une hiérarchie de droits et de principes constitutionnels où la dualité canadienne et la société distincte du Québec ont préséance sur le multiculturalisme. D'après eux, l'article 16 de l'Accord ne représente pas une protection adéquate.[28]

Ils soulignent que le droit à l'égalité protégé par la Charte ne fait pas partie de ceux protégés par l'article 16, et que l'article de la Charte portant sur le multiculturalisme, bien que mentionné dans l'article 16, constitue une règle d'interprétation qui ne s'applique qu'à la Charte; alors que celle de la dualité et de la société distincte s'applique à l'ensemble de la Constitution (y compris la Charte). Il en découle, selon eux, une subordination du multiculturalisme à la dualité linguistique et au caractère distinct du Québec. Ils craignent donc que le Québec, de par ses nouvelles attributions constitutionnelles (de protéger et de promouvoir son caractère distinct), puisse en toute légitimité limiter l'épanouissement du multiculturalisme à l'intérieur de la province au profit de la culture et de la langue françaises. A l'inverse, les représentants de la Fédération des groupes ethniques du Québec soutiennent plutôt que l'Accord ne fait pas une place suffisante au caractère français du Québec:

> Dans notre optique, la mention d'une société distincte ne reflète pas suffisamment et adéquatement le visage du Québec et ne reconnaît pas formellement la spécificité du Québec.... Nous croyons qu'il faudra faire ressortir dans le futur texte constitutionnel, dont l'élaboration a été confiée aux juristes, la réalité fran-

---

27 Ma Lilian (Chinese Canadian National Council), *Procès-verbaux et témoignages du Comité mixte spécial du Sénat et de la Chambre des communes sur l'Entente constitutionnelle de 1987*, jeudi 13 août 1987, fascicule no.7, p.62.
28 Pour une description de l'article 16, *supra* note 22.

cophone du Québec, le fait français au Québec, la réalité française au Québec, sa langue, sa culture, ses traditions, et assurer et garantir la survie de cette spécificité.[29]

Enfin, l'autonomie plus grande des provinces en matière d'immigration leur fait craindre l'élaboration de politiques disparates d'une province à l'autre, ce qui pourrait avoir pour effet de rendre l'immigration et le regroupement des familles plus difficiles.

3) La minorité anglo-québécoise

L'article de l'Accord décrivant la dualité canadienne et reconnaissant le Québec comme une société distincte fut le plus pris à partie par les commentateurs Anglo-Québécois.

Tout d'abord, la formulation de l'article sur la dualité canadienne, quoique reconnaissant formellement la communauté anglophone du Québec comme une caractéristique fondamentale du Canada, n'est guère appréciée par le groupe Alliance-Québec, principal porte-parole de cette communauté. Ce dernier soutient qu'elle ne reconnaît pas l'historicité de leur présence au Québec: "Nous ne sommes pas un prolongement ou une intrusion du Canada anglais au Québec. Nous sommes une partie intégrante de la société québécoise et de son histoire."[30]

Mais, chose plus importante, cet article est surtout dénoncé en raison du peu d'effet qu'il aura pour les minorités linguistiques. C'est-à-dire que le rôle des gouvernements fédéral et provinciaux de protéger la dualité canadienne est, à leur avis, nettement insuffisant. C'est pourquoi Alliance-Québec, lors de sa comparution devant la commission de l'Assemblée nationale, a recommandé qu'à ce rôle de protéger soit adjoint celui de promouvoir la dualité canadienne.

Toutefois, le principal objet de préoccupation de la minorité anglophone au Québec porte sur l'impact qu'aura l'article reconnaissant le caractère distinct du Québec sur la Charte des droits et libertés. Pour cette communauté, la Charte a d'ores et déjà prouvé, par des jugements rendus à l'endroit de la loi 101, son

---

29 Bagdjian, Kevork (Président de la Fédération des groupes ethniques du Québec), *Procès-verbaux de la Commission permanente des Institutions de l'Assemblée nationale du Québec sur l'Accord du lac Meech*, mardi 12 mai 1987, pp.R 3129-R3130.

30 Goldbloom, Michael; Maldoff, Eric; et Weil, Kathleen, "Le caractère distinct n'a pas besoin d'être défini; la protection du français n'implique pas l'uniformité linguistique et culturelle", *Le Devoir*, 22 mai 1987, p.11.

efficacité à protéger certains de leurs droits linguistiques (individuels). Ils redoutent donc de voir cette efficacité de la Charte se dissoudre au profit de la promotion de la société distincte. Ce que l'ancien sénateur Eugene Forsey juge concevable sous les auspices de l'Accord du lac Meech:

> The role of preserving and promoting the distinct identity of Quebec could also mean that the government of Quebec could take administrative action, and the Quebec legislature could pass laws that would perpetuate existing restrictions on the rights of English-speaking Quebecers that would otherwise be in violation of the Canadian Charter of Rights and Freedoms.[31]

Il est à noter qu'il prend ainsi à contre-pied la position mise de l'avant par la plupart des experts québécois (francophones), à savoir que l'article sur la société distincte ne saurait prévaloir sur la Charte. Pour les commentateurs anglo-québécois, cependant, rien ne saurait justifier une telle assertion. Ils interprètent plutôt l'article sur la société distincte comme autorisant le gouvernement québécois à maintenir l'interdiction de l'anglais dans l'affichage, afin de s'acquitter de son rôle de protéger et de promouvoir le caractère distinct du Québec; ou encore à utiliser, avec une légitimité accrue, la clause dérogatoire (nonobstant) de la Charte, et suspendre ainsi certains de leurs droits fondamentaux.

En somme, leur plus grande appréhension face à cet Accord est qu'il ouvre des brèches dans leur protection constitutionnelle, les mettant ainsi à la merci du gouvernement du Québec en ce qui regarde l'exercice de certains de leurs droits fondamentaux, et au premier plan ceux touchant la langue.

Ils dénoncent par conséquent les dispositions de l'article 16 de l'Accord, qui spécifient que seuls les droits constitutionnels des peuples autochtones et des groupes multiculturels canadiens seront à l'abri de l'article sur la dualité canadienne et la reconnaissance du caractère distinct du Québec. Alliance-Québec recommande donc qu'une clause soit introduite réaffirmant la primauté de la Charte dans son entier.

En fait, peu de gens parmi la communauté anglo-québécoise ne s'opposent au statut de société distincte pour le Québec. Leur souci est plutôt de faire en sorte que l'exercice de ce caractère distinct se fasse en conformité avec la Charte des droits et libertés.

---

31 Forsey, Eugene, "Was the Price for Meech Lake Deal Intolerably Steep?", *The Gazette*, 12 May 1987, p. B3.

C) "THEMES SECONDAIRES"

En marge du débat public au Canada anglais, qui fut monopolisé par l'impact de l'Accord du lac Meech sur l'unité canadienne et sur la Charte des droits et libertés, certains autres groupes exprimèrent des inquiétudes particulières. Les principaux groupes sont les suivants: les minorités francophones, les peuples autochtones et les Territoires du Nord-Ouest et le Yukon.

1) Les minorités francophones hors Québec

L'inquiétude exprimée par les francophones hors Québec vis-à-vis l'Accord du lac Meech porte sur l'article sur la dualité canadienne. Etant donné qu'avec l'Accord les différents gouvernements n'ont pour rôle que de protéger la dualité linguistique, et non de la promouvoir, ils estiment que cela les prive d'un appui légal pour acquérir de nouveaux pouvoirs. En fait, puisqu'aucun gouvernement n'a le mandat de faire leur promotion, ils considèrent que cela les confine au *statu quo* perpétuel.

Il persiste également dans la communauté francophone hors Québec un certain sentiment d'insécurité par rapport à la dynamique que va engendrer l'Accord du lac Meech. Ainsi, certains prédisent déjà un impact fort inégal de l'Accord pour les différentes minorités francophones, suivant leur poids démographique et leur signification politique:

> Il est probable que les francophones de l'Ontario et du Nouveau-Brunswick profiteront également, même si c'est à un degré moindre [que les anglo-québécois] de cette disposition relative au principe de la dualité, dans la mesure où elle vient renforcer certains droits déjà acquis. Mais dans le cas des autres minorités francophones, dont la faiblesse numérique n'a pas permis jusqu'à présent qu'elles obtiennent de leur parlement provincial des droits véritables, on voit mal comment la reconnaissance de la dualité canadienne pourrait changer leur sort de façon significative.[32]

De plus, pour les Acadiens du Nouveau-Brunswick l'Accord du lac Meech nie leur caractère collectif. Ils en sont réduits à ne plus être que "la présence hors du Québec, de Canadiens d'expression française". Le Nouveau-Brunswick étant en outre la seule province officiellement bilingue, en vertu des articles 16 à 20 de la Charte, il semble donc anormal, pour plusieurs, que cette communauté

---

32 Woehrling, José, "Le poids juridique de la spécificité du Québec; les Anglo-Québécois pourront mieux défendre les avantages qu'ils ont déjà, mais les francophones n'obtiendront pas plus facilement les droits qu'on leur a refusés jusqu'à maintenant", *Le Devoir*, 14 mai 1987, p.11.

francophone soit traitée de la même façon que les autres à travers le pays. Ainsi, pour le constitutionnaliste Pierre Foucher, il est impérieux que l'Accord du lac Meech soit amendé, de sorte que l'égalité des deux communautés linguistiques du Nouveau-Brunswick soit reconnue dans la Constitution comme étant une caractéristique fondamentale du Nouveau-Brunswick, que les gouvernements du Canada et du Nouveau-Brunswick auraient pour rôle de protéger et de promouvoir.[33]

L'Accord du lac Meech a également révélé un autre aspect préoccupant pour les francophones hors Québec. Il a mis en évidence le fait que les intérêts des francophones du Québec, tels que perçus par leur gouvernement, ne coïncident pas toujours avec ceux des francophones à l'extérieur de cette province. De cette façon, le gouvernement du Québec a été appelé à poser des gestes et à prendre des positions qui, selon le professeur Woehrling, jouent en défaveur des francophones hors Québec:

> Ce qui est évident dès maintenant, par contre, c'est que la présence d'une distinction entre protection et promotion d'une part, l'existence de la clause générale de sauvegarde d'autre part, l'une et l'autre dues à l'insistance du Québec, réduisent énormément les avantages qui étaient susceptibles de découler de l'accord constitutionnel pour les minorités francophones.[34]

De tout cela, on craint que n'émerge un Québec distinct, de plus en plus français, à côté d'un Canada tout aussi unilatéralement anglais. Ce qui, pour les communautés francophones hors Québec, ne laisse augurer rien de bien réjouissant.

2) Les peuples autochtones

Les peuples autochtones, Amérindiens, Métis et Inuïts, perçurent l'Accord du lac Meech comme une seconde rebuffade constitutionnelle en moins de trois mois. On se rappellera qu'au mois de mars 1987, les négociations constitutionnelles concernant les droits des autochtones échouèrent lamentablement. A ce moment, Jim Sinclair, porte-parole du Ralliement national des Métis, fit figure de prophète en déclarant à la délégation québécoise qu'elle obtiendrait ce

---

33 Foucher, Pierre, "La réconciliation des majorités", *Le Matin*, 8 juin 1987, p.7.
34 Woehrling, José, "Les ambiguïtés de l'Accord d'Ottawa", *La Presse*, 16 juin 1987, p. B3.

qu'elle voudrait lors des négociations sur le Québec, puisque "they can't leave out their own". [35]

Les porte-parole des peuples autochtones voient dans cet Accord une politique de deux poids deux mesures. Alors que la majorité des premiers ministres refusèrent obstinément d'inscrire la notion de gouvernement autonome pour les Autochtones sans qu'elle ne soit définie au préalable, ils acceptèrent unanimement celle de société distincte, sans autre forme d'éclaircissement.

En outre, les leaders autochtones estiment qu'au niveau de l'interprétation future de leurs droits et de leur statut, l'Accord comporte de graves lacunes. Notamment en raison du fait que la nouvelle règle interprétative de la Constitution ne reconnaît pas leur présence comme une caractéristique fondamentale du Canada, et également parce que seul le Québec a acquis le statut de société distincte. Selon les chefs autochtones, cela est admettre implicitement qu'il n'y a pas d'autres sociétés distinctes au Canada, sinon elles auraient été spécifiquement identifiées. Ils ne voient donc rien dans l'Accord du lac Meech qui, d'un point de vue constitutionnel, leur permettrait de faire avancer leurs droits: les clauses interprétatives ayant été ciselées sur mesure pour les Canadiens d'expression française et anglaise et pour le Québec.

Le professeur Tony Hall explique cet état de choses en ces termes:

> What prevents the First Ministers from extending to native peoples the constitutional tools they require to promote actively the vitality and distinctiveness of their own society is the premiers' fear that the practice of aboriginal rights will undermine the jurisdictional basis of provincial control over natural resources.
>
> So French-speaking rights, because they can be associated with the advancement of provincial rights, are actively promoted at the same time as aboriginal rights are being denied by most of Canada's First Ministers. [36]

Le caractère décentralisateur de l'Accord fait aussi craindre aux représentants autochtones un délaissement du fédéral de ses responsabilités constitutionnelles à leur endroit. Et comme les peuples autochtones bénéficient largement des programmes socio-économiques du fédéral, ils désirent ardemment maintenir l'accès à ces programmes, malgré les retraits éventuels de leur province de résidence.

Une autre source d'inquiétude pour les Autochtones est l'élargissement de la règle de l'unanimité requise pour modifier certaines clauses de la Constitu-

---

35 Cité *in* Morriset, Jean-Maurice, "Le welfare constitutionnel; l'invocation du Québec comme berceau d'une société distincte équivaut de facto à la revendication fondamentale des Autochtones", *Le Devoir*, 6 mai 1987, p.9.

36 Hall, Tony, "First Ministers Revealed Their Biases in Accord", *Toronto Star*, 19 June 1987, p. A1.

tion. Ainsi, à leur avis, l'objectif qu'ils convoitaient d'accroître leur représentativité dans les institutions centrales, plus particulièrement au sein d'un Sénat réformé, vient de disparaître. Il en va de même pour la création de provinces dans les territoires où ils forment la majorité.

En plus, l'ajout de l'article 16 dans l'Accord constitutionnel du 2-3 juin, qui affirme que la règle interprétative (reconnaissant la dualité canadienne et la société distincte du Québec) n'a pas pour effet de porter atteinte aux droits constitutionnels déjà assurés aux Autochtones, n'a pas fait adhérer les chefs amérindiens à l'Accord. Le chef George Eramus, de l'Assemblée des premières nations, a d'ailleurs commenté cet article de la façon suivante:

> L'inclusion des dispositions générales sur le patrimoine autochtone dans cet accord, loin de répondre à nos aspirations, vient simplement tenter de contrer nos contestations devant les tribunaux.[37]

Dans l'ensemble, l'élément le plus négatif de l'Accord du lac Meech pour les Autochtones est qu'il renvoie aux calendes grecques une de leurs requêtes les plus chères, soit le droit à l'autonomie gouvernementale.

3) Le Yukon et les Territoires du Nord-Ouest

Absents lors des négociations de l'Accord constitutionnel du lac Meech, les porte-parole de ces régions ont le sentiment qu'ils seront absents encore longtemps du processus politique fédéral canadien.

L'article de l'Accord qui leur fait le plus problème est la nouvelle formule de modification qui donne un droit de veto à chaque province concernant la création de nouvelles provinces. Ainsi, sans avoir été engagés le moins du monde dans cet arrangement, les résidants du Yukon et des Territoires du Nord-Ouest voient néanmoins leurs aspirations à devenir un jour résidants de province s'évanouir, pour une période que certains n'hésitent pas à qualifier de toujours.

Les effets d'une telle perspective, c'est-à-dire demeurer territoires *ad vitam aeternam*, sont lourds de conséquences avec l'Accord du lac Meech. Par exemple, aucun résidant de ces régions ne pourra accéder à des postes de juges à la Cour suprême, puisque ceux-ci seront proposés par les gouvernements provinciaux. Pareillement, les gouvernements du Yukon et des Territoires du Nord-Ouest ne pourront participer pleinement aux conférences annuelles des premiers ministres sur la Constitution et l'économie, lesquelles sont appelées

---

37 Cité *in* Clavet, Roger, "Les autochtones s'en disent étonnés; la soudaine unanimité sur la Constitution," *Le Droit*, 5 juin 1987, p.3.

à devenir des centres décisionnels importants. C'est pourquoi les gens des territoires nordiques s'estiment, avec l'Accord du lac Meech, confiner à être des Canadiens de deuxième classe.

Les gouvernements du Yukon et des Territoires du Nord-Ouest ont donc, en désespoir de cause, fait appel à leurs Cours suprêmes respectives afin que soit modifié l'Accord du lac Meech. Ils visent à démontrer par cette manoeuvre que le gouvernement fédéral, en prenant part à l'entente, "a abusé des droits démocratiques des résidents territoriaux et de [leurs] droits selon la Charte des droits et libertés."[38] Ils désirent en outre une déclaration de leurs Cours spécifiant si leurs droits contre la discrimination, tels que protégés par la Charte, ont été respectés. Toutefois ces démarches juridiques tournèrent court puisque la Cour suprême du Canada refusa, sans expliquer sa décision, d'entendre la requête des Territoires du Nord-Ouest et du Yukon, dont ce dernier avait été, dans un premier temps, débouté par sa propre Cour d'appel.

LE DEBAT AU QUEBEC: UN MINIMUM VITAL

La majorité des experts et observateurs québécois qui ont passé l'Accord du lac Meech au crible ont évalué celui-ci à la lumière des objectifs constitutionnels historiques du Québec, et en ayant à l'esprit les pertes subies lors du rapatriement de 1982. Dans les circonstances, tenant compte de la dynamique politique et du rapport de force actuels, ils ont majoritairement jugé l'Accord comme étant un minimum vital, au-dessous duquel le Québec ne pourrait adhérer à la *Loi constitutionnelle de 1982* sans abdiquer, par la même occasion, des droits historiques fondamentaux et la foi en une culture québécoise rayonnante et distincte à l'intérieur de la fédération canadienne. Outre le Parti québécois et autres groupes indépendantistes qui, pour des raisons évidentes, comptent bien tirer profit d'un second échec constitutionnel, certains autres groupes et individus se sont opposés à l'Accord parce que celui-ci n'assurerait pas une protection linguistique suffisante pour le Québec et parce que le pouvoir de dépenser du fédéral, tel que circonscrit dans l'Accord, constitue une intrusion du fédéral dans des domaines de compétences exclusives du Québec.

Pour le Québec l'Accord constitutionnel du lac Meech avait pour principal objectif de remédier aux reculs subis lors du rapatriement de la Constitution en 1982 et d'assurer la protection et l'épanouissement (culturel, linguistique, politique et économique) de la société québécoise au sein de la fédération

---

38 Pennikett, Tony, "Le Yukon rejette l'entente du lac Meech", *Le Devoir*, 3 juin 1987, p.9.

canadienne. La discussion publique au Québec s'est déroulée exclusivement selon cette perspective.

Tout d'abord, quels étaient les reculs ou les effets de la *Loi constitutionnelle de 1982* que le Québec devait rectifier à son avantage? La perte la plus évidente était celle de son droit de veto à toute modification constitutionnelle. Non seulement s'agissait-il d'un droit historique que le Québec avait déjà utilisé par le passé (1965 et 1971), mais en plus, en raison de son déclin démographique, il lui était de la plus haute importance d'exercer un veto sur toute modification constitutionnelle touchant aux institutions centrales et à l'évolution du fédéralisme canadien.

L'Accord du lac Meech modifie à cet effet deux aspects de la formule de modification de 1982. Ainsi, le consentement unanime des gouvernements fédéral et provinciaux est maintenant requis pour toute modification s'appliquant aux articles 41 et 42 de la *Loi constitutionnelle de 1982*. De cette façon, le Québec (comme toutes les autres provinces) obtient un droit de veto en ce qui regarde, en autres, une réforme du Sénat, la Cour suprême, la création de nouvelles provinces et le principe de la représentation proportionnelle des provinces à la Chambre des communes. Ensuite, l'extension du droit de retrait des provinces avec "juste compensation" financière à toute modification constitutionnelle transférant des compétences législatives provinciales au Parlement fédéral, permet au Québec de sauvegarder ses compétences législatives et d'éviter ainsi toute centralisation abusive.

Ces changements à la formule de modification apportées par l'Accord du lac Meech, associés aux articles sur la participation des provinces aux nominations des sénateurs et des juges à la Cour suprême ont été considérés par les observateurs québécois comme rétablissant en bonne partie le veto que le Québec avait perdu en 1982, tout en lui assurant un certain contrôle sur l'évolution des structures du système fédéral.[39] Par conséquent, ces articles de l'Accord du lac Meech ne furent pas l'objet de polémiques ou de discussions controversées.

La *Charte canadienne des droits et libertés* est un autre élément du processus constitutionnel de 1982 dont le Québec espérait réorienter les effets. A cet égard nous devons souligner que la perception québécoise de la *Charte canadienne des droits et libertés* diffère de celle qui prévaut au Canada anglais. Sans dénier l'importance de la protection des droits et libertés individuels (le Québec a d'ailleurs promulgué sa propre Charte des droits et libertés de la personne dès 1975) la majorité des observateurs québécois considère toutefois que

---

39 Décary, Robert, cité *in Le Québec et le lac Meech* (un dossier du *Devoir*), Montréal, Guérin littérature, 1987, p.71.

la Charte canadienne outrepasse la simple protection de ces droits et insuffle une dynamique centralisatrice et uniformatrice dans la fédération canadienne. Certains jugent même que la Charte diminue l'ensemble des pouvoirs du Québec: "... l'enchâssement en 1982 d'une Charte des droits dans la Constitution a ratatiné tous les pouvoirs du Québec, du premier au dernier, et d'une manière continue.[40]

On allègue également que cette Charte impose des contraintes injustifiées au gouvernement québécois dans l'élaboration de sa politique linguistique en faveur du français. Or, pour une société qui tente tant bien que mal de maintenir et de promouvoir son caractère distinct, il était primordial de chercher à contrebalancer ces forces centripètes et homogénéisatrices.

A) L'ARTICLE SUR LA SOCIETE DISTINCTE

L'article de l'Accord du lac Meech qui traite de la société distincte a été en partie conçu pour répondre à cet objectif. Le ministre Rémillard mentionne à ce sujet:

> ... cette règle d'interprétation, cette déclaration selon laquelle le Québec a le rôle de protéger et de promouvoir le caractère distinct du Québec, de la société québécoise, cela pourra avoir beaucoup de conséquences. Bien sûr qu'une première conséquence, M. le Président, est en relation directe avec l'application de la Charte canadienne des droits et libertés.[41]

Toutefois, le libellé de cet article sur la société distincte est la source d'inquiétudes et de divergences profondes quant à sa portée réelle, et à son aptitude à défendre et promouvoir le caractère français du Québec. Les points de désaccord se résument à trois thèmes dominants: a) le concept de société distincte doit être précisé—de façon à inclure le caractère français du Québec; b) le concept de société distincte doit demeurer ouvert; et c) quelle sera la préséance de la société distincte sur la dualité canadienne et sur la Charte des droits et libertés?

40 Tremblay, Guy, *Procès-verbaux de la Commission permanente des Institutions de l'Assemblée nationale sur l'Accord du lac Meech*, vendredi 22 mai 1987, p. R-3036.
41 Cité *in* Conseil de la langue française, *Les compétences linguistiques du Québec après l'accord du lac Meech*, (Avis au Ministre responsable de l'application de la Charte de la langue française), Québec, p.33.

1) La nécessité de définir le concept de société distincte

Sous sa forme actuelle l'article se rapportant au caractère distinct du Québec ne comporte aucun énoncé descriptif. Il y est simplement mentionné que le "Québec forme au sein du Canada une société distincte". Plusieurs au Québec discernent dans cette imprécision un risque flagrant à la sécurité culturelle tant recherchée.

Pour Léon Dion, notamment, l'article reconnaissant le Québec comme société distincte n'offre aucune garantie s'il n'est pas précisé. Bien qu'il soit d'accord avec le ministre Rémillard que de définir la société distincte risque de laisser de côté certaines de ses caractéristiques, il est néanmoins d'avis que, sans nécessairement définir, il faille à tout le moins préciser certains objectifs qui font consensus au sein de la société québécoise, surtout en ce qui a trait à la langue française. Ainsi, il propose un amendement à l'article sur la société distincte dans lequel le mot "rôle" est remplacé par "responsabilité", et où la spécificité francophone est mentionnée:

> (3) L'Assemblée nationale et le gouvernement du Québec ont la responsabilité de protéger et de promouvoir le caractère distinct de la société québécoise mentionné au point 1(B).
> Cette responsabilité inclut nécessairement la protection et la promotion du français, composante principale et essentielle de cette société, sur l'ensemble du territoire du Québec de même que toute autre composante de cette société considérée sous le même angle (droit civil, écoles, économie, etc.). La protection et la promotion des institutions anglophones au Québec seront soumises à cette priorité principale et essentielle de la langue.
> (4) Cette responsabilité particulière du Québec sera reconnue par le gouvernement fédéral et les gouvernements des autres provinces.[42]

En fin de compte, ce que les partisans d'une précision du concept de société distincte visent, c'est d'obtenir la certitude que l'interprétation future de cet article ne puisse porter atteinte à la progression du français au Québec (maintenir l'intégrité de la loi 101). Pour ces derniers cet article doit être un tremplin pour l'épanouissement culturel et linguistique du Québec, et non un moyen détourné d'imposer le bilinguisme.

Or, si l'ambiguïté quant à sa signification persiste, non seulement rien ne garantit comment sera interprété cet article, mais c'est mettre entre les mains des tribunaux l'avenir du Québec. C'est-à-dire qu'en dernière instance ce sera la Cour suprême qui définira cette société distincte. Ce qui, à leurs yeux,

---

42 Dion, Léon, "Le Québec, une société distincte; qu'on me dise aujourd'hui ce qu'on entend par cette expression", *Le Devoir*, 21 mai 1987, p.11.

outrepasse les pouvoirs du domaine judiciaire, et constitue un pari hasardeux à cause de la majorité anglophone des juges qui y siègent, et du poids politique décroissant du Québec au sein de la fédération canadienne. Sans autre forme de précision ou de balises, le caractère distinct du Québec peut être interprété comme étant bilingue et multiculturel, puisque la présence anglaise est considérée comme une caractéristique fondamentale (ce que d'aucuns considèrent comme donnant préséance sur la société distincte)[43] et que la promotion du multiculturalisme est protégée par l'article 16.

Pour d'autres intervenants, parmi l'aile nationaliste, il n'est pas tout de préciser le caractère français du Québec, encore faut-il que cela coïncide avec l'acquisition de nouveaux pouvoirs. L'article sur la société distincte doit donc accorder au gouvernement du Québec des pouvoirs et des responsabilités linguistiques et économiques élargis, de manière à ce qu'il soit en mesure d'orienter et de développer ce caractère distinct.

Enfin, un groupe d'experts constitutionnels québécois a proposé de remplacer le concept de "sociéte distincte" par celui de "peuple distinct", lequel serait défini "nécessairement mais non limitativement par référence à la langue française."[44] Selon eux, du point de vue juridique et du droit international, le concept de peuple est beaucoup mieux circonscrit que celui, plutôt flou, de société.

C'est en partie à la suite de ces appréhensions, exprimées principalement lors des audiences de la commission parlementaire québécoise, que le gouvernement du Québec envisagea et finalement acquit, lors des négociations de l'édifice Langevin, l'insertion d'une clause de sauvegarde spécifiant que l'article sur la dualité canadienne et la société distincte: "n'a pas pour effet de déroger aux pouvoirs, droits ou privilèges du Parlement ou du gouvernement du Canada, ou des législatures ou des gouvernements des provinces, y compris à leurs pouvoirs, droits ou privilèges en matière de langue." De cette façon, les pouvoirs linguistiques du Québec sont "consolidés", et aucun article de la Constitution (entre autres, celui de la dualité canadienne) ne peut être utilisé pour les diminuer. Cependant, certains objectent déjà que c'est le règne du *statu*

---

43 Morin, Jacques-Yvan, "Les conséquences inavouées de l'entente du lac Meech", *Le Devoir*, 20 janvier 1988, p.9.
    Woehrling, José, "Les clauses de l'Accord relatives à la dualité linguistique et la reconnaissance du Québec comme société distincte", in Forest, Réal-A. (dir.), *L'adhésion du Québec à l'Accord du lac Meech*, Montréal, Editions Thémis, 1988, pp. 30-31.
44 Arbour, Maurice J., *et. al.*, "Le Québec ne peut accepter tel quel le projet du Lac Meech", *Le Devoir*, 27 mai 1987, p.9.

quo, et qu'il sera difficile dans l'avenir pour le Québec d'obtenir de nouveaux pouvoirs linguistiques sur la base de son caractère distinct:

> Lorsqu'à l'avenir la Cour suprême devra interpréter ce partage [pouvoirs linguistiques entre le fédéral et le Québec] pour venir le préciser dans une "zone grise" (par exemple en ce qui concerne l'application de la loi 101 aux entreprises d'incorporation fédérale, à l'égard desquelles la compétence linguistique des provinces est douteuse et controversée), la clause de sauvegarde empêchera presque certainement les juges de s'appuyer sur le caractère distinct du Québec pour reconnaître à celui-ci une compétence plus large que celle qu'il possédait déjà avant que soit adopté le nouvel accord constitutionnel. La clause de sauvegarde, du fait qu'elle bénéficie également au fédéral, exclut par conséquent que le caractère distinct du Québec puisse être utilisé comme fondement d'une croissance éventuelle des pouvoirs linguistiques de celui-ci.[45]

2) *La nécessaire imprécision du concept de société distincte*

A ceux qui affirment que le concept de société distincte doit être précisé, d'aucuns rétorquent invariablement: "Quand on énumère dans un article de droit, l'on restreint toujours".

Ils estiment en effet que de décrire ou de préciser, de quelque manière que ce soit, le concept de société distincte, c'est restreindre indubitablement sa portée. Ainsi, le juriste québécois L. Yves Fortier soutenait devant la commission parlementaire de l'Assemblée nationale que la meilleure façon d'assurer l'entière plénitude de cette expression est de ne point la définir:

> L'absence de définition est, selon moi, la meilleure garantie de la reconnaissance par les tribunaux du Québec et du Canada de tous ses éléments distinctifs, sans exceptions.[46]

Il base cette affirmation sur la règle selon laquelle le législateur n'est pas présumé parler pour ne rien dire, et sur la possibilité, en cas de recours devant les tribunaux, "de recourir à la preuve pour démontrer les attributs de cette 'société distincte'". Il soutient également que les tribunaux, au cours de l'histoire, ont interprété les expressions non définies de la *Loi constitutionnelle de 1867* d'une manière satisfaisante; et que l'article sur la société distincte, en

45 Woehrling, José, "Les ambiguïtés de l'Accord d'Ottawa", *La Presse*, 16 juin 1987, p.B3.
46 Fortier, Yves L., "Reconnaître l'"existence" de la société distincte; l'absence de définition précise est la meilleure garantie de la reconnaissance par les tribunaux de tous ses éléments distinctifs, sans exception", *Le Devoir*, 26 mai 1987, p.11.

tant que règle d'interprétation de la Constitution, "s'imposera au juge dans l'interprétation de toutes et chacune des dispositions de la constitution".

De plus, on considère que la reconnaissance du statut majoritaire des francophones au Québec (dualité canadienne) et la possibilité de recourir à la clause dérogatoire de la Charte des droits et libertés (article 33) constituent des moyens efficaces pour défendre la langue française. Toutefois certains ont émis des réserves quant à la validité de ces deux arguments. Tout d'abord, le professeur Guy Tremblay soutient que la société distincte du Québec, telle que décrite dans l'Accord du lac Meech, n'est pas nécessairement en majorité francophone; et ensuite le professeur Woehrling souligne que l'article 33 de la Charte des droits et libertés peut être abrogé sans le consentement du Québec.

> Le professeur Tremblay:
> ... il se trouve dans la rédaction de l'entente de principe un trou béant: on ne précise pas que les francophones sont majoritaires au Québec! Imaginons qu'en l'an 2027 il n'ait plus que 40% de francophones au Québec et qu'il en reste encore 2% ailleurs au Canada. La clause du lac Meech serait toujours respectée parce que le Canada francophone serait toujours concentré mais non limité au Québec, et que le Canada anglophone serait toujours concentré dans le reste du pays mais présent au Québec. En d'autres termes, la société distincte du lac Meech n'est pas nécessairement en majorité francophone.[47]

> Le professeur Woehrling:
> Soulignons cependant qu'il existe au Canada anglais un fort mouvement d'opinion en faveur de l'abrogation de l'article 33, considéré comme incompatible avec une véritable protection des droits et libertés. Or, cette abrogation n'exigerait pas l'accord de toutes les provinces, mais seulement de sept d'entre elles (ainsi que l'accord du parlement fédéral) et en outre, il est douteux selon nous qu'une province puisse exercer le droit de retrait à l'égard d'un amendement abrogeant l'article 33. Autrement dit, rien n'assure au Québec que la possibilité de déroger à certains des droits et libertés garantis par la Charte sera maintenue à l'avenir.[48]

Malgré cela le gouvernement québécois reste persuadé que le concept de société distincte doit demeurer ouvert. En fait, il entend utiliser "l'élasticité" de cet article pour étendre sa marge de manoeuvre dans tous les domaines possibles, et non la confiner uniquement à la langue et à la culture.

---

47 Tremblay, Guy, *op. cit.*, p.R-3039.
48 Woehrling, José, "L'incidence de la Charte sur les pouvoirs du Québec", *La Presse*, 17 juin 1987, p.B3.

3) La préséance de la société distincte

Un autre aspect de l'article sur la société distincte qui a soulevé des questions au Québec a trait à l'équilibre instable qu'il établit entre droits collectifs et droits individuels. Les gains anticipés par la reconnaissance constitutionnelle du caractère distinct du Québec pourront être éventuellement neutralisés, pense-t-on, si l'article en question n'a pas préséance sur le principe de la dualité canadienne et la Charte des droits et libertés.

a) La dualité canadienne. La reconnaissance du Québec comme société distincte n'est pas la seule règle d'interprétation de la Constitution entérinée dans l'Accord du lac Meech. Le principe de la dualité canadienne, lequel constitue une "caractéristique fondamentale du Canada" est également sanctionné à cet effet. De ces deux règles découlent que le Parlement fédéral et les législatures provinciales ont le "rôle" de "protéger" cette caractéristique fondamentale, et que l'Assemblée nationale et le gouvernement du Québec ont le "rôle" de "protéger" et de "promouvoir" ce caractère distinct.

Dans la première version de l'Accord du lac Meech, l'entente du 30 avril, il était question pour les gouvernements fédéral et provinciaux d'un "engagement" à l'égard de la protection de la dualité canadienne, et d'un "rôle" pour le Québec vis-à-vis la protection et la promotion de son caractère distinct. Plusieurs au Québec voyaient dans ce libellé une subordination de la clause sur la société distincte à celle sur la dualité canadienne. D'autant plus que le principe de la dualité canadienne est consacré "caractéristique fondamentale du Canada", ce qui n'est pas le cas de la société distincte. Il ne faisait donc pas de doute, à leur avis, que l'impact juridique d'une telle terminologie serait défavorable au Québec. Le professeur Jacques-Yvan Morin résume cette interprétation de la façon suivante:

> Lequel de ces deux critères d'interprétation, dualité ou société distincte, l'emportera en cas de conflit entre les droits de l'anglais et ceux de la langue majoritaire? Entre une "caractéristique fondamentale" qui fait l'objet d'une obligation [entente du 30 avril] et une caractéristique non fondamentale protégée par un "rôle", on peut deviner que les tribunaux auront vite fait leur choix.[49]

Les rectifications apportées à cet article lors des négociations du 2-3 juin n'eurent pas l'heur de plaire totalement à l'aile nationaliste québécoise. Ils préfèrent une formulation qui ne prête à aucune équivoque; qui soit contraignante. Que l'on reconnaisse la clause sur la société distincte comme

---

49 Morin, Jacques-Yvan, "Nous sommes devant un nouveau piège; le premier ministre devra trouver le courage de dire non une fois de plus", *Le Devoir*, 20 mai 1987, p.9.

une caractéristique fondamentale, au même titre que la dualité canadienne; et que le gouvernement du Québec et l'Assemblée nationale prennent l'"engagement" (terme plus entreprenant que celui de "rôle") de protéger et de promouvoir la spécificité québécoise.

Malgré le fait que les deux clauses font maintenant l'objet de "rôle" (bien qu'une ait toujours la particularité d'être une caractéristique fondamendale), et qu'une clause de sauvegarde soit venue confirmer certains pouvoirs du Québec, il reste que la primauté de la clause sur le caractère distinct du Québec n'est pas évidente.

Beaucoup d'intervenants demeurent perplexes à l'idée que le Québec doive simultanément protéger la dualité canadienne et promouvoir son caractère distinct. Lequel finalement l'emportera en cas de conflit:

> Ces deux rôles se relativisent mutuellement et, même si l'on peut insister sur la distinction entre protection et promotion pour essayer de démontrer que le rôle de promotion du caractère distinct doit primer le rôle de protection de la dualité, on ne peut aller jusqu'à prétendre que le premier annule le second.[50]

Ainsi, l'effet escompté de l'article sur le caractère distinct du Québec demeure, pour plusieurs, entièrement aléatoire.

b) La Charte des droits et libertés. Le problème se pose en termes similaires en ce qui a trait à la Charte des droits et libertés. Qu'arrivera-t-il si des droits protégés par la Charte entrent en conflit avec des lois promouvant le caractère distinct du Québec? Qui aura préséance? Les droits individuels ou les droits collectifs?

A ce sujet, plusieurs experts québécois craignent que certains articles de la Charte amenuisent la portée de l'article sur la société distincte, particulièrement en ce qui concerne la promotion de la langue française. Ils se réfèrent, entre autres, aux articles 2 (libertés fondamentales), 6 (liberté de circulation et d'établissement) et 27 (multiculturalisme) de la Charte des droits et libertés.

Ainsi, sur la base de l'article 2 (libertés fondamentales), la Cour supérieure du Québec a déjà invalidé certaines dispositions de la loi 101 relatives à l'affichage unilingue français. Ceux parmi la communauté anglophone du Québec qui ont commenté l'Accord du lac Meech (principalement le groupe Alliance-Québec) redoutent que ce jugement puisse être renversé au bénéfice de la clause sur la société distincte. Toutefois, la majorité des spécialistes qui ont témoigné devant la commission parlementaire québécoise, ont admis que la clause sur le caractère distinct du Québec ne pourrait prévaloir sur la Charte.

---

50 Woehrling, José, "Jusqu'où va la primauté du caractère distinct?", *La Presse*, 18 juin 1987, p.B3.

M. Reed Scowen, député à l'Assemblée nationale, mentionne d'ailleurs à ce propos:

> The experts who have testified at the National Assembly committee have argued unanimously, and sometimes regretfully, that this is not the case. The right to use English as well as French on signs is protected by the Charter of Rights.[51]

Un autre article de la Charte des droits et libertés, l'article 6 sur la liberté de circulation et d'établissement, pourrait également diminuer la marge de manoeuvre du Québec dans la promotion de son caractère distinct. Par exemple, advenant une contestation de la politique de francisation des entreprises sur la base qu'elle restreint la liberté de circulation, il n'est pas assuré, selon le professeur José Woehrling, que la clause sur la société distincte ait préséance:

> ... il est impossible, selon nous, de prétendre que les tribunaux feront nécessairement primer le caractère distinct du Québec sur la liberté de circulation. Ce serait oublier que l'accord constitutionnel du 3 juin continue d'investir le Québec du rôle de protéger la dualité canadienne....[52]

Enfin, l'article 27 de la Charte stipulant que "toute interprétation de la présente Charte doit concorder avec l'objectif de promouvoir le maintien et la valorisation du patrimoine multiculturel des Canadiens" peut, selon certains, relativiser les ordonnances de l'article relatif à la société distincte.

Il semble que de l'avis majoritaire des experts québécois la portée de l'article sur la société distincte est manifestement restreinte par le principe de la dualité canadienne (caractéristique fondamentale), tel qu'inscrit dans l'Accord du lac Meech, et par certaines prescriptions de la Charte des droits et libertés. En somme, selon eux, il sera difficile de faire prévaloir le français sur les autres langues au Québec en s'appuyant sur cet article.

Cependant, pour le gouvernement québécois, le fait que la Constitution (y compris la Charte des droits et libertés) devra désormais être interprétée de manière à concorder avec le caractère distinct du Québec constitue un bouclier efficace contre les effets centralisateurs de la Charte. En outre, il soutient que la reconnaissance constitutionnelle du Québec comme société distincte, qu'il aura le rôle de protéger et de promouvoir, constitue une assise juridique solide qui lui permettra de faire des gains tant au niveau linguistique que dans les "zones grises" du partage constitutionnel des compétences. Ainsi, le ministre Rémillard déclarait à l'Assemblée nationale:

51 Scowen, Reed, "'Distinct Society' Is No Spur to Independence; Would Quebec Join Canada as a Step Toward Leaving It?", *The Gazette*, 22 May 1987, p.B3.
52 Woehrling, José, *op. cit.*

Il y a des dizaines de causes chaque année partout au Canada concernant le partage des compétences législatives. Nous avons là avec la reconnaissance du Québec comme une société distincte, un outil fondamental, un outil premier pour interpréter ce partage des compétences législatives.... Ce que nous avons maintenant avec la reconnaissance du Québec comme société distincte, c'est la possibilité d'utiliser cet élément d'interprétation constitutionnelle, ... pour démontrer que Radio-Québec est un outil essentiel pour le développement culturel du Québec et que, par conséquent, nous avons compétence en matière d'éducation.... Nous devons avoir des outils pour plaider que les caisses populaires sont vraiment de compétence provinciale.... nous voulons la possibilité de nous exprimer très clairement sur la scène internationale en fonction de notre spécificité.[53]

C'est en se basant sur cette argumentation que le gouvernement québécois s'est opposé à ceux qui prétendent qu'avec l'Accord du lac Meech le Québec s'enferme dans une "camisole de force constitutionnelle", à l'intérieur de laquelle il lui sera impossible d'étendre ses pouvoirs législatifs et linguistiques. Le gouvernement estime d'ailleurs que l'article sur la société distincte va au-delà de la simple interprétation; aux dires du ministre Rémillard il s'agit "d'une véritable déclaration de pouvoir, qui est même plus qu'une règle d'interprétation."[54] Cela s'adresse évidemment à ceux qui soutiennent qu'en tant que règle d'interprétation l'article sur la société distincte ne sera utilisé que selon le bon plaisir des juges.

Cette approche tranche avec l'attitude traditionnelle des gouvernements québécois précédents pour qui l'ahésion à tout changement constitutionnel était liée à l'extension des pouvoirs ou compétences législatives du Québec. Le gouvernement actuel semble toujours favoriser cet objectif (étendre les compétences législatives du Québec), mais au lieu de procéder uniquement par des amendements constitutionnels, comme c'était le cas auparavant, il ouvre, avec l'Accord du lac Meech, un deuxième front via la voie judiciaire. Cela reflète, selon nous, une appréciation réaliste de la dynamique politico-constitutionnelle actuelle, où les provinces, fortes de leur affermissement des dernières années et de leur sentiment d'égalité, s'opposeront (et se sont déjà opposées) à ce que le Québec seul élargisse ses compétences. Face à cette obstruction systématique et paralysante, il importait au gouvernement québécois d'ouvrir une voie par laquelle le Québec pourrait éventuellement accroître ses compétences, et être mieux à même de défendre la langue et la culture françaises, sans pour autant avoir à convaincre six gouvernements provinciaux plus le gouvernement fédéral de son bien-fondé. Pour le gouver-

---

53 Cité *in* Conseil de la langue française, *op. cit.*, pp.42-43.
54 *Ibid.*, p.33.

nement du Québec il ne fait aucun doute que l'Accord du lac Meech, et notamment l'article sur la société distincte, constitue une assise juridique qui lui permettra d'atteindre plus facilement certains objectifs constitutionnels.

B) LE POUVOIR DE DEPENSER

Le deuxième élément de l'Accord du lac Meech qui fut amplement débattu au Québec est l'article sur le pouvoir de dépenser du gouvernement fédéral. Le gouvernement du Québec recherchait par cet article à limiter et à circonscrire ce pouvoir du gouvernement fédéral (ce qui constitue un objectif constitutionnel historique pour cette province). Toutefois, la façon dont cet article a été évalué par la majorité des observateurs québécois s'inscrit en faux contre cette interprétation.

Tout d'abord, les premières réactions ne manquèrent pas de souligner que pour la première fois le Québec reconnaît, et se dit prêt à enchâsser dans la Constitution, le pouvoir du gouvernement fédéral de dépenser dans des domaines de compétence provinciale exclusive. Cette reconnaissance constitutionnelle légitimera dorénavant l'établissement par le fédéral de programmes à frais partagés dans des champs de juridiction exclusive des provinces (surtout dans les domaines sociaux). Ce qui était autrefois un exercice litigieux pour le gouvernement fédéral deviendra un acte entièrement licite.

De plus, le fait d'autoriser le versement d'une "juste" compensation financière aux provinces se retirant d'un programme national à frais partagés dans un domaine de compétence provinciale, qu'à la condition que la province mette en place un programme ou une mesure compatible avec les objectifs nationaux (définis par le gouvernement central), représente pour plusieurs une perte d'autonomie législative des provinces.

En somme, on interprète cet article comme permettant au gouvernement fédéral de faire indirectement ce qu'il ne peut faire directement, soit de réglementer des domaines de compétence provinciale exclusive. Les professeurs Andrée Lajoie et Jacques Frémont ont résumé ce point de vue de cette façon:

> Ce qui, à première vue, peut sembler une concession du fédéral faite au Québec et aux provinces doit se révéler après un examen plus détaillé une victoire majeure du fédéral qui, par ce biais, réussira enfin à faire ce qu'il cherchait à accomplir depuis de nombreuses années, à savoir d'acquérir l'autorité constitutionnelle

d'investir et de contrôler à toutes fins utiles tous les domaines de juridiction provinciale exclusive.[55]

Cette interprétation d'un affermissement, ou d'un accroissement, des pouvoirs du fédéral a été mise de l'avant par plusieurs spécialistes québécois qui, du même souffle, en dénonçaient vivement les implications centralisatrices. Pour la majorité de ces intervenants, l'article sur le pouvoir de dépenser représente une porte ouverte à l'intrusion du fédéral dans les domaines exclusifs des provinces. Cela contredit la position historique du Québec en matière constitutionnelle et pour certains cela signifie un net recul, puisque le Québec avait déjà obtenu des compensations entières lors de retraits précédents. Maintenant non seulement les provinces n'obtiennent qu'une "juste" compensation, mais pour y avoir droit elles doivent se conformer à des objectifs définis par le gouvernement central et s'appliquant à la grandeur du pays. Ce qui, sous certains aspects, dilue la notion d'une société distincte agissant souverainement dans ses domaines de juridiction exclusive.

Face à ces critiques le gouvernement du Québec recherra et obtint, lors des négociations du 2-3 juin à l'édifice Langevin, l'insertion d'une clause à l'article sur le pouvoir de dépenser, affirmant que: "le présent article n'élargit pas les compétences législatives du Parlement du Canada ou des législatures des provinces".

Selon le gouvernement québécois, en introduisant cette "clause de sauvegarde" l'article sur le pouvoir de dépenser ne fait que reconnaître le droit de retrait des provinces d'un programme à frais partagés et ne reconnaît aucunement le pouvoir du fédéral de s'immiscer dans les compétences provinciales. Le ministre Rémillard est d'ailleurs catégorique à ce sujet:

> ... l'article 106A est rédigé de telle manière que l'exercice pour le Québec de son droit de retrait n'entraînera pas une reconnaissance du pouvoir fédéral de mettre en oeuvre des programmes dans des domaines provinciaux. En effet, cet article ne dispose que du droit de retrait sans reconnaître ni définir le pouvoir fédéral de dépenser. Pour effacer tout doute à cet égard, un deuxième alinéa complète l'article 106A et confirme que les pouvoirs législatifs du Fédéral ne sont pas modifiés par cette disposition. Le Québec conserve donc intacte, par exemple, sa faculté de contester judiciairement tout usage du pouvoir de dépenser qui serait inconstitutionnel.[56]

55 Lajoie, Andrée; Frémont, Jacques, "Le pouvoir fédéral de dépenser; des amendements inacceptables", *Le Devoir*, 14 mai 1987, p.11.
56 Rémillard, Gil, "L'Accord constitutionnel de 1987 et le rapatriement du Québec au sein du fédéralisme canadien", cité *in* Forest, Réal-A., *op cit*, p.198.

En outre, ceux qui, à l'instar du gouvernement québécois, souscrivent à l'article sur le pouvoir de dépenser soutiennent que l'imprécision des termes "mesures compatibles" et "objectifs nationaux" donnent aux provinces une flexibilité, une marge de manoeuvre, dans la manière dont elles entendent utiliser la compensation financière (au lieu d'être contraint par des normes ou des critères stricts). De cette façon, les provinces seront à même de respecter leurs priorités tout en bénéficiant des programmes à frais partagés.

Pour les tenants de cette thèse, cela implique qu'avant d'intervenir dans des domaines de compétence provinciale, le gouvernement fédéral devra consulter les provinces et être clair à propos de ses objectifs. La formule du "à prendre ou à laisser" ne sera plus de rigueur. Ainsi, le fédéral ne pourra plus imposer, par le biais de son pouvoir de dépenser, des programmes à frais partagés "clé en main", comme c'était le cas auparavant.

Malgré ces arguments, la majorité des observateurs québécois demeurent sceptiques quant à la réelle limitation que l'Accord du lac Meech apporte au pouvoir de dépenser du gouvernement fédéral.

CONCLUSION

A la lumière de ce que nous venons d'observer, il appert que la différence de perception qui existe entre le Canada anglais et le Québec francophone par rapport à l'Accord du lac Meech trouve sa source dans trois facteurs principaux:

1. Tout d'abord, la place et le rôle que la Charte des droits et libertés (avec tout ce qu'elle incarne de symbolisme et de vision de la société et du fédéralisme canadien) occupe dans l'inconscient collectif de chacune de ces communautés a fortement influencé leur appréciation de l'Accord. Ainsi, au Canada anglais la Charte représente l'emblème et l'instrument de développement d'une nation canadienne, de même que le rempart absolu de la protection des droits et libertés individuels; au Québec, par contre, ce sont plutôt ses conséquences politiques négatives (visées uniformisatrices et atteintes à la politique linguistique, entre autres choses) qui sont l'objet de préoccupations. De cette façon, tout changement qui risque de perturber l'interprétation de la Charte est perçu comme un crime de lèse-majesté au Canada anglais, alors que pour le Québec il s'agit d'un objectif crucial afin de maintenir un certain contrôle sur son développement social. Par conséquent, l'Accord du lac Meech, en portant "atteinte" à la Charte trouve un écho différent dans chaque communauté.
2. Ensuite, la façon dont les deux communautés perçoivent les gouvernements provinciaux et leur rôle a également influencé leur réaction face à l'Accord. Ainsi, l'élite canadienne-anglaise perçoit généralement les

gouvernements provinciaux d'un oeil beaucoup moins favorable que les Québécois francophones qui, pour des raisons culturelles, s'identifient plus volontiers à cet ordre de gouvernement. Cette méfiance qui prévaut à l'égard des gouvernements provinciaux est particulièrement vivace auprès des intellectuels libéraux de l'ouest du pays, qui ont, depuis plusieurs années, à transiger avec des gouvernements provinciaux conservateurs et peu enclins envers les droits des minorités, des femmes, des programmes sociaux, etc. Or, l'Accord du lac Meech, en permettant aux provinces d'exercer une plus grande influence au sein des institutions nationales (Sénat et Cour suprême) et d'avoir une marge de manoeuvre plus étendue dans l'établissement des programmes sociaux nationaux (retrait avec compensation), soulève des craintes et des oppositions au Canada anglais, où l'on considère que le gouvernement fédéral ne pourra plus être en mesure de faire contrepoids aux provinces. Au Québec, en revanche, cette marge de manoeuvre est jugée minimale et essentielle.

3.   Enfin, le troisième facteur qui explique l'attitude divergente du Canada anglais et du Québec francophone par rapport à l'Accord du lac Meech, est l'évaluation opposée qu'ils font d'un échec de ce dernier. Au Canada anglais, à l'exception d'une minorité qui prêcha dans le désert, les conséquences d'un échec de l'Accord furent soit ignorées, soit mésestimées. Ainsi, dans un éditorial, le journal *The Ottawa Citizen* allègue qu'un échec de l'Accord aura au Québec les conséquences suivantes: "Disappointment, yes, and political turmoil certainly, but we are used to that".[57] Il est donc compréhensible qu'avec une pareille désinvolture on n'hésite pas à recommander des amendements ou le rejet pur et simple de l'Accord.

Toutefois, penser qu'un échec n'entraînera pas de séquelles sérieuses c'est méjuger profondément, à notre avis, la raison d'être de l'Accord et le contexte historique dans lequel il s'insert (ce qui fut d'ailleurs une caractéristique du débat public au Canada anglais). Mme Solange Chaput-Rolland témoigna avec éloquence sur ce sujet devant le comité mixte spécial du Sénat et de la Chambre des communes sur l'Entente constitutionnelle de 1987:

Le Canada anglais s'en fichait déjà un mois après [du référendum] et cela m'a blessée, ainsi que tous ceux qui se sont battus si fort pour rester au Canada, de nous trouver à l'extérieur du Canada. Vous savez, c'était un geste très dramatique,

57 The Ottawa Citizen, "Second Thoughts on Meech Lake -3", *The Ottawa Citizen*, 7 May 1988, p. B2.

monsieur Hamelin, quant M. Lévesque a mis le drapeau du Québec en berne le jour où vous fêtiez tous ici. Mais nos coeurs étaient en berne aussi ce jour-là, parce que nous avions été exclus d'un pays où nous avions choisi de rester. Alors l'Accord du lac Meech nous a paru un "incredible" geste d'amitié.

C'est la première fois, depuis que le téléphone a sonné chez nous et qu'un ami m'a téléphoné du lac Meech pour me dire "c'est fait", que j'ai relevé la tête, en ayant l'impression que je n'avais pas trompé mes compatriotes lorsque, avec l'équipe du clan du "NON", on leur a dit "il y a de la place pour le Québec dans le Canada de demain. Il y aura de la place pour les Québécois francophones dans les institutions fédérales du Canada, et la Fédération du Canada va se rajeunir".

Et je voudrais beaucoup que l'on sache bien que pour nous, les Québécois, et comme pour tous les autres ici et ailleurs, les accords du lac Meech, ce n'est pas une finalité, mais c'est l'amorce d'un grand processus, je pense. Mais je dois vous dire que pour moi c'est vraiment la première fois que je me sens en possession de ce référendum avec la sensation, OUI, de l'avoir gagné.

Vous savez sûrement tous que si, pour une raison ou pour une autre, l'Accord du lac Meech tombe à l'eau... il ne pourra plus y avoir de négociations, plus de justifications. Si le Québec a encore une fois l'impression qu'il est plus difficile d'entrer dans la Confédération canadienne que de demeurer à l'écart, vous savez fort bien que cela ne pourra mener qu'à une autre forme d'indépendance, cette fois non pas choisie par un parti politique québécois, mais peut-être choisie et imposée au Québec de l'extérieur.[58]

Ainsi, la majorité des commentateurs québécois s'accorde à reconnaître qu'un rejet de ces demandes minimales du Québec apporterait de l'eau au moulin du mouvement indépendantiste (qui appelle de tous ses voeux un tel échec). C'est pourquoi certains d'entre eux, plutôt tièdes vis-à-vis l'Accord, n'en désirent pas moins sa ratification afin d'éviter pareille éventualité. Le professeur Léon Dion est un de ceux-là:

C'est là l'un des tournants imprévisibles de la politique, que nombre de ceux-là qui s'objectaient aux termes de cet accord, notamment en raison de l'imprécision de l'expression "société distincte"—et j'étais de ceux-là—estiment aujourd'hui que si cet accord n'est pas retenu sous sa forme actuelle par tous les responsables, il pourrait s'ensuivre une grave secousse ayant une fois de plus son épicentre au Québec et pouvant même aboutir à une nouvelle flambée du sentiment indépendantiste: si le Canada anglais repoussait les cinq propositions des plus raisonnables

58 Chaput-Rolland, Solange, cité *in* Rapport du comité mixte spécial du Sénat et de la Chambre des communes, *L'entente constitutionnelle de 1987*, Ottawa, Imprimeur de la Reine, 1987, pp. 143-144.

du Québec malgré les exhortations pressantes et même angoissées du premier ministre Bourassa et du ministre Gil Rémillard, il serait bien téméraire celui qui espérerait que tout rentrerait dans l'ordre et qu'après pareil affront le Québec capitulerait en apposant sa signature à la constitution de 1982 qui le laisse sous des aspects essentiels à la merci des autres provinces et même d'un éventuel gouvernement québécois imprévoyant.[59]

Il va de soi qu'un rejet de l'Accord du lac Meech placerait l'élite fédéraliste québécoise à court d'argument, et laisserait le terrain libre à l'élite politique indépendantiste qui aurait beau jeu d'évoquer les événements de 1981-82 comme étant une "seconde conquête" imposée au Québec par le reste du Canada.

De plus, même si l'on fait abstraction de la menace indépendantiste, il n'en demeure pas moins qu'un échec de l'Accord perturberait sans aucun doute l'évolution constitutionnelle du pays, et mettrait en suspens des questions d'importance telles que le statut constitutionnel des autochtones, la réforme du Sénat, etc.

Ceux qui rejettent l'Accord parce qu'il heurte leur conception fondamentale du pays, malgré les conséquences possibles de ce choix, ont à tout le moins le courage de leurs convictions. Les autres, par contre, qui réclament des amendements à l'Accord tout en souscrivant à la lettre et à l'esprit du texte, démontrent ou bien une incompréhension de la signification de l'Accord pour le Québec, ou bien une opposition camouflée derrière de nobles principes.

Car il est bien évident qu'à ce stade-ci le Québec ne peut accepter aucun amendement à l'Accord du lac Meech. Plusieurs raisons furent mentionnées à cet effet (toile sans couture, boîte de Pandore, etc.), mais la raison fondamentale est que les principaux amendements revendiqués (protection et promotion des minorités linguistiques par tous les gouvernements et préséance absolue de la Charte des droits et libertés sur l'article sur la société distincte), se trouveraient à anéantir la raison d'être de l'Accord pour le Québec (marge de manoeuvre accrue à l'intérieur de la Charte et promotion exclusive de son caractère distinct).

En fait, c'est la signification de l'Accord pour le Québec qui fit le plus grand défaut au débat public au Canada anglais; tout comme le débat au Québec demeura insensible aux valeurs pan-canadiennes.

59 Dion, Léon, "Défence du français, défence d'une société; 2) Le rejet de l'accord du lac Meech pourrait entraîner une nouvelle flambée du sentiment indépendantiste au Québec", *Le Devoir*, 27 mai 1988, p.9.

IV

The Combined Impact

SEVEN

The Federal-Provincial Social Contract[1]

Thomas K. Shoyama

L'auteur de ce chapitre développe une thèse en trois volets sur l'actuel "contrat social fédéral-provincial". Les trois volets portent sur: 1) l'Accord du lac Meech, 2) l'Accord sur le libre-échange, et 3) la réforme fiscale. L'auteur soutient que ces trois initiatives affectent l'équilibre fédéral-provincial dans un sens favorable aux provinces.

S'ajoutent à ces trois volets, trois autres cas où le gouvernement fédéral a perdu du terrain face aux provinces: 1) les accords énergétiques avec les provinces maritimes et de l'ouest; 2) la nouvelle stratégie fédérale de développement régional; et 3) le domaine de la réglementation des marchés financiers.

L'auteur conclue en soutenant que le "fédéralisme compétitif", tel que défini par Albert Breton, constitue un modèle offrant de meilleures garanties de démocratie et d'efficience économique que celui du "fédéralisme coopératif" en vogue au cours des trois dernières années. L'ascendant pris par les provinces au dépens du fédéral déstabilise l'équilibre entre les deux ordres de gouvernement et nuit à une gestion efficace du système fédéral canadien.

The agenda that I propose to examine is the contemporary federal-provincial social contract. This may seem a mouth-filling phrase, but I think its meaning will become clear in what follows. In this context, I advance a unifying, if overly simplified thesis that is comprised of three parts.

First, in my view over the past three years, the federal-provincial social contract has been tending more and more toward a serious imbalance. That imbalance stems from a broad devolution of power, control and responsibility toward the provinces with a commensurate erosion of the presence and leadership capacity of the federal government. Second, that erosion is singularly inappropriate for a unified nation-state, as we move into a period of intensifying

---

1 This chapter is based on an address delivered to the Association of Professional Economists of B.C., Vancouver, B.C., 26 February 1988

globalization of nearly every aspect of economic, social and political national life. Third, even domestically at home and apart from these external pressures, the loss of competitive power at the broad federal level to countervail against narrower, provincially-bounded interests, increases the potential for significant welfare loss (in economists' terms) for Canadians as a whole. This play in three acts, together with an epilogue is intended to argue this three-part thesis.

Act One concerns the Meech Lake Accord. That accord was the product of a protracted negotiation on the part of the Prime Minister and the ten provincial premiers. It was, of course, the culmination of a lengthy series of consultations. These focussed in the first instance on the conditions which the Quebec government had set out as the basis for agreement to subscribe to the *Constitution Act of 1982*. The crunch sessions were held behind closed doors at Meech Lake in the Gatineau Hills. They carried on into the early hours of the morning, and according to reports, the agreement finally reached depended in large part upon the bargaining tactics and skill of the Prime Minister himself. The draft accord was later amplified in a further formal session with the premiers and subsequently set out in formal constitutional language. It has been endorsed in that form by a Parliamentary Committee, by all three parties in Parliament, and by a number of the provincial legislatures. If and when it receives unanimous approval by all of the latter, it will become an integral part of the Constitution of Canada.

Assuredly the Accord is a matter of great symbolic and political importance, ending as it does the constitutional isolation of the province of Quebec. In my view, however, and in those of numerous critics, it contributes to a significant dilution of federal authority in at least four explicit ways. It also opens the door to further concessions to provinces in three other directions. First, it confers upon Quebec the special status of a "distinct society". Just what that may mean is far from clear, but it is accepted that the words and their context must imply both weight and significance, reserving aspects of law and policy in Quebec from the common reach of federal jurisdiction. Indeed, the concern that the phrase itself may limit or encroach upon the spirit and equality provisions of the Charter of Rights itself has excited not a little legal controversy and lies at the centre of the opposition voiced by women's groups.

Next, the adoption of provincial nominations to both the Senate and the Supreme Court breaks new ground in a similar direction. So too with the constitutional mandating of agreements with provinces in the concurrent area of immigration. It is suggested that notwithstanding the transfer of administrative authority to the provinces, crucial elements of policy will remain with Ottawa. However, it is well known that hands-on administration inevitably plays a crucial role in policy decisions. One has only to recall the story on the barriers to Jewish refugees in the late 1930s. It is interesting in this connection to read the *Financial Post* report on the federal-provincial conflict already at hand because of the competition among the provinces to attract so-called entrepreneurial immigrants with capital to invest, even to the extent of offering incentive guarantees to underwrite such investment. Finally there is the dilution of the federal spending power, by the acceptance of the right of a province to opt out but to receive fiscal compensation whenever there is federal initiative to launch a shared-cost programme in an area of provincial jurisdiction. Admittedly the essence of that notion was present in the *Constitution Act of 1982*, but it was carefully confined to matters of an educational or cultural nature deliberately to ward off as much as possible the threat of "checkerboard Canada." Now there is no such restriction.

As to the other avenues of political erosion of federal authority, one can refer to the agreement for further constitutional discussions on jurisdiction over "seacoast and inland fisheries" and on longer-run Senate reform. In both areas, the obvious push will be for further transfer of power to the provinces—which may well be merited. Where is the suggestion of a *quid pro quo* which would help to preserve the federal-provincial balance. The essential difficulty is that we seem to be launched on a one-way street, down a steep and slippery hill and with gathering momentum. We are likely to see more of that as the last element of the Meech Lake Accord comes into play—the new constitutional requirement for an annual conference on the economy. In substance that can mean either a great deal or a great deal of nothing. Politically, however, the theatrics of a wailing wall for premiers, or gang-up of ten provinces demanding more and larger fiscal transfers, regional and sectoral subsidies, new forms of trade protection, and made in-Canada interest rates point to a potentially rough time for any prime minister, glass-jawed or otherwise.

Well, what about Act Two, the intermezzo of the bilateral free trade agreement. Here, at first glance, the federal power seems to have emerged intact, especially after Premier Peterson seems to have thrown in the towel on the issue of provincial authority over the pricing of wine. It is obviously true that given federal jurisdiction over most aspects of international trade and external economic relations, the federal government has been very much in the driver's seat. It was at least heartening to witness the Prime Minister at last November's economic conference in Toronto reply to a complaint from Premier Pawley that Canadian trade policy was not going to be determined by a committee of premiers.

Nevertheless the imprint of their influence and input is readily apparent. It appeared first in the extensive and protracted consultative process which preceded and proceeded at every step and every level of the negotiation. It is an all too short step for a government, obsessed with political reconciliation and fearful of competitive confrontation, to acquiesce in a provincial demand for full-fledged seats at the international bargaining table. Or if not right at the table, then certainly in the next room, as was sought during the recent talks. Perhaps this is all too fanciful, but the venue is already at hand in the multilateral negotiations of the "Uruguay" round of talks on the General Agreement on Trade and Tariffs (GATT).

Moreover, it is revealing to note some of the most prominent derogations from the ambit of the arrangements with the U.S., where provincial concerns seemed to have shaped the final outcome. The exclusion of the brewing industry has been highlighted in this connection. A second case is the retention of import restrictions on commodities governed by supply-management marketing boards, where provincial quotas are deeply entrenched. A further instance is the extra precautions taken with regard to the Auto Pact, and the restriction of access to its benefits to the Big Three manufacturers, almost exclusively concentrated in southern Ontario. There is, as well, the current conflict with the U.S. over the special measures being taken to protect the textile and garment industry, largely located in Quebec. Finally, one observes that despite the trade-offs in government procurement, there is no reference or application to purchasing at the provincial level. Careful study of the text of the agreement would no doubt reveal additional instances of a very tender regard for provincial pressures—and I know from past personal experience that that was far from being a natural or instinctive bent of Canada's chief negotiator.

This brings us to Act Three—the unfolding story of Tax Reform, still very much centre stage, and especially as regards the second shoe still to be dropped as a National Sales Tax (NST), or Value Added Tax (VAT). For the moment, however, I think the crucial question concerns the future of the relatively harmonized income tax system that we have known in Canada throughout the postwar period. As you will all know, central to this harmony has been the willingness of nine of ten provinces to accept the tax base pretty much as defined by federal law, and to set their rates either directly as a percentage of that base in the corporate income tax field, or as a percentage of basic federal tax in the personal income tax field. This latter is important since it also means that the agreeing provinces accept the rates of progression built into the federal tax structure.

A large part of the harmony is also achieved through the mechanics of the tax collection agreements, which help to contain both collection and compliance costs for administrative machinery and taxpayers alike. At the same time the acceptance of various forms of surcharges and tax credits in different provinces has provided a helpful degree of flexibility for the provinces. That flexibility was stretched to a new and even incompatible degree by the introduction in Saskatchewan two years ago of a special flat tax, levied not on taxable income but upon net income.

Understandably the whole system has always come under strain whenever major changes are attempted in the federal tax structure, and of course if provincial revenues are affected. The federal budget papers of last June and December contend that given the intended revenue neutrality of the changes taking effect in 1988, provincial revenue levels in the aggregate are also essentially maintained. Nevertheless, it can be fully expected that provinces are likely to press for a radical shift in the structure of the system. The direction of that shift has been frequently discussed in the past, and perhaps is even foreshadowed by the Saskatchewan development already mentioned.

It could thus appear in the form of a provincial demand to switch from the present concept of "provincial tax on federal tax" to that of a provincial tax levied on taxable income. In other words, even if the base continues to be defined largely by federal law, provinces would be free to establish their own rate levels and structure. This is appealing to the political level since the apparent rate numbers would come down, even if the actual tax loads were increased. Moreover, by defining their own tax brackets and roles, provinces would establish the degree of progressivity to serve their own social or economic objectives. All of this, of course, falls squarely within their constitutional right to levy direct taxes, as Quebec has done, and the only constraint available to the federal government has been through the pressure to take advantage of the collection agreements.

Potential variability among the provinces need not necessarily be disadvantageous for Canadians as a whole, particularly if extremes are avoided either by constraints imposed as part of a continued unified collection system or by the competitive influences of other provinces. However, it would probably raise again in more extreme form the contentious issue of the appropriate mechanism for allocation of revenues among the provinces, presently determined in large part on the simple basis of compromise and saw-off. More seriously, however, are we once again on a one-way street heading down a steep and slippery slope? The next step to variable rate structures levied against an agreed-upon base is to move to variation in defining the base itself. If that is so, the ghosts of Rowell-Sirois hacking their way through the tax jungle of the 1930s can still be called to mind. This may be nothing but scare-mongering. In my observation, I regret to say there is nothing shorter than a provincial memory. Even a turnover of bureaucrats can lead to a re-write of history. Further, in this instance, unlike the external trade arena, the constitutional defences available to Ottawa are much less clear and substantial, if they exist at all. That is why a powerful political presence and role at the centre is all the more vital.

So much for Act Three, but may I throw in an epilogue as well by reference to three other areas where the federal government has given ground to the provinces or is being further challenged. Recall first, the case of the energy agreements, and especially offshore oil and gas where the constitutional rulings clearly support federal authority. Nevertheless, both the Newfoundland and Nova Scotia accords surrender not only major potential revenues to the provinces, but also important measures of policy and administrative control. At the same time, the recipient provinces are also largely sheltered from the downward adjustment of fiscal equalization payments which would be required under an objective application of the basic principles underlying the equalization system. Naturally these two Atlantic models set out the minimum features of provincial ascendancy which the provincial government will inevitably demand in a B.C. Accord, extending over federal constitutional rights in the Pacific exclusive economic zone.

A second case is the curious jigsaw now put in place for defining and administering federal regional development policy. From its explicit roots in the 1950s, up to and including the establishment of the Department of Regional Economic Expansion (DREE) or its successor, the Department of Regional Industrial Expansion (DRIE), regional development policy had evolved as a broad national programme. The approach was to maintain coherence and co-ordination, based upon country-wide economic relationships and relativities, and working through essentially parallel programmes, adjusted for *measured* regional differences in employment, productivity and income. Now, however, there remains a vestigial DRIE, forecast to be transformed into the Department of Industry, Science and Technology (DIST), overlain by three regionally located development agencies, each with separate minister, policy planning groups, and bureaucratic structures. Ottawa observers also note that in addition to the Atlantic Canada Opportunities Agency (ACOA), the Western Diversification Initiative (WDI), and FEDNOR (the Northern Ontario agency), there is a Prime Ministers Office for Quebec, with its *own appropriate minister*. This fractured structure is rationalized as a special effort to respond to unique provincial situations. They may be valid, but it is hard to discern any potential for a coherent national or sectoral economic strategy or the retention of a balanced economic perspective.

Finally, the federal authority and presence is being challenged and threatened in the sensitive arena of the capital markets. No doubt there are important benefits to be gained in the deregulation of financial institutions. However, the erasure of boundaries around the four pillars is not without potential costs, and it has brought to the fore the latent struggle between federal and provincial regulation over these institutions and their functions. The constitutional aspects, as I understand them, remain somewhat obscure and the old tacit working understandings regarding banking and securities are under great strain. Obviously this has spilled over immediately into the international arena, where the emergence of particularized provincial voices in conflict with each other or with the federal view suggests an unfortunate prospect of disorder and disarray. It is hard to imagine any worse approach to a sphere of global activity normally characterized at best by volatility and rapid change.

This last point emphasizes why I think there is cause for concern about the implications of a weakened and eroded central authority for our external financial and economic relations. I suspect that a specialist in international political relationships could outline causes for parallel disquiet in our over-all foreign policy. At a minimum, it can be taken for granted that a less successful economic performance and status also weakens the forcefulness of an international political role and influence. Looking out to the pace of change and the rise of the Pacific profile in the world today, that is surely unfortunate.

Let me turn now to a concluding comment on the domestic scene. Here I borrow a perspective from a supplement to the Macdonald Royal Commission report submitted by Commissioner Albert Breton. He has been prominent in that school of economists who have worked in the application of economic theory to analyze the operations of political, as distinct from economic markets.

Breton's supplement points to the marriage of the British parliamentary system with a federal structure of government, and argues that a model of competitive federalism conduces to optimum welfare for Canadians. This can only follow if both horizontal and vertical competition are relatively efficient. Efficient horizontal competitions—i.e. between and among provinces—depends upon many factors, not least of which is some degree of equality among the provinces. While this is difficult to achieve in Canada, it is nevertheless underpinned by constitutional political power and status, and by the equalizing economic and fiscal role of the federal government and Parliament. Vertical competition—i.e. between the federal and provincial levels—is perhaps even more crucial given the *de facto* interdependence both within and among assigned areas of constitutional jurisdiction, and the resulting interplay between the two levels in every part of the country.

In this model, competitive federalism rather than the collusive behaviour implicit in so-called co-operative or executive federalism is not only more democratic and accountable. It is also likely to be economically optimum for citizens,—again provided that the competition is reasonably efficient. That in turn requires a balance of competitive strength in the political market place. As one who has observed this competitive struggle in many applied areas, I find this theoretical perspective quite persuasive. As this article has tried to suggest, I believe the aggressive ascendancy of the provinces at the expense of the federal authority over the past three years undermines the competitive balance, or the social contract, essential to the optimum management of our federal-provincial system.

Perhaps all of this has just been an alternative way of phrasing what is often described as the balkanization of the country—with its obvious implication of a loss of power and control at the centre. Indeed, the current disaffection with the political scene in Ottawa suggested by the public opinion polls may reflect this perception. However, the rather dismal picture I have painted of a growing provincial-federal imbalance—a fractured social contract—is probably something of a minority view. That is likely to be so in those parts of the country geographically distant, and often legitimately disaffected, from Ottawa. Many would argue that much of the Canadian inspiration comes not from the centre but from the insights and imagination to be found in the provinces and provincial political parties. My 18 years in Saskatchewan strongly suggests that view. However, to be effective for the country as a whole my experience also suggests that there must be a coherent, strong federal presence. That is why its apparent substantial shrinkage over the past three years is disquieting to say the least.

It is fair to ask, then, if I think anything can be done to stem the tide and reassert a more convincing federal role. I really have no answer other than to stress—as any good academic would—the importance of recognition, analysis and reflection. Beyond that the repair of the contract obviously lies in the political process and the democratic participation of citizens. Perhaps the most helpful instrument available lies in those national interest groups with broad-ranging concerns and longer-run perspectives on that familiar issue. Are we a community of regionally and provincially-based communities or is the whole really greater than the sum of the parts?

EIGHT

Round Table Discussion: Executive Federalism, Public Input and Public Interest

EDITORS' NOTE

Throughout the discussion of the Meech Lake Accord, the character of the process has continually been an issue of contention. The secrecy involved in the negotiations and the perceived lack of public input has been severely criticized, particularly by interest groups. These are features of an intergovernmental process first described by Donald V. Smiley as "executive federalism". The Meech Lake Accord represented a pure example of executive federalism at work. However, the adverse public reaction to the process has forced those involved to rethink the procedural issues and to try to devise ways of obtaining greater and more routine public input. The need to bring the general and interested public into the decision-making process at various stages seems to be increasingly essential both for the legitimacy and the ultimate success of efforts and constitutional revision such as the Meech Lake Accord.

The problems and prospects of welding public interest and input to the practical realities of executive federalism was the subject of the annual meeting of the advisory council of the Institute of Intergovernmental Relations held 24-26 May 1988. The council consists of senior officials from intergovernmental affairs agencies, leading academic experts of federalism and intergovernmental relations, and a number of others with an interest in federalism issues. The regular members of the council were joined on this occasion by a number of guests, including Chris Speyer, MP, co-chairman of the Special Joint Committee of the Senate and House of Commons on the 1987 Constitutional Accord, and Charles Beer, chairman of the Ontario Select Committee on Constitutional Reform. Also present as observers were three graduate students in political studies at Queen's University, Keith Brownsey, Hugh Mellon, and Avigail Eisenberg. What follows is their record of the proceedings and a commentary on the future of executive federalism in Canada, possible means of obtaining greater public input into a hitherto closed process, and the consequences of opening up the process, in terms of serving the public interest.

Report on Round Table Discussions

Keith Brownsey
and Hugh Mellon

La réunion annuelle du Conseil consultatif de l'Institut des relations intergouvernementales porta sur les difficultés d'établir un consensus dans les domaines des modifications constitutionnelles et de l'élaboration des politiques économiques. Plus précisément, les discussions abordèrent l'héritage de l'administration Trudeau, les limites à la participation du public, et l'interaction entre les groupes d'intérêt et la structure institutionnelle du fédéralisme canadien. Les participants s'attardèrent à la complexité relevant du recoupement des clivages territoriaux et sociétaux. Leurs réflexions concernant les rapports entre une négociation réussie et la participation du public jettèrent une lumière sur les négociations fédérales-provinciales qui menèrent à l'Accord du lac Meech et sur la coordination d'une politique économique nationale.

INTRODUCTION

As the focus of this volume indicates, two events dominated the Canadian federal-provincial agenda in 1987 and 1988—constitutional reform and trade negotiations with the United States. Both agreements have proven to be controversial not only in terms of their content but in terms of the processes by which they were negotiated.

At first sight the unanimous agreement reached at Meech Lake by the Prime Minister and the ten premiers was hailed as a remarkable achievement. It soon became apparent, however, that there was considerable opposition to it from many individuals and groups.

Opposition to the Accord has focussed not only on its content but the method by which it was reached. Critics as well as supporters are asking whether secret and closed negotiations are an appropriate method for changing the constitution in a liberal democracy. They are asking whether those opposed to the Accord are attacking the process by which it was negotiated because they are angry at being excluded from this process or because they are dissatisfied with the outcome. They are searching for a method of constitutional change that will include provision for public input.

The Canada-U.S. Trade Agreement poses different, but no less serious, problems for the processes of Canadian federalism. These discussions potentially involved broad areas of provincial jurisdiction. Yet several governments, especially British Columbia, Alberta, and Saskatchewan appeared willing to support this intrusion into provincial jurisdiction in exchange for the perceived benefits of greater trade with the United States. By contrast, several provinces have been vehemently opposed to the agreement. Prince Edward Island, Ontario, and until recently Manitoba all opposed the deal claiming it impinged on provincial jurisdiction. Even those provinces that supported a Canada-U.S. trade arrangement demanded that certain sectors of the economy be excluded from the talks, that provincial governments be consulted by the federal government on the progress of the talks, and that the provinces be given a veto over any final agreement. Quebec has gone so far as to insist that those areas of the federal implementing legislation which impinge on provincial jurisdiction must receive the approval of the National Assembly independent of the Federal Parliament. The provinces have, in effect, attempted to legitimize the process of executive federalism within the broad area of economic policy-making—the same process which has been the focus of criticism concerning Meech Lake.

The discussions of the Advisory Council of the Institute for Intergovernmental Relations of 24-26 May 1988 were divided into two sections. The first session entitled "The Future of Executive Federalism: Processes of Constitutional Reform", was chaired by Institute Director Peter Leslie. The discussion panel included Chris Speyer, MP, co-chairman of the Special Joint Committee of the Senate and the House of Commons on the Constitutional Accord 1987 and Charles Beer, MPP, chairperson of the Ontario Select Committee on Constitutional Reform. Both Speyer and Beer outlined the general problems they confronted when faced with a negotiated agreement which sought public input after the intergovernmental negotiations had been completed. These first-hand observations set the direction for the discussion. Several proposals for increased public input into the constitutional reform process were examined. Council members were sensitive to criticism that the Meech Lake accord was "reached by 11 men sitting around a poker table in the dead of night." Greater public input was deemed a necessary part of any future constitutional debate although there was some ambivalence about the appropriate extent.

The second session dealt with "The Future of Executive Federalism: Issues Relating to the Economy". Chaired by Jack Mintz of the Department of Economics at Queen's University the discussion began with reference to the paper "Strategic Choices for Provincial Governments" by Peter Leslie.[1]

---

1 This paper is available as an Appendix in Peter M. Leslie, *Federal Leadership in Economic and Social Policy* (Kingston: Institute of Intergovernmental Relations, *Reflections*, No. 3, 1988), pp. 27-33.

The focus of this session was on the ability of the federal and provincial governments to harmonize their various economic policies. The question of the harmonization of federal and provincial economic policies reflected a concern with the effectiveness and efficiency of the federal system in terms of industrial and economic policy. The issue of public input into the processes of executive federalism arose here too in the realm of economic affairs from concerns about the legitimacy of the process of executive federalism and the outcomes of that process.

Although the similarities with the previous session's discussions were stressed, it was recognized that there are major differences between economic policy-making and constitutional reform. In the economic field each order of government can to some degree work within its own areas of jurisdiction; in the constitutional field it is the definition of the areas of jurisdiction that characterizes nearly all disputes. With regard to economic problems, common action may be desirable but may not be necessary; in the realm of constitutional reform this choice does not arise: common action is a prerequisite. Public input has always been essential to economic policy-making; in constitutional reform during the past decade it has become an increasingly important although still not a completely welcomed factor.

MEECH LAKE AND THE CONSTITUTIONAL REFORM PROCESS

A fundamental aspect of the discussion in the first session was the search for a means of balancing our heritage of complex, and occasionally bitter, federal-provincial negotiations with the need for periodic constitutional revisions. There was widespread recognition that the politicians who sought to run the constitutional gauntlet faced a multitude of dangers and potential roadblocks. As a senior government figure put it, "my great fear is paralysis." Those who sought to fashion an agreement had to move with dexterity. Whether such constitutional re-fashioning required a level of confidentiality beyond what some might regard as acceptable, constituted a further conundrum. The intricacy of reaching consensus in an environment marked by deep cleavages and serious downside risks was thus a consistent theme of discussion.

The memories of 1980-82 were obviously a critical feature of the backdrop to current debates and interest group sensitivities. While various participants stressed that the Meech Lake Accord represented a fulfillment of 1982, there were cautious reminders that observers should acknowledge that the needs of 1987-88 were not those of 1982. One speaker warned of "mythologizing" the process which led to the 1982 settlement and thereby devaluing the wisdom of the Meech Lake process. In 1981, native rights and the concerns of women's groups were belatedly recognized following extensive public pressure. Another speaker argued that Canadians should be aware that constitutional amendment does not always represent a major political transformation. In general, the multi-dimensional legacy of 1981-82 contained valuable lessons about complex trade-offs and future agendas, while also spawning uncertain analogies and tenuous parallels.

It was suggested that a basic misunderstanding of many in the aftermath of the *Constitution Act, 1982*, was the expectation that no federal-provincial agreement on subsequent reforms was likely to be politically possible. This skepticism was seen as having kept many groups on the sidelines until the Meech Lake process had generated significant momentum. Not until the late spring of 1987 did many groups sense that negotiations were making real progress and become concerned at the lack of attention to their own particular interests. At that point, certain organizations took up the issue of openness and accessability as the means of signifying their discontent at having had no input. This anger was cited by various participants as becoming a feature of subsequent media coverage. The impact of such coverage upon public perceptions, upon the Meech Lake ratification debates and upon the possibilities for future amendment received extensive attention in the Advisory Council discussion.

Council discussion grappled with these concerns and the over-arching challenge of relating the mechanics of executive federalism to the dynamic tableau of political pressures and realities. The full dimensions of this challenge can be understood through reference to the four basic questions raised during the session:

1. Is the "Meech Lake process" best understood as a unique phenomenon or as a model for future revisions?
2. What mechanisms are potentially available for opening up the process of constitutional debate and reform?
3. What lessons can be drawn from the "Meech Lake process" on the place of interest groups and their involvement in constitutional discussions?
4. What factors are shaping the future of Canada's constitutional agenda?

THE "MEECH LAKE PROCESS"—IS IT BEST UNDERSTOOD AS A UNIQUE EVENT OR AS A MODEL FOR FUTURE REVISIONS?

Participants identified five key steps in what they labelled as the "Meech Lake process"—1) the Mont Gabriel discussions of May 1986; 2) ten months of informal, mainly bilateral, discussions among governments; 3) the meeting of the First Ministers at Meech Lake, 30 April 1987; 4) the follow-up meeting of First Ministers in Ottawa 2 June through 3 June; and 5) the ongoing steps of final ratification by Parliament and the provincial legislatures. Speakers were careful to emphasize the inter-locked nature of these steps.

Participants who were practicing politicians were, perhaps, most aware of the two-edged nature of the process and its associated momentum. Progress in moving the process from one phase to another was a complicated task. Participants spoke of the laborious efforts of the Quebec and federal governments in preparing the way for constitutional talks. There was agreement that in the 1986-87 period even inaction had been deemed by all the players to be preferable to failure. The dangers posed by failure were on the minds of all participants: "imagine what would have happened had they (the First Ministers) failed. This is the central question." Concerned figures in both federal and provincial governments sensed, however, that inattention to the deep-rooted constitutional objectives of Quebec could not be a viable option.

Foremost among the positive attributes cited by various speakers concerning the pursuit of agreement was the careful and painstaking cultivation of views and positions away from the glare of publicity. Participants applauded the efforts to avoid confrontational politics or assorted forms of grandstanding. This requires a recognition of the discretion, tact and responsible leadership shown by various governmental officials and politicians. It was observed by several speakers that without this willingness for effective compromise, the opportunity for an agreement would have been lost.

Several participants highlighted the useful preparatory steps taken by the Government of Quebec during the 1985-1987 period. Representations were made throughout the country to both levels of government. Recognition of this should lead, it was argued, to an awareness of Quebec's commitment to the current Meech Lake understandings. It was also suggested that the Government of Quebec has the most to lose if Meech Lake fails the ratification gauntlet.

The perceived liability of this cautious agreement-oriented approach was that public participation was not a prominent feature of its early steps. Speakers lamented that various public observers of the Meech process criticized it as being burdened by excessive secrecy and private covenants. It was strongly asserted by one concerned academic, however, that such rhetorical flights missed fundamental realities. The First Ministers were the elected leaders of legitimately elected governments. Furthermore, the various legislatures at both levels had ample opportunity to hear concerns of citizens. Given that, it was feared that the perpetuation of such criticisms might seriously misrepresent the traditions of our constitutional practices. Despite these points, doubts remained about reconciling the interventions of interest groups with the realities of serious federal-provincial negotiation. One senior provincial government participant observed, "whether these interventions are compatible with a negotiated process is the key question."

Several participants reminded the meeting of the widespread lack of interest in constitutional matters during 1985 and 1986 outside Quebec. There appeared to be no widespread public efforts aimed at fostering extensive debate, and there were a number of other issues which ranked ahead of constitutional reform on the public agenda. The resulting *hiatus* in public demands may have permitted frank and open federal-provincial negotiations. It was speculated by one participant that some groups were actually using complaints over procedural openness to obscure their group's earlier inattentiveness to constitutional matters during the 1985-86 period.

It was also suggested that the process which produced the Constitutional Accord was as fundamental a part of the substance of the Accord as any of its formal provisions. Thus debates over Meech Lake's credibility involve discussions of process. The process of constitutional change is a complex topic at any time. Complexity was intensified in the case of the Meech Lake Accord because it attempted to rectify the limitations of the 1981-82 constitutional agreement. Seen in that light, issues of open access become secondary to alleviating the perceived dangers borne of Quebec's apparent isolation. This was illustrated by the highly limited range of amendments which the federal government would even consider. The decision to restrict amendments to "egregious errors" was recognized as having served to spark vigourous calls for true openness and flexibility. It is noteworthy that the Special Joint Committee of the Senate and the House of Commons on the Accord observed:

> The side agreement not to propose changes in the absence of "egregious errors" is binding only on First Ministers. It does not bind Parliament or the provincial legislatures. The whole Accord, or any part of it, can be amended or rejected. But practical politics being what they are, it is clear that flexibility *after* First Ministers have made a decision will always be limited and, therefore, in future the emphasis must be on a more open process *before* First Ministers meet to discuss constitutional issues.[2]

WHAT MECHANISMS ARE POTENTIALLY AVAILABLE FOR OPENING UP THE PROCESS OF CONSTITUTIONAL DEBATE AND REFORM?

Both the federal parliamentary hearings and those of the province of Ontario found themselves dealing with questions about openness and accessability. Despite the extensive work of selected committees in both sets of hearings, it was invariably the case that the limited opportunity for amendment represented by a formal multilaterally negotiated text had raised controversy. It was observed that having an agreed-upon text served to direct discussion into

2 The Report of the Special Joint Committee of the Senate and the House of Commons, *The 1987 Constitutional Accord* (Ottawa: Queen's Printer, 1987), 132. Emphasis in original.

profitable channels yet also limited the opportunity for subsequent amendment. It was suggested that Quebec avoided some of these difficulties by having its hearings prior to the final Ottawa First Ministers' meeting, but even here the tension between political practicalities and optimum openness was apparent. While the momentum for an agreement could have adapted to hearings in one province at this step, a commentator queried whether this momentum could have dealt with multiple governmental hearings and the cross-referencing of questions and positions across hearings. Speculation about the useful limits of openness and flexibility further intensified when it was pointed out that without a formal text, discussion would, of necessity, be vague and groups might opt for a "wait and see" posture.

Were such concerns over the process simply delaying tactics? Some thought this might be possible. One participant suggested that the complaints about process were really limited to those who felt themselves to be losers under the terms of Meech Lake. Others responded by arguing that there was a general lack of evidence that the Constitutional Accord would actually penalize the interests of any group. Furthermore, there was a degree of skepticism about both the knowledge base and representativeness of various groups. One speaker bluntly queried, "why should interest groups be more representative or democratic" than governments? While agreeing that the Accord did not penalize any particular group, some suggested that it was not really the crux of the issue. The key feature was that in the post-Charter environment, certain groups felt they held a certain right to involvement in any subsequent constitutional revisions. Thus, process complaints from these groups were expressions designed for recognition of their "status".

Considerable time was spent discussing the potential for new mechanisms to facilitate federal-provincial discussions and decision-making. One speaker made reference to procedural distinctions made in certain other countries between partial and extensive constitutional changes. Partial changes can be accomplished incrementally on a simpler, more frequent basis.

Most of the discussion, though, was concentrated upon the possibility of having ongoing or permanent constitutional review committees in the federal and provincial legislatures. Ongoing committees would serve to prepare both the general public and the media for future items on the constitutional agenda. They might also serve to educate concerned legislators. These committees might sufficiently de-mystify the constitutional amendment process to permit review of such alternative amending procedures as discussed in the preceding paragraph. Noting that "nothing precludes any legislature from reviewing constitutional proposals", one speaker suggested that it would be "interesting to see if any constitutional legislative committees develop in advance" of future talks on the Senate, fisheries, or native rights.

Ongoing committees would also provide an avenue for interest group participation. Groups could be heard well in advance of any serious federal-provincial negotiations. One speaker noted the apparent difficulty in generating public interest without a "final text". Periodic group presentations might mean little to these groups without the opportunity to comment on agreements in process.

In future we might think of setting a "constitutional agenda" for a particular period of time. However, the more the process is formalized, the more it gives rise to fears of limited room for negotiations or concessions. There were also questions raised as to where and when such legislative committees might be set in motion. One speaker used the Ontario committee that dealt with the Ombudsman as an example. It was suggested this might serve as a model. Another made reference to Quebec's process for dealing with the Meech Lake proposals before the final text was agreed upon a month later. This gave rise to some concern about the possibilities of interest groups winning concessions from one government and then springing it upon the other governments.

The debate over the Meech Lake process was a useful inquiry into the pitfalls of federal-provincial decision-making in an open society with eager interest groups. Is it possible that efficiency and legitimacy are becoming more difficult to reconcile? Deliberation upon this dilemma sparked heated debate over the place and role of interest groups.

WHAT LESSONS CAN BE DRAWN FROM THE DEBATES ABOUT THE MEECH LAKE
PROCESS ON THE PLACE OF INTEREST GROUPS AND THEIR OPTIMAL RELATIONSHIP TO
CONSTITUTIONAL DISCUSSIONS?

There was widespread agreement that interest groups were now important parts of our political landscape. While several speakers questioned the representativeness of such groups, their vitality and access to media voices was uniformly recognized. Their ability to gain media attention was regarded as a vital part of their political strength.

One speaker lamented that interest groups had taken from political parties the practical responsibility for organizing people and expressing their views to public servants and legislators. This was seen as a serious problem due to the uncertain and parochial agendas of such groups. There were also concerns raised about the actual representativeness of the agendas put forth by interest group leaderships. Where such agendas were the work of a small circle there was seen to be a greater danger that their concerns would be inadequately representative.

Despite the variations in the structure and openness of interest groups, it was widely agreed that these groups now played a major role in public debate; and yet, it was also acknowledged that these groups were, to a degree, marginalized in the interests of completing the unfinished agenda from 1981-82 and "bringing Quebec in". A number of interest groups, particularly in English Canada, complained of excessive secrecy and of governmental rigidity. Such complaints were countered by seminar participants who emphasized the political mandates of the First Ministers. Various participants also argued that negotiations only produce fruitful results when the players at the table can "deliver the goods". While interest groups can offer a voice for the concerns of some or all of their members, they are not governments. This point prompted a government figure to warn against "polluting the negotiation process" with players who have no mandate "to reach a deal". It was submitted that this limited the value of interest groups as prospective participants in delicate constitutional negotiations.

The key question becomes one of finding a way for these groups to have input without undermining the potential for compromise. If such a way is not found, confrontation results. Such confrontation could be strong enough to endanger the entire process. Perhaps more importantly there is the conundrum that interest group input is most useful before the actual terms of agreement are reached. Yet this is also the stage where it is most difficult for groups to argue definitely because their opinions will, of necessity, be conditional upon acceptance of a final text. Future consultative mechanisms will undoubtedly continue to encounter this. One solution proposed was for ongoing constitutional committees where, over time, there would develop greater sensitivity not only to certain group interests, but also to the imperatives of selected trade-offs. One participant spoke of the difficulties of a group seeking to defend and represent their constitutional concerns in the period before the April meeting at Meech Lake. The serious limitations imposed on their preparations due to uncertainty about the ultimate text and their own financial limitations were of considerable concern to their members.

Some participants cautioned against according interest groups unjustified importance. Analogies to labour-management relations were provided to support the position that places "at the table" should be reserved for those who could deliver "the goods" (i.e., formal legislative consent as required by the constitutional amending formulas). The suitability of such an analogy was questioned by some given the principles of public participation upon which our understanding of liberal democracy is based.

Nonetheless accommodations between governments and interest groups are seen as imperative. Lowell Murray, for example, has "suggested to the Special Joint Committee, [that] in future there could be an opportunity for parliamentary and public consideration of the issues before governments reach agreement on amendment texts, and this may make management of the negotiation process more complex".[3] Constitutional talks will thus become even more cumbersome. It was accepted by conference participants that governments now needed to be extremely sensitive to interest groups as representatives of certain segments of society. If such respect is not granted there would be political costs to bear. One participant reminded the group that "governments defeat themselves"; the way to overcome such a political liability was to arrange a means for ongoing group input. One speaker speculated that complaints from particular groups over process were simply ways of saying to governments: "Ignore us and we can make your lives miserable".

WHAT FACTORS ARE SHAPING THE FUTURE OF CANADA'S CONSTITUTIONAL AGENDA?

Whatever changes are made or mechanisms adopted, the nature of reform to the constitutional process will ultimately rest upon the substantive agenda items. Senate reform and fisheries jurisdiction stand as two current examples. It is clear that there are important constitutional issues and questions to be faced in the future months and years. Conference participants engaged in some useful speculation upon possible future trends and concerns.

There were two basic schools of thought about future constitutional discussions. The first was composed of those who expressed fears of an endless series of provincial efforts to put forth "pet issues". One speaker made a critical reference to the possibility of Canada developing a constitution resembling those of various American states. Perhaps too many items had been made constitutional. The second school was more concerned about the possibility of paralysis, as demands for openness submerged the possibilities of reaching agreements regarded by provincial governments as important to their citizens.

Certain speakers made reference to a recent public speech by Senator Lowell Murray who spoke of federal recognition that various provinces will have particular issues which they deem of critical importance. It was Senator Murray's hope that the constitutional negotiating process would be sufficiently flexible to permit provinces to take the lead in shaping debates about their critical issues in a manner similar to that played by Quebec in the case of Meech Lake. While flexibility was generally endorsed, certain individuals feared the development of a band-wagon of provincial complaints gaining the status of

---

3   Senator Lowell Murray, "The Process of Constitutional Change in Canada: The Lessons of Meech Lake," *Choices* (February, 1988), 6.

constitutional issues. One academic lamented, will "every province get to have an issue?"

Despite their differences, most participants saw Meech Lake's ratification as a positive step. It would deal with a major aspect left unfinished in 1981-82 and allow Canada to complete that chapter of its evolution. Attention could then be directed toward the challenges posed by other public issues.

ECONOMIC POLICY-MAKING AND COORDINATION

In the second session the debate moved on to the inter-relationship of contemporary federalism to economic policy-making. Despite the new terrain, the contours of discussion and reflection remained similar. Central to both sessions was the search for an effective yet generally accepted means of improving the conduct of public business in an era of changing constitutional and political conditions. While the discussion about the Meech Lake Accord had concentrated upon the process of constitutional renewal, the economic policy discussions centred upon the renewed search for co-ordinated direction in an environment shaped by the constitutional division of powers and by evolving global threats and opportunities. As a senior academic declared, the question "is how far to go in developing common policies or complementary action and whether, to the extent that this effort is made, this freezes out interest organizations or reduces citizen involvement in processes of policy-making and correspondingly reduces government accountability." The search for answers to both of these policy challenges has been complicated by the dynamic nature of events and political pressures. The *Constitution Act, 1982*, was up for significant revision only five years after its proclamation. Economically, fears of growing global protectionism and of "subsidy wars" were apparently propelling policy-makers to evaluate new trade relationships and co-ordinating mechanisms. Both the national economic and constitutional agendas were undergoing strong pressures for change and adaptation. Participants in the Advisory Council discussions felt it critical that Canadians gain an appreciation of both these fundamental policy fields.

As with the Meech Lake session, the economic discussions covered several key questions:

1. What is the basic nature of the regional cleavages which constrain effective policy co-ordination?
2. How much federal-provincial co-ordination is actually desirable in economic matters?
3. What is the optimal relationship between private interests, public input and policy-making?

4. What are the future options for policy co-ordination within our evolving federal system?

WHAT IS THE BASIC NATURE OF THE REGIONAL CLEAVAGES WHICH CONSTRAIN
EFFECTIVE POLICY COORDINATION?

From the outset of this session, attention turned to the problems posed by regional rivalries. The opening speaker argued for emphasis upon policy harmonization as the best means of avoiding costs due to inefficiencies. In order to demonstrate this point, he asserted "look at aerospace—hardly an advertisement for efficiency in the way national policy has gone." The speaker criticized the use of procurement and other government decisions for regional development objectives. This, he suggested, promoted inefficiency and excess costs. Furthermore, it constrained Canada's efforts to be competitive on a global scale.

This stark interpretation was viewed critically by many participants. While accepting that the promotion of regional development may run counter to strict efficiency considerations, many felt this to be too restricted a perspective. One line of critical response addressed the apolitical nature of such commentary. Governments are political institutions and therefore their decisions, be they about procurement or about the location of the new national space agency headquarters, will always have to reflect not just economic efficiency but political forces. People believe governments should defend territorial interests. As one speaker put it—in Canada debate is not simply about "Jobs! Jobs! Jobs!" (to echo a comment attributed to the Prime Minister), but rather "Location! Location! Location!".

Discussion continued with the aerospace sector as a focus. A senior government figure asserted that "having picked the aerospace sector the first speaker had picked a terrific sector that illustrates that there is no international competitive paradigm that can be pointed to. Every government in the world has engaged in one form or another of subsidizing the aerospace industry." Canada was far from alone in attempting to balance economic support with regional pressures.

Interprovincial rivalries were also seen as forcing certain issues onto the policy agenda. Questions were raised, however, about the ability of the Canadian economy to tolerate such pressures. The international environment was seen by some as becoming potentially perilous for Canadian interests. U.S. economic leadership may be ebbing and thus greater attention needs to be paid to protectionism and the relative strength of a united Europe or a resurgent Far East. Some observers argued that it was vital that provinces overcome their rivalries and set clear objectives with the federal government. However, most cautioned that the actual elements of provincial or regional rivalries were deep-rooted and therefore not amenable to quick solutions. Furthermore, if constitutional debates emphasized decentralization and provincial priorities, this would reinforce regional rivalries. Attention thus turned to the nature of interprovincial rivalries and their impacts.

Procurement fights received the most attention as examples of the complex factors involved in regional cleavages. The fight among Atlantic governments for a new Litton plant was highlighted as an example of the serious danger posed by interprovincial competition. Some asserted that incremental policy-making intensified such problems since it sacrificed comprehensive planning for case-by-case announcements. While perhaps true, others argued that the problem went deeper than this.

Concentration upon the question of regional cleavages moved to the twin issues of internal barriers to trade and the recent history of confrontation in federal-provincial relations. The process of policy co-ordination amid this atmosphere of confrontation has been awkward and hesitant. One speaker, a senior provincial official, lamented the lack of a neutral advisory body with the confidence of the federal and provincial governments; "when just governments are involved you run up against barriers. This type of process needs some sort of a back-up..." An advisory group of this sort could offer input on the trade-offs involved in major decisions and offer advice as to possible compromises which might prove beneficial in promoting harmony and making losses easier to bear.

The issue of internal barriers to trade strikes at the heart of debate over regional or provincial cleavages. Provincial figures spoke of the dilemma posed in attempting to protect provincial interests yet recognize the benefits of economies of scale and of national (or even regional) co-ordination. Insight into such difficulties was provided by reference to the record of achievement displayed by the Council of Maritime Premiers. While that Council has encouraged the joint provision of certain services, differences remain due to conflicting views and interests. Major economic choices too often have winners and losers without clearly compensatory trade-offs.

Persuading political leaders to put regional or national co-ordination before the fight for their province or region is thus a very difficult challenge. Coupled with strong territorial identities, the confrontational style of executive federalism may exacerbate cleavages. However, most participants concluded that the fundamental problem arose more from a long history of regional distrust and the "zero sum" public perception of economic decision-making. The mechanisms of federal-provincial negotiations were undoubtedly important, but they were not seen as decisive in shaping regional discontent. They reflected underlying perceptions and suspicions, rather than creating them. Given this conclusion, attention turned to assessing how much co-operation was desirable.

Assessing the optimal degree of compromise and/or co-ordination would then lead to an assessment of the place of public input, and of desired future policy directions.

HOW MUCH FEDERAL-PROVINCIAL COORDINATION IS ACTUALLY DESIRABLE IN ECONOMIC MATTERS?

Participants grappled with the task of delineating the degree and types of co-operation which they felt desirable on matters of economic policy. Strong co-ordination was favoured by some. Others argued for the benefits of intergovernmental competition. Discussion also covered the criteria for assessing the benefits (or costs) of co-operation. Some asserted that the size of governments was a pivotal indicator, others felt the better measuring tool was the size of observable economic challenges, while still others wanted to use strict guidelines based upon program outputs and productivity indicators. Obviously, given the range of ideological differences and divergent perceptions of the challenges ahead, disagreement was more prevalent than consensus. This should not however blind us to the importance of the question as a whole and its relation to the broader agenda of discussion.

Given the participants' prevailing interest in federalism, comments were related to trends in federal-provincial and interprovincial relations. Central to the discussion were the competing perceptions of the values or costs of inter-governmental competition. Relying upon the insights of Albert Breton in the Macdonald Commission and a predisposition to a limited state, some argued that rivalry and competition should be encouraged. This rivalry prevented governments from taking economic growth for granted. Incentives for business such as low taxes and lax environmental standards were seen as restraining growth of governmental activity. This restraint was valued by some participants.

Others argued that such an approach overlooked efficiency costs and the growing international challenges and threats. These observers emphasized that Canada was only a middle-sized power with an economy dependent upon market access to other nations. Canada could no longer be hamstrung by parochial outlooks or interprovincial squabbles and ill-fated giveaways. Canadians could no longer smugly anticipate prosperity. Far from endorsing small governments as an answer, this group supported policy co-ordination and extensive consultation.

Overall, this portion of the debate is least amenable to a brief summary. The issues and disputes are complex and deep. Thus, one will find strands of this debate in subsequent sections. Perspectives on co-operation and the role of governments involve ideological and economic values and understandings.

Nonetheless there was widespread recognition of rapidly changing economic circumstances and of the values of reasoned restraint. Debate arose when one faced the choice of adapting the system to deal with these matters. Some saw the answer in large-scale, coordinated planning; others saw it in lean, competing governments. Both, however, saw a need for adaptation in order to achieve international market competitiveness.

WHAT IS THE OPTIMAL RELATIONSHIP BETWEEN PRIVATE INTERESTS, PUBLIC INPUT AND POLICY-MAKING?

Central to both the debates on Meech Lake and those on economic questions was the issue of public access to the process. One speaker argued that the central matter was the availability of relevant information. Public or group input without adequate, timely knowledge would be of limited value. Given the general reluctance of governments to part with sensitive information, some felt there was reason for pessimism about effective co-operation. One long-time observer of federal-provincial dealings declared that "Canada is not short of governmental institutions. The issue is one of information." Participants strongly agreed that governments should provide more information in the interests of policy education and longer term planning. One participant characterized the central dilemma as being how to merge openness with the closed-door sessions which feature cautious bargaining and deliberation upon compromises. Policy-making was thus compared to a regulatory board process whereby "first the facts are heard" and then behind closed doors decisions are reached. One speaker complained that currently intergovernmental conferences "are almost always closed, but leaky"—possibly the worst of both worlds.

By contrast with the preceding constitutional debate, participants in this discussion saw public input on economic matters as being a task for interest groups. Economic policy-making and co-ordination was seen in a very different focus. Major economic interest groups were seen as vital players, whose involvement was essential to successful policy-making. The question became one of finding an appropriate model to facilitate such involvement. Some argued for new intergovernmental mechanisms or for modified forms of industrial re-structuring. One speaker advocated an intergovernmental forum "between the two orders of government and business". Such ideas did not seem to win strong support, though. One participant suggested that the Macdonald Commission had made clear the limited possibilities for corporatism or new intergovernmental mechanisms. Competition and liberalized markets had therefore been promoted. While no one else took up the reference to the Macdonald Commission, the issue of freer trade and its implementation received extensive debate.

Many participants had at least some degree of "first-hand" knowledge about the consultative efforts which had accompanied the Canada-U.S. trade deal negotiations. These consultations appeared to receive general support as a positive step in the road to improved policy planning. While provinces were consulted and listened to, speakers hastened to acknowledge that "being listened to" and "winning their point" were quite different phenomena. Yet, in terms of the overall consultative process, many seemed impressed.

This spirit of support for current consultative processes waned, however, when it came to the sectoral and other consultative bodies designed to deal with issues such as internal trade barriers or the regulation of financial institutions. These groups were seen as having the most difficult task—developing agreement upon issues of fierce and fundamental conflict. It was asserted by various speakers, however, that although one could simply be skeptical about the workings of these groups serious reflection did indicate that their labours were productive. One positive example cited by a senior provincial figure was the work of the Canadian Council of Resource Ministers.

Several speakers elaborated upon the complex inter-relationships of existing federal-provincial forums. First Ministers' Conferences were seen as serving three roles: 1) resolving conflict 2) publicizing important issues and 3) promoting and approving the labours of the various consultative mechanisms. First Ministers' Conferences may promote the efforts of these mechanisms, for example by holding the federal and provincial sectoral ministers accountable. Action is therefore encouraged as a means of avoiding the censure of the First Ministers.

There is thus the ongoing dilemma of providing the optimal channels for interest group input into the growing federal-provincial machinery. Many seem to regard the recent trend toward widespread consultations and federal-provincial information-sharing as a positive direction. Such assessments are, of course, difficult to prove conclusively. Various participants spoke of the significant improvements made to the trade deal between its initial preliminary text and the final, public legal text. It was claimed that attentiveness had helped the federal government to sense problem areas in advance and make appropriate adjustments. Consultation had worked and unnecessary confrontation was avoided. One example of such federal sensitivity was believed to be the moderate wording of the reserve powers section of the federal legislation implementing the Free Trade Agreement.

Despite the apparent progress some serious concerns about the existing input mechanisms and their operations were voiced. One participant said that private consultations weakened the strength of small provinces and the interests dependent upon them. Some acknowledged that "in those private sessions there is a lot of bullying that goes on" and that the interests of smaller provinces may be relegated to a secondary position on the agenda. The interests of industry associations would be enhanced at the expense of the interests of smaller provinces. Another participant advocated greater study of the support provided by Canadian governments to various interest groups. He argued that we had not sufficiently thought through the best means of co-ordinating such support. Finally, there were concerns that we still lacked sufficient, neutral information on over-arching national economic trade-offs. Governments had developed better consultative mechanisms without also fostering feelings of collegiality and shared responsibility.

Overall, participants felt much more favourably disposed toward interest group involvement on matters of economic policy. Even those advocating more limited government intervention in the economy, supported consultation as a means toward better government. The two most commonly identified problems were the persistent interregional conflict over procurement or other forms of government largesse, and the need for new policy strategies to cope with the evolution of international competition.

WHAT ARE THE FUTURE OPTIONS FOR POLICY COORDINATION WITHIN OUR EVOLVING FEDERAL SYSTEM?

Debate on this critical point had been stimulated by the "discussion paper" circulated by Peter Leslie in advance of the session.[4] Professor Leslie suggested that recent trends in American-Canadian economic relations may result in strengthened pressures for consultation. International irritants such as the softwood lumber dispute and the new institutions such as the dispute settlement mechanism were seen as having the potential to seriously alter the policy environment. Such changes deserved careful consideration. This consideration was seen as revolving around the following "strategic choices"—1) improving the policy-making capabilities of federal-provincial conferences, 2) altering the division of powers under the *B.N.A. Act*, and/or 3) clarifying the range of bilateral and multilateral responses available when areas under provincial jurisdiction were threatened by international pressures.

The complexity of such choices was intensified when speakers debated whether the proposed Canada-U.S. trade deal would allow integrated national planning or would restrict such efforts to a sectoral basis. Federal-provincial relations would have to take Washington into account. This brought into play differing Canadian and American perceptions and traditions about the relation-

---

4   The reference for this paper appears in the introduction.

ship between trade and foreign policy. Unlike Canada, the U.S. was seen as regarding these as being fundamentally linked.

In the end, the participants agreed that there were future dilemmas to be faced. The experience of the softwood lumber deal convinced many that in the future, trade and economic issues would be dominated as they had been in recent years, by "political hardball".

Commentary

Avigail Eisenberg

Les discussions du Conseil consultatif de l'Institut des relations intergouvernementales sur les modifications constitutionnelles et l'élaboration des politiques économiques ne permettent pas de tirer des conclusions précises quant au meilleur mécanisme pour y parvenir.

En ce qui concerne la politique économique, le débat s'articula autour de deux visions de développement économique: l'une favorisant la coordination entre le fédéral et les provinces, et l'autre penchant plutôt pour un "fédéralisme compétitif". Les conférences annuelles des premiers ministres furent considérées comme un forum offrant des possibilités intéressantes pour la planification économique. Pour ce faire, il faudra toutefois que le rôle décisionnel des premiers ministres soit accru et que les groupes d'intérêt puissent y participer d'une manière effective.

Pour ce qui est des questions touchant les modifications constitutionnelles (et ici l'Accord du lac Meech servit d'exemple), le dilemme majeur qui se pose est de trouver le juste équilibre entre les besoins de discrétion d'une part et de participation du public d'autre part. A cet égard, l'auteur, à l'instar de quelques autres intervenants, suggère que la meilleure solution pour intégrer les groupes d'intérêt est une utilisation accrue des institutions intermédiaires, telles que le Parlement ou les comités parlementaires.

While the future may necessitate playing "political hardball" when it comes to forming economic policy, the present reflects far too much indecisiveness and dissent to make this possible. Conclusions, or "lessons to be learnt" from the Advisory Council's discussions of current processes employed to facilitate economic change are not clear cut because so many questions remain unanswered. The same is less true for the discussions of process related to constitutional change and Meech Lake. This is partly because there are certain rules of the constitutional game that all players and analysts recognize as being important. Participants share a similar "language" when it comes to discussing the place of executive federalism in the process which led to the Constitutional Accord, even if they do not agree on all particulars of the outcome.

The rules for managing economic change were not shared as widely. This was due to a number of important factors. First, a discussion about process and economic change, even when circumscribed to a number of central questions, seemed to invite too many diverse examples and therefore diverse analyses. The direction of economic change and the role of government in this change are matters that in part depend on which sector of the economy is being scrutinized. Yet this is the crux of a basic problem; sectoral diversity makes a co-ordinative industrial policy difficult to formulate.

A second reason for the difficulties is that the level of disagreement among participants was fundamental. Some participants opted for a more competitive strategy while others argued for one which necessitated more co-ordination. Those who argued for co-ordination were generally more concerned with responding to international market forces while those who argued for the competitive strategy were generally focussing upon the trade barriers within Canada. This in turn coloured each group's attitude towards the extent to which federal-provincial co-ordination mechanisms had to be improved and how this should be accomplished.

In the discussions there was a definite split between those participants who argued for controlling federalism so as to make co-ordination of economic policy possible and those who favoured the idea of competitive federalism. Participants who favoured co-ordination argued that federal-provincial conflict creates inefficiency, reducing Canada's ability to compete internationally. Lack of co-ordination has also left the door open to foreign multinationals who exploit the domestic politics of Canadian federalism to their own economic advantage. There is a need to assign priority to the sectors of our national economy and on the basis of these priorities to work out a more economically efficient industrial policy.

Yet, economic efficiency cannot be the only goal of an industrial policy in Canada. The location of jobs and industries, and not simply the efficiency of those industries, is a central concern. Participants recognized that the question of location cannot always be decided on the basis of efficiency. Political and social concerns are imperative as well. Even when concerns involving economic efficiency dominate decisions, it should be recognized that political harmony and stability may themselves be prerequisites for the achievement of this efficiency. Therefore, trade-offs which occur within the economy inevitably involve social and political trade-offs. It is not simply a matter of giving the contract to the lowest bidder. The federal government must take care to treat the regions fairly, answering the economic concerns of poorer regions in order to promote the country's social welfare as well as to promote the government's political welfare.

Participants who expressed their preference for competitive federalism did not address their arguments directly to those made by their opponents. Instead they pointed to the conclusions of the Royal Commission on the Economic Union and Development Prospects for Canada which also support a combination of federalism and economic competition.[5] Constructing industrial policy may in some ways be easier on the provincial level because the federal government is much more constrained given the range of factors it needs to consider. Yet provincial economies do not operate in isolation from each other. Dealing with these spill-over effects as they arise, that is incrementally, is costly in terms of efficiency and may be too high a price to pay simply in order to avoid framing a broader industrial plan.

As for the type of forum that would facilitate rational economic planning, First Ministers' Conferences (FMCs) were thought to have promise even though they were characterized as having numerous drawbacks. Conferences should be able to incorporate both efficacious participation by the public and effective decision-making by the executives. The conferences should have two phases. The first would be one in which the public contributes its perspective and is able to get information from the government. The second phase should be less open in order to be more conducive to decision-making.

While in principle FMCs seem to be able to meet the objectives of openness and decisiveness, there were many complaints voiced about how FMCs actually operate. Some participants complained that the resources available at FMCs were not being used to their maximum utility. Reports prepared for the conferences are often not scrutinized sufficiently by the First Ministers. Whether as a cause or effect of knowing that the conferences will not be used for decision-making, many people involved in FMCs do not take them seriously. However, it is not clear why the conferences and their participants are not using the forums for what they were intended. Or are they? One participant argued that the purpose of FMCs had more to do with accountability than decision-making; they are forums from which the governments can jointly communicate to the public. Yet, if this is the case, conferences should be planned and judged on this basis. It is ridiculous to centre decision-making machinery and information around an institution that is not being used to make decisions.

One point upon which all participants agreed is that interest group involvement in economic decision-making is essential. A similar consensus was not expressed regarding interest group participation in the constitutional process

---

5   Albert Breton, "Supplementary Statement", Royal Commission on the Economic Union and Development Prospects for Canada, *Report*, v.3 (Ottawa: Canadian Publishing Centre, Supply and Services Canada, 1985) 486-526.

and the Meech Lake Accord. The health of the economy was seen to involve the public directly in the sense that the public is largely responsible for creating a healthy economy and the public is ultimately the judge of the economy's health. Yet, for most participants, the health of the Constitution was seen to be the charge of government in both these respects.

The discussions about the process leading to the Meech Lake Accord are easier to assess partly because there exists a coherent body of scholarly literature on the process associated with executive federalism. One would expect that the conclusions generated about executive processes within this literature could be supported or refuted by the Meech process. The literature on executive federalism is most applicable to areas of policy in which it is possible to minimize variables connected to public participation and thus focus primarily on relations between governments. In this respect constitutional change is better suited than economic change (at least in Canada), to test some of the conclusions in the literature about executive federalism.

There is little said in that literature about how a particular issue around which executive discussions are centred affects the process. Rather the literature dwells on how the executive process affects the way issues are defined by guiding debate to focus on territorial cleavages rather than other cleavages which the public is more apt to introduce. On this latter point there seems to be ample evidence in the case of the Constitutional Accord negotiations that this tendency is real; the focus on provincial autonomy and the francophone/anglophone cleavage dominated the negotiations. The concerns of women and Native Canadians were not voiced until the public later became involved in the process.

The obverse possibility, that the nature of the issue is apt to affect the process, is one worthy of serious investigation. In the case of the Meech Lake Accord, getting Quebec to be party to the *Constitution Act, 1982* was seen to be of such import by the other executive participants that there was a reluctance to invite full participation from arenas where it was felt that the importance of the cause was not appreciated. For example, that interest groups did not appreciate the importance of the Constitutional Accord but rather were guided by their own interests carried the implication that their participation in this particular process was less than fully legitimate. It was not simply lamented that certain interest groups would make effective resolution of the Accord more difficult. Rather, it seemed that certain objections to the Accord could never be justified in the eyes of the executives who supported the Accord. If the interest groups "really" understood how essential it was to secure Quebec's agreement they would not be opposing the Accord for self-interested reasons. The fact that provincial legislatures are likely to impede the process of constitutional amendment was cited as a possible reason to temper their participation in the amendment process as well.

A third problem also relating to the nature of the issue is that the more complicated the issue the less fruitful public participation. Complexity arises from the very nature of some issues, particularly constitutional amendments. It also arises from the tendency of the public to add to the agenda by "jumping on the constitutional bandwagon" with their own pet concerns. This, in turn, leads to a more trying negotiation process. The more complicated the negotiation process is the less likely public participation in the process will be invited.

It is possible, given the complicated and wide ranging nature of the issue, that little could have been done about this latter problem in the case of the Constitutional Accord. It was suggested that in the future, amending the Constitution should proceed more incrementally and that the deals between the governments reflect efforts at partial revisions rather than total change. Public participation in the amending process might be a necessity which governments must become used to dealing with effectively. However, not all amendments need be subject to extensive public debate. An example cited was the revision of section 43 on education rights in order to ascribe these rights to Pentecostal schools in Newfoundland. It may be worth our while to use more extensively different amendment procedures for extensive amendments and for narrower revisions.[6] However, doing so gives rise to the question of who decides when an issue is of one nature rather than another.

As for the executives' role, their monopoly over the decision-making process with regards to the Accord was subjected to only mild criticism in the Advisory Council discussions. It may be true that the executives were too concerned about retaining or extending the power of each of their governments while at the same time bringing Quebec into the constitutional fold to forge a deal that would be more acceptable to the public. However, it was also felt that the Accord would not have come very far if it were not for the executives' leadership role and the discreteness of the process. Evidence to substantiate each side of

---

6   Switzerland uses two different amendment procedures to revise its constitution, one for partial revisions and the other for total revisions. The Swiss Federal Constitution was totally revised in 1874 and since then has undergone over 80 partial revisions. There have been efforts since the mid 1970s to totally revise the Constitution once again. A great impediment to these efforts has been the procedure which must be followed in the case of total revisions. Among other things, this procedure requires a substantial amount of consent directly from the citizenry and from the cantons making consensus on extensive total revision difficult to achieve. See: *Federal Constitution of Switzerland*, article 119 and 120; J. Murray Luck, ed., *Modern Switzerland*, (California: The Society for the Promotion of Science and Scholarship Inc., 1978); Charles F. Schultz, *Revising the Federal Constitution of Switzerland* (Ottawa: Department of Political Science, Carleton University, 1983).

the argument was drawn from the 1982 agreement. The executives forged the final deal with the inclusion of section 33, linguistic rights, and the amending formula. Public interest groups, on the other hand, pushed for the inclusion of gender rights and Native rights. Yet, regardless of whether it is more desirable to rely on the leadership of the executives or the public interest groups to introduce the relevant considerations in the constitutional reform process, there is a need for executives to recognize that in 1981-82 the public became part of the amending process and today some participation on their part is unavoidable.

Public participation becomes much more problematic when secrecy and complexity are part of the process as well. One hypothesis put forward by Don Smiley in "An Outsider's Observations of Federal-Provincial Relations Among Consenting Adults" is that a reliance on the executives in decision-making processes will tend to shroud an issue in secrecy and contribute to the complexity of the issue, thus removing it from public understanding. [7] The tendency towards secrecy in executive negotiations is illustrated by the discussions which led to framing the Constitutional Accord. As one participant in the Advisory Council meeting observed, the process of constitutional amendment must be demystified in order to facilitate effective public and legislative participation. As for the charge of complexity there seem to be two types to distinguish. First is the complexity ushered in by those members of the executive who find it necessary to reinforce agreements with a myriad of technicalities due to the legal nature of these agreements. This type of complexity is often criticized because it places the matter beyond the public's reach by translating the agreement into a language not shared by the public. Second there is the type of complexity which itself results from widespread public participation. The public's tendency to jump on the constitutional bandwagon with additional issues complicates attempts at constitutional amendment. Thus, constitutional amendments seem destined to be complicated by whichever process the government chooses to follow.

Another Smiley observation may be pertinent here: executive federalism perpetuates conflict between the two orders of government. [8] The tendency on the part of each executive to extend the powers of its government as an end in itself rather than as a means to a desired end is truly a worrying prospect. However, in the case of the Meech Lake Accord, this tendency did not exist nor

---

7 D. Smiley, "An Outsider's Observations of Federal-Provincial Relations Among Consenting Adults", *Confrontation and Collaboration; Intergovernmental Relations in Canada Today*, Richard Simeon ed., (Mississauga: Institute of Public Administration of Canada, 1979), p. 105-6.

8 *Ibid.*, p. 106.

was it considered to be a worry by the participants. If anything, the worry was directed to the absence of conflict between the premiers and the Prime Minister in contrast to the apparent conflict among various sections of the public. It seems that just as too much conflict is undesirable, so is the appearance of too little conflict.

Many of the problems which the executives faced in the Meech Lake process ought to have been handled by the mediating institutions. One of the most important roles of Parliament and parliamentary committees is to facilitate communication between the public and executives. Yet, in the case of the Constitutional Accord, performing this role was riddled with problems. The committees were thought to be rubber-stamps to a deal that was beyond revision. This perception made it difficult for the committees or the legislatures to create a mood in the public arena in favour of the Accord. The function of selling the Accord to the public could not be performed. Yet, in this case, that is exactly what the executives needed—an institution, trusted by the public, that would sell the Accord to the public. This need was particularly felt given that the media was seen to be perpetuating a "misinformation" campaign regarding the Accord. Thus, the executives acted contrary to their own interests by not consulting with their legislatures at an earlier point in the process. By following a route to decision-making that relied primarily on their own input, the executives created the perception that the legislatures and their committees would be unable to alter the Accord. This in turn meant that the public would be less inclined to trust the information and opinions of legislators and committee members. This serves as a good example of the concrete way in which the credibility (or lack thereof) of the process shapes the credibility of the issue.

As previously explained, reliance on the legislatures and parliamentary committees in the decision-making process may complicate the amendment procedure and in the case of the Meech Lake Accord, may in the end make its implementation unattainable. Partly this is because legislative committees involved in the process are likely to proceed on the basis of their own province's interests rather than the interests of the country as a whole. Yet, in the case of wide-ranging constitutional amendments such as the *Constitutional Accord, 1987*, there may be a need for the committees to be exposed to a broader-than-provincial perspective in order to assess the issue fairly. Unfortunately, suggestions to hear testimony from outside the province may provoke a political backlash from within the province.

A suggestion has been put forth by both the House of Commons Select Committee on Constitutional Reform and the Ontario Select Committee on Constitutional Reform to establish a standing committee on constitutional and intergovernmental affairs within each province. Such standing committees may allow the legislatures to be more adept participants in the decision-making process. In addition, the continuity of such committees may allow for a broader-than-provincial perspective to be represented within each province. The committees may be able to travel to different provinces at times when there is not a pressing and politically volatile issue on the agenda. However, the mere existence of such committees will not guarantee their legitimacy in the eyes of the public. Only an efficacious role for these committees in the decision-making process will accomplish this.

A final issue of marked controversy in the Advisory Council discussions was the role of interest groups in the process of negotiating constitutional amendments. Interest group involvement in the Meech Lake Accord process was particularly criticized. Interest groups were criticized for overcomplicating the process by adding too much to the an agenda which was directed at a specific set of objectives. In some instances they were approaching the Accord from a very self-interested perspective and were seen as not appreciating the importance of what was at stake should the Accord not succeed. The groups were thought to be misinformed at times. This would partly be the product of the secrecy of the process and partly the product of poor information coming from the media. Lack of accurate or complete information tended to make it difficult for interest groups to assess the Accord and resources were wasted by some groups who attempted to "cover all the bases" rather than deal with a discrete set of issues.

Establishing a standing committee as described above may help to remedy the problem of accurate and sophisticated information getting to the public. In addition, the need for accurate information and "a precise text from which to work" means that it is not necessary or desirable to involve the public in the process from the very start. Interest groups need a solid starting point from which to build their case and must have input before a final form is negotiated. In general, it seems that the quality not quantity of participation is what matters.

The problems attached to interest group involvement may go beyond anything the government can do. Exclusion of interest groups from the decision-making process may be justified on the basis of evidence which suggests that these groups are generally unrepresentative of the public sentiment. Unlike the premiers or the Prime Minister, interest groups are not elected. Yet, they may be very well organized and well funded. Their input into the constitutional amendment process may perpetuate or institutionalize constitutional instability. What seems to be needed is a way to temper their involvement without freezing them out of the process. The best vehicles to accomplish this are the mediating institutions. The political party is one type of institution that could be used for this function. Should this prove insufficient, increased reliance on parliamentary committees may be imperative.

Overall, the issues arising from the Constitutional Accord negotiations seem to have been better handled by the participants of the Advisory Council meeting than the issues involving economic change. Some useful prescriptions for the course of future processes involving consitutional change were set forth and examined. These might warrant further investigation.

As for the discussion about economic policy-making, what seems to be needed is more discussion centred around specific questions. Exactly which strategy should inform our industrial policy, one which mixes co-ordination within federalism or one which opts for competitive federalism? Is sectoral planning possible given the social, political and economic realities in Canada? What type of forum should be used to facilitate economic decision-making? What is the purpose of First Ministers' Conferences on the Economy and how can they be improved in light of their purpose? Which institution will be able to handle the problems which arise out of a trade agreement with the United States? Should the Advisory Council participants choose to focus on these questions in upcoming meetings they will spend their time most productively.

V

Chronology

NINE

Chronology of Events 1986-1987

Darrel R. Reid and Christopher Kendall

A list of recurring entries begins page 250

1986

8 January
Environment—Acid Rain—Canada-U.S. Relations

Special Canadian envoy on acid rain, William Davis, and his U.S. counterpart Drew Lewis recommend in their Joint Report of the Special Envoys on Acid Rain, that the United States government spend $5 billion over a five year period on pollution control technology. The report was commissioned in March of 1985 when Prime Minister Mulroney and U.S. President Ronald Reagan met in Quebec City for their "Shamrock Summit." Noting the 75-year history of environmental co-operation between Canada and the United States, the two leaders agreed each to appoint a personal Special Envoy to examine the acid rain issue and report back before the next summit in the spring of 1986.

The report, which places emphasis on U.S. action and voluntary development of technology rather than mandatory action by polluters, is criticized by the provinces for failing to set targets for actually reducing the environmentally destructive rains. The $5 billion is to be provided equally by the U.S. government and U.S. manufacturers and spent on technology as recommended by industry. Responding to criticisms that the report is inadequate, Davis is quick to point out that it is the first declaration by any American envoy that acid rain is indeed a problem.

20 January
Elections—Quebec

Quebec Premier Robert Bourassa returns to the Quebec National Assembly by winning a by-election in the Montreal-area riding of St.-Laurent. He easily defeats nine other candidates, capturing 83 per cent of the popular vote in the riding. Although his Liberal Party had swept to power in the 2 December provincial election, Bourassa had been defeated as the candidate for the riding of Bertrand.

31 January
Crown Corporations—Privatization

The Crown Corporation De Havilland Aircraft of Canada Ltd. is sold by the federal government to Boeing Co. of Seattle for $90 million.

1 February
Regional Development—Canada-Alberta Subsidiary Agreement

Federal Transport Minister Donald Mazankowski and Alberta Agriculture Minister Leroy Fjordbotten sign, in Edmonton, a $50-million, five-year agreement to provide financial assistance to Alberta firms that process agricultural equipment. The deal—the *Canada-Alberta Subsidiary Agreement*—is a continuation of a former ten year, $145-million agreement and provides assistance in three areas: capital assistance, non-capital assistance, and public information and technical services.

7 February
Fisheries—Assistance

Federal Fisheries Minister Tom Siddon announces in Ottawa that the federal government will terminate the Fishing Vessel Assistance Program as of 31 March 1986. The programme, first introduced in 1942, was designed to aid fishermen in covering the costs of replacing fishing vessels. It provided up to 25 per cent of the costs of replacing the vessels. The federal subsidy has amounted to a yearly average of $6 million during the past ten years. Siddon explains that the elimination of the subsidy will serve to weaken the case of American fisheries in their fight to impose countervail duties on Canadian fish sold in the United States. He points out as well that the programme has outlived its usefulness and has led to the building of too many boats.

14 February
Federal-Provincial Fiscal Relations— Established Programs Finance

Despite strong opposition from the provinces, Finance Minister Michael Wilson tables *Bill C-96*, a measure to amend the *Federal-Provincial Fiscal Arrangements and Federal Post-Secondary Education and Health Contributions Act, 1977*. It is designed to reduce the rate of growth in federal transfers to provincial governments. Under the legislation, which was first proposed in Mr. Wilson's 1985 budget, the growth of Established Programs Finance payments is to be reduced from seven per cent per year to five. The measure is expected to save Ottawa about $2 billion annually by the 1990-91 fiscal year.

The provinces are upset because the legislation was imposed earlier than they had expected. In his May, 1985 budget Mr. Wilson had tabled a chart showing no changes in EPF payments during the fiscal year 1986/1987, which begins 1 April 1986. However, Anne Park, director of federal-provincial relations announced that the new measures will take effect as of 1 April 1986. The provinces argue that more consultation is needed to ease predicted revenue shortfalls—some provinces predict total reductions of as much as $350 million—caused by the new legislation.

14 February
Hydroelectricity— Exports

Manitoba Minister of Energy William Parasiuk announces that Manitoba has negotiated the largest hydro-power export deal in Canadian history. The record breaking deal with the Upper Mississippi Power Group will bring in revenue of $4.3 billion to Manitoba Hydro. Revenue from the sale will be placed in a Manitoba Energy Foundation, which will receive 50 per cent of the profits from the sale. The money will be used to ensure that Manitoba power rates remain the lowest in Canada. The other 50 per cent will be allocated to Manitoba Hydro. Under the terms of the deal, the Upper Mississippi Power Group has agreed to purchase 550 megawatts of power annually over 16 years, beginning in 1996.

17-18 February
Francophone Summit

The first Francophone Summit opens in Versailles, France, with the Canadian delegation consisting of Prime Minister Brian Mulroney, Quebec Premier Robert Bourassa and New Brunswick Premier Richard Hatfield. Notwithstanding the presence of the two premiers representing provinces with large francophone populations, Mr. Mulroney asserts that, in international matters, he alone "speaks for the people of Canada, at all times and in all circumstances." Under an agreement reached in late 1985 between the provinces and the federal government, the premiers may speak on any subject providing they receive approval from the Prime Minister and their remarks are consistent with the federal position. This entente is soon broken, however, when on the first day Premier Bourassa proposes, on behalf of Quebec, the examination of a substantial plan for alleviating food shortages in the Third World—without the approval of Mr. Mulroney. Although the Prime Minister makes no mention of Mr. Bourassa's failure to secure prior federal approval for his initiative while in France, once back in Canada he makes it clear that such behaviour will not be tolerated in the future, stating of his Quebec counterpart's actions: "Blindside me once and you have a problem the next time we have a meeting."

Among other issues discussed at the summit is sanctions against South Africa, with the 40 summit delegations passing a resolution condemning that country's policy of apartheid. Also, the French-speaking nations agree to the creation of an energy institute to assist Third World countries to draw on the expertise of the developed countries in coping with energy problems.

26 February
Budgets, Federal

Finance Minister Michael Wilson presents his second budget, this one aimed primarily at deficit reduction. According to Mr. Wilson, the main vehicle for reducing the deficit will be the generation of increased tax revenues over the next five years. The measures contained in the budget are expected to cost individual taxpayers $5.2 billion over the next five years, consumers $6 billion, and business $1.5 billion.

Included in the budget is an increase in the federal sales tax/surtax. Effective 1 July, a three per cent surtax is added to individuals federal tax payable. For business, the three per cent surtax comes into effect 1 January 1987. In addition, federal sales taxes on goods and services rise 1 April by one percentage point.

With respect to income taxes, the budget provides families earning less than $18,000 a year with a refundable sales tax credit of up to $50 per adult and $25 per child. Families receiving a child tax credit are to receive a $300 pre-payment in November, the balance being payable when tax returns are filed the following spring. Corporate tax rates drop by two per cent and the seven per cent investment tax credit for business is to be phased out by 1989.

Announcing his government's determination to cut down on spending, Mr. Wilson reduces future rises in government spending to two per cent annually. This includes the placing of a 2.75 per cent cap on military spending increases for 1986-87 and a two per cent annual limit on the growth of future outlays. The deficit forecast for the fiscal year beginning 1 April is to drop to $29.8 billion from $32.7 billion.

6 March
Constitution—
Charter of Rights
and Freedoms—
Quebec

Quebec Minister of Intergovernmental Affairs Gil Rémillard, announces that the province of Quebec will no longer systematically exempt its laws from the *Charter of Rights and Freedoms*. As Mr. Rémillard explains, "we want Quebecers to have the same protection of their fundamental rights as other Canadians." Further, since the Liberals were elected in Quebec in 1985, their government has quietly allowed the five-year "notwithstanding" clause, inserted into every law by the previous PQ government, to expire rather than renewing it for each law as required by the Constitution. The PQ government began inserting the clause in 1982 to mark Quebec's refusal to sign the 1981 constitutional agreement.

11 March
Ministerial Task Force on Program Review

Deputy Prime Minister Eric Nielson tables his Ministerial Task Force on Program Review, an analysis of government spending. Comprising 21 volumes, the $3.7-million report evaluates the purpose, delivery and record of a broad range of programmes, and proposes an equally broad range of legislative and regulatory reforms. The Task Force, established as part of the government's commitment to making the government expenditures process more efficient, involved the efforts of 221 people and studied a total of 1000 programmes during 1985. Among the Task Forces' substantive findings are the following:

- Ottawa spends billions each year on programmes that have outlived their purpose, that duplicate other programmes or that overlap services offered elsewhere;

- structural problems within government hinder efforts to improve the situation;

- there are few incentives for public service managers to accomplish new or difficult tasks, to try innovative approaches, to provide better services or to do more with less;

- the federal government would be able to wipe out its annual deficit, estimated at $29.5 billion in the 1986-87 fiscal year, if it cancelled all "tax expenditures"—such as tax breaks for individuals and subsidies for business, which cost the government an estimated $35 billion a year in lost revenue;

- Canada is over regulated;

- one of the few areas where government should not alter its approach is social assistance as, contrary to popular myth, there is little evidence of individual abuse of the system; and

- subsidies for agriculture should be eliminated or greatly reduced.

18-19 March
Canada-U.S. Relations—Summit; Environment—Acid Rain; NORAD

Prime Minister Mulroney and U.S. President Ronald Reagan meet for a two-day summit in Washington. Items on the agenda include acid rain, NORAD, Free Trade, and U.S. space initiatives.

With respect to acid rain, Mr. Reagan announces that he fully endorses the Davis-Lewis report released in January and that he will ask Congress to spend an extra $100 million annually for the next five years to clean up factories that release acid rain-causing pollutants. He announces the appointment of U.S. Secretary of State George Schultz as his U.S. representative on a joint administrative body that will monitor progress on the acid rain programme. Mr. Mulroney names Minister of External Affairs Joe Clark as Canada's member on the board.

As expected, the Canadian government agrees to a five-year renewal of its North American Air Defence Command (NORAD) agreement with the U.S.

As well, Mr. Mulroney announces that Canada will spend $800 million over the next 15 years to build a service centre for the manned space station planned by the United States. The programme is expected to generate over 10,000 jobs for Canada and $15 million in revenues.

19 April
Health—Canada Health Act—Quebec

Federal Health Minister Jake Epp announces that Quebec is to be paid the $14 million in penalties which has been imposed by Ottawa in a dispute over medical user fees. The money represents medical grants that have been withheld under the *Canada Health Act* during the last two years. The money is to be returned because Quebec medical fees are no different than the daily "room and board" fees for chronic patients which are charged by other provinces and which do not violate the *Canada Health Act.*

21 April
Elections—Prince Edward Island

Voters in Prince Edward Island bring to an end seven years of Progressive Conservative rule and sweep Tory Premier James Lee out of power by giving Joe

Ghiz's Liberal party 21 seats in the 32-seat legislature. The Conservatives retain 11 seats.

1 May
Language Policy—
Bilingualism;
Supreme Court—
Language Policy

In a ruling expected to have broad implications for language policy in Canada, the Supreme Court of Canada rules that courts in Quebec and Manitoba can issue unilingual summons.

In one case, the Court dismisses an appeal by businessman Duncan Macdonald of Montreal to overturn a 1981 unilingual traffic summons from a Montreal Municipal Court because it was written in French, ruling that the *Constitution Act, 1867* allows a Quebec Court to issue a document in "either of the official languages."

In a second case the Court rules that Roger Bilodeau, a Manitoba francophone, had no right to a speeding summons in French, with the Court dismissing the argument that the *Manitoba Summary Convictions Act* and the *Highway Traffic Act* are invalid because they were not published in French.

8 May
Elections—Alberta

Don Getty and his Progressive Conservatives are returned to power in Alberta, but with a significantly reduced majority as the NDP and the Liberals make a strong challenge to win seats from the Tories. Final standings in the legislature after the election are as follows: Progressive Conservatives 83, NDP 16, Liberal 4.

9 May
Constitution—
Quebec

At a symposium at Mont Gabriel, sponsored by the Institute of Intergovernmental Relations, Quebec Minister of Intergovernmental Relations Gil Rémillard makes explicit for the first time his province's five conditions for signing the *Constitution Act, 1982*. They are as follows:

• recognition of Quebec as a distinct society;

• a greater provincial role in selecting immigrants;

• a role for Quebec in appointments to the Supreme Court of Canada; limitations on the federal spending power; and

• a veto for Quebec on future constitutional amendments.

21 May
Aboriginal
Peoples—Claims

Bill C-110, the *Grassy Narrows and Islington Indian Bands Mercury Pollution Claims Settlement Act,* is passed in the Commons. The legislation provides a $16.6-million settlement for two northern Ontario Indian bands affected by mercury pollution. The settlement was reached between the federal government and the two bands in November, 1985 to compensate their members for mercury contamination band members received through eating fish from the Wabigcan-English River system. The contamination was discovered in the early 1970s and the source traced to a Dryden Ontario paper mill owned by Reed Inc. Under the provisions of the bill, the Grassy Narrows band will receive $8.6 million and the Islington band $8 million. Ottawa is to contribute $2.75 million, the Ontario government $2.176 million, Reed Inc. $5.75 million, and Great Lakes Forest Products Ltd., who bought the Mill in 1979, $6 million.

22 May
Canada-U.S. Trade
Relations—Ex-
ports; Forestry—Ex-
ports

United States President Ronald Reagan announces a stiff five-year tariff against Canadian imports of cedar shakes and shingles on grounds that they are hurting the U.S. industry. The new tariff—set at 35 per cent for the first 30 months—is expected to be a crippling blow to the British Columbia lumber industry.

23 May
Canada-U.S. Trade
Relations—Ex-
ports; Forestry—Ex-
ports

The federal government demands that the United States immediately lift the newly-proposed tariffs on British Columbia cedar shakes and shingles. Prime Minister Mulroney states in the Commons that the tariffs run counter to joint commitments he and President Reagan made at the Quebec City and Washington summits to fight protectionism, adding that "actions like these make it extremely difficult for anyone, including Canadians, to be friends with the Americans from time to time." The Canadian government sends a diplomatic note to Washington registering its "profound disappointment" over the incident.

29 May
Western Premiers'
Conference;
Canada-U.S. Trade
Relations—Exports;
Agriculture—Sub-
sidies

The four western premiers meet in Swan River, Manitoba, where international trade—particularly Canada's trade with the United States—dominates discussions. The premiers express their concern about the United States' imposition of trade barriers while the two countries are discussing lifting such restrictions. In a communiqué issued at the end of the talks, the premiers request the rollback of tariffs imposed by the U.S. on shakes and shingles and a freeze on any similar measures while the free trade talks continued. The premiers also urge the federal government to take action to counteract the massive subsidies given by the European Economic Community and the U.S. to their agricultural sectors to the detriment of Canadian farmers.

2 June
First Ministers'
Meetings—Free
Trade

The ten premiers meet with Prime Minister Mulroney to discuss free trade and, following their meeting, give him their approval to open negotiations with the United States without direct provincial participation. They win from Mr. Mulroney an agreement that meetings will be held every three months to review the process and keep the provinces up to date on events of relevance to them. Many of the premiers had been demanding that they have representatives participating in the trade talks, but Mr. Mulroney had previously announced his position that the federal government would be alone at the table. He allows, though, that "a great deal of provincial involvement" will be required to ratify any agreement with the United States.

Canada-U.S. Trade
Relations—Imports

Finance Minister Michael Wilson announces that Canada will impose duties of about $80 million against U.S. products in retaliation for the American tariff on Canadian shakes and shingles. The duties are announced on U.S. books, periodicals, computer parts and semiconductors; in addition, already existing tariffs are increased on a number of other imports.

4 June
Interprovincial
Trade Barriers

Federal and provincial Regional and Economic Development ministers meet in Belleville, Ontario for a two day meeting and pledge to reduce trade barriers between the provinces. To aid in reducing inter-provincial trade barriers, the provincial and territorial representatives agree to a three point plan that includes:

- a moratorium on new barriers;
- the establishment of a permanent mechanism for reducing barriers; and
- the establishment of a process to take an inventory of all existing barriers.

12-13 June
Eastern Canadian Premiers and New England Governors

The five Eastern Canadian premiers and six New England governors meet for their yearly conference, this one in Lowell, Massachusetts. Although free trade is not formally on the agenda, which includes such issues as housing and economic development, the premiers and governors give a vote of support to the Canada-U.S. negotiations, although not without some disagreement. The conference participants record their concern over the recent U.S. tariffs on Canadian lumber products and the retaliatory measures taken by Canada. Both premiers Buchanan of Nova Scotia and Bourassa of Quebec put forth plans to sell energy to their New England counterparts—Buchanan through sales of natural gas and the building of coal-fired plants, and Bourassa through the joint funding of new Quebec power plants.

17 June
Aboriginal Peoples—Self-Government

Bill C-93, which allows for self-government on the part of the Sechelt Native Community of British Columbia, is given final reading in the House of Commons. The purpose of the bill is to allow the Sechelt Indian Band to assume a municipal-style control over its land, resources, health, social services, education and local taxation. Much of the bill was drafted by the Indian band itself and is seen as a model for future initiatives in this field. It is the first of its kind in Canada.

International Trade—Wine and Liquor—GATT

Following a federal-provincial meeting of ministers of trade in Winnipeg, federal Trade Minister James Kelleher announces that the provinces have agreed to reduce markups on imported wine and liquor as they had promised in 1979. The original agreement had been reached after complaints by the United States and European Economic Community to the General Agreement on Tariffs and Trade about discriminatory markups by some provinces on imported beverages. According to Mr. Kelleher, it had been agreed in 1979 that such markups should be no more than five per cent by 1988; some provinces, though, have been slow to implement the new pricing policies.

19 June
Federal-Provincial Fiscal Relations— Equalization

Finance Minister Michael Wilson tells his provincial counterparts after a one-day federal-provincial meeting of finance ministers in Victoria that they should not expect much in the way of increases in equalization payments. The meeting marks the tenth time the ministers have met since January in an attempt to reach a consensus on a mutually-acceptable equalization formula by 31 March 1987, the date the federal government's new formula is to go into effect.

Health—Canada Health Act—Ontario

After 43 days of often-heated debate, extra-billing by doctors becomes illegal in Ontario as *Bill 94* is given final reading and passed. Passed by a vote of 69 to 47, the law prohibits physicians from charging more for their services than the Ontario Health Insurance Plan provides and prescribes a penalty of $250 for a first offence. Ontario's incentive to end the practice came from the federal *Canada Health Act* which withheld the amount extra-billed by any province's doctors from federal health grants to a given province. Ottawa had been withholding $100 million in such funds from Ontario.

20 June
Federal-Provincial Fiscal Relations— Equalization

Federal Finance Minister Wilson meets with his provincial counterparts in Victoria to discuss their concerns over the federal government's proposed tax transfer guidelines. The provinces—especially Quebec and Newfoundland—contended that Ottawa had already been chipping away at money for the provinces and that those losses should be made up when the new equalization plan is put forward in nine months. Mr. Wilson tells the ministers not to expect much in the way of an increase in transfers—already reaching $5.5 billion, although he announces his willingness to consider new ways of dividing up existing funds among the provinces.

24 June
Transportation—
Railways—
Newfoundland

Transport Minister Don Mazankowski announces $36.4 million for Newfoundland's troubled railway industry. The money is to be spent over the next four years to convert fully the railway's boxcars to containers and to upgrade the Island's narrow gauge track system.

26 June
Canada-U.S. Trade
Relations—Exports; Forestry—Exports

The United States International Trade Commission votes 5-0 in Washington that imports of pine and other softwood lumber from Canada are injuring the U.S. lumber industry, and that the low stumpage fees that lumber companies pay for their trees constitute an unfair subsidy.

4 July
Deregulation—
Quebec

Quebec's Task Force on Deregulation releases *Regulate less: regulate better (Réglementer moins et mieux)*, its report on deregulation in the province. In it, the Task Force proposes major changes to Quebec's labour and occupational health laws, together with the deregulation of the construction, trucking and inter-city bus travel industries. Task force chairman Reed Scowan asserts that if the report's recommendations are implemented it would create tens of thousands of jobs and reduce the costs to consumers of numerous items from houses to auto repairs to inter-city bus tickets.

21 July
Constitution—
Quebec

A spokesman for Prime Minister Mulroney announces that a letter has been sent to nine premiers urging them to be sympathetic to renewed attempts to bring Quebec into the Constitution. In it, he asks the premiers to "keep a very open mind" on the issue and to be "sympathetic to the new process " the Prime Minister wants to get underway.

10-12 August
Annual Premiers'
Conferences; Con-
stitution—Quebec;
Free Trade

The ten premiers meet in Edmonton for the 27th Annual Premiers' Conference. First on the agenda is a discussion of Quebec's constitutional situation and, in response, they release the "Edmonton Declaration," affirming that their first constitutional priority is to commence constitutional negotiations based upon the five conditions put forth by Quebec (see entry for 9 May). The importance of bringing Quebec back into the Constitution is to take precedence over the specific constitutional concerns of other provinces on such issues as Senate reform, fisheries and property rights, which are to be discussed in future conferences.

The premiers also draft a communiqué on free trade with eight of the ten urging the federal government to go "full speed ahead" on the free trade talks. Premiers Pawley of Manitoba and Peterson of Ontario refuse to support the deal.

On trade-related matters, premier Grant Devine of Saskatchewan fails to secure the backing of the other provinces for his request for a $5-billion federal assistance package for western farmers.

20 August
Western Separatism

Alberta premier Donald Getty warns that support for western separatism is increasing because of frustration over the federal government's regional policies. Prime Minister Mulroney replies: "I don't know that you will find a government that has responded so quickly and so completely to the needs of western Canada."

26 August
Energy Policy—
Canada-Nova
Scotia Offshore
Petroleum Resour-
ces Accord

Prime Minister Brian Mulroney, Nova Scotia Premier John Buchanan and their respective energy ministers sign the Canada-Nova Scotia Offshore Petroleum Resources Accord, a long-term agreement on joint management of offshore oil and gas exploration. In essence, the deal gives Nova Scotia two federal grants worth a total of $225 million, equal jurisdiction with Ottawa over offshore developments and the permanent right to set its own oil and gas royalties. The agreement also contains a clause which states that Ottawa will compensate Nova Scotia for taking away its back-in rights in 1985. Back-in rights, as set out in the National Energy Program, allowed both governments to buy into offshore wells at pre-discovery prices after oil and gas had been found. Under the new pact, if offshore oil or gas goes into production, Ottawa will repay the province for the profits it would have enjoyed from the back-in.

7 September
Canada-U.S. Trade Relations—Exports; Forestry—British Columbia

British Columbia Forest Minister Jack Kempf announces that his province might be prepared to give in to certain U.S. demands in order to forestall the imposition of countervailing duties on Canadian exports of softwood lumber. This position is opposed by other provinces, most notably Ontario.

10 September
Council of Maritime Premiers; Deregulation—Transportation

The Council of Maritime Premiers meets in Mill River, Prince Edward Island. Foremost among the Council's deliberations is the operations of the Council itself, with the premiers agreeing to examine carefully how the 15-year-old organization spends its time and its budget of $11 million per year. The premiers also express their concern about the federal government's proposed deregulation of the transportation industry, maintaining that the legislation does not take regional disparities into account. They request a meeting with federal Transportation Minister John Crosbie to express their concerns.

1 October
Energy Policy—National Energy Program

The federal government's Petroleum and Gas Revenue Tax (PGRT) is officially taken off the books. The tax was first implemented as a tax on excessive profits in 1980 as part of the National Energy Program. In 1984, it was agreed that the tax would be scrapped as part of the Western Accord signed on 28 March 1985. Provincial governments had wanted the tax removed immediately thereafter, but the federal government was not prepared to forego such a large source of revenue at one time. Its abolition will marginally improve the cash flow of the larger oil companies.

*Health—Canada
Health Act—Alberta*

Extra-billing ends in Alberta. The province was the last holdout against the provision of the *Canada Health Act, 1982*, which banned extra-billing by doctors and authorized the federal government to withhold federal payments to provinces in the amount extra-billed by doctors. Unlike Ontario (see entry for 19 June), doctors who extra-bill will not be fined. Those found guilty of extra-billing will be given an initial warning and if they persist will be forced out of the Alberta Health Care Insurance Plan. A total of $29.03 million in federal funds withheld from the province is to be returned by early December.

16 October
Canada-U.S. Trade Relations—Exports—Softwood Lumber; Forestry—Exports

The United States Commerce Department (USCD) rules that imports of Canadian softwood lumber are to be penalized because they are unfairly subsidized. The ruling finds that timber pricing practices in British Columbia, Alberta, Ontario and Quebec constitute subsidies because they are provided "at preferential prices to a specific industry or group". The USCD imposes a 15 per cent import duty on most of the $4 billion of annual Canadian lumber exports to the United States. Under U.S. trade laws, the Commerce Department has until 30 December to make a final ruling on the decision. Until the issue is resolved, Canada must pay post bonds in anticipation of the 15 per cent duty.

In Ottawa, Minister of International Trade Pat Carney responds, charging that the ruling infringes on Canada's right as a sovereign nation to set its own resource policies, and fires off a strongly-worded diplomatic note attacking the duty.

20 October
Elections—Saskatchewan

Premier Grant Devine leads his Progressive Conservative party back to power—albeit with a reduced majority—in Saskatchewan, capturing 38 of 64 legislative seats. The New Democratic Party will form the official opposition with 25 seats, and the Liberals capture one.

22 October *Elections—British* *Columbia*	Premier Bill Vander Zalm leads his Social Credit Party to victory in British Columbia, winning 49 seats in the 69-seat provincial legislature. The New Democrats form the official opposition with twenty seats.
31 October *Government* *Procurement*	The federal government awards Canadair Ltd. of Montreal a $103-million contract to maintain Canada's fleet of front-line CF-18 jet fighters, despite the fact that the runner up, Bristol Aerospace of Winnipeg submitted the lower bid and had more evaluation points on technical competence from a team of 75 civil servants. Amid the outcry in Manitoba and western Canada generally, Manitoba Premier Howard Pawley demands an immediate explanation from the Prime Minister.
Crown Corpora- *tions—Privatization*	Canadair Ltd. is sold by the federal government to Bombardier Inc. for $120 million plus a possible $120 million in royalties.
3 November *Government* *Procurement*	Manitoba Premier Pawley leads a delegation of Manitoba's political, business and labour leaders to a meeting with the Prime Minister to express their anger over the awarding of the CF-18 contract to Canadair of Montreal. In addition to the premier are Winnipeg Mayor Bill Norrie and John Doole of the Winnipeg Chamber of Commerce. Ninety minutes of discussion fail to bring about any significant results, with Mr. Mulroney emerging to insist that he had acted in the best interests of the country as a whole.
18 November *Canada-U.S. Trade* *Relations—* *Softwood Lumber;* *Forestry—Exports*	At a federal-provincial meeting on the Canada-U.S. lumber dispute in Ottawa, International Trade Minister Pat Carney fails to settle an interprovincial dispute between British Columbia and Ontario over the means by which Canada should respond to the U.S. Commerce Department ruling on softwood lumber. British Columbia wants to negotiate a compromise with the U.S. before the legal deadline of 30 November, while Ontario takes the position that the tariff should be fought through legal means. No consensus is reached. The next day, over the objections of the

British Columbia government, Ontario mounts a legal challenge in the United States to the ruling, filing a notice of objection in the U.S. Trade Court.

21 November
Canada-U.S. Trade Relations—Softwood Lumber; Forestry—Exports

Ottawa and the provinces meet in Ottawa to discuss the U.S. lumber ruling. The federal government and those of the major lumber-producing provinces agree that, pending U.S. approval, a 15 per cent export tax will be placed on all lumber exports in return for the dropping of the import duty by the U.S. Ottawa and governments of Quebec and British Columbia endorse the plan, while those of Ontario, Nova Scotia and New Brunswick object. Details of the plan are delivered to the U.S. Department of Commerce on 26 November.

2-3 December
Council of Maritime Premiers; Deregulation—Transportation

The Council of Maritime Premiers meets in Fredericton, N.B. Foremost on the agenda is the federal government's transportation deregulation plans, which they criticize as being detrimental to the interests of Atlantic Canadians. Once more, the premiers seek a meeting with federal Transportation Minister John Crosbie to seek changes to the proposed legislation, including the insertion of a clause ensuring that regional development would take precedence over a profitable transportation service when the two conflict. Regarding the Atlantic Canada Opportunities Agency, the details of which had not yet been released, the premiers express their skepticism that the programme would produce lasting benefits to the region, citing a long history of failed regional development initiatives in Atlantic Canada.

4 December
Deregulation—Financial Institutions—Ontario

Ontario Financial Institutions Minister Monte Quinter announces in the Ontario Legislature the province's plans to relax its ownership restrictions on the securities industry effective Spring 1987 to allow unlimited competition in the capital market. Under the new rules foreigners, banks and trust companies will be permitted to take over stock brokerages in the province in moves that the government hopes will give the financial services industry the capital it needs to compete in the highly-competitive international market. The new legislation will permit banks, trust companies and other non-financial firms to buy 100 per cent of stock brokers as of 30 June 1987; foreign interests will be able to buy 50 per cent of investment dealers, and 100 per cent a year later.

9 December
Agriculture—Assistance

Prime Minister Mulroney announces at the end of the annual Agricultural Outlook Conference in Ottawa that Canadian farmers will get a preliminary payment of $300 million from the $1-billion federal farm assistance programme. Under the Special Canadian Grains Program, the maximum payment per farmer will be $25,000 with growers of spring and durham wheat, barley and oats, rye, mixed grains, grain corn, soybeans, canola, flax and sunflower seeds eligible. The remaining $700 million is to be paid in the spring.

18 December
Supreme Court—Sunday Shopping—Ontario

The Supreme Court of Ontario rules that an Ontario law restricting Sunday shopping is valid, although it infringes upon constitutional guarantees of freedom of religion to some extent. The Court rules that, although the law infringes upon the rights of those for whom Saturday is the Sabbath—most notably Jews and Seventh-Day Adventists—this infringement is reasonable and, under Section 1 of the Charter of Rights and Freedoms, " demonstrably justified in a free and democratic society". The Justices rule that the Ontario law is essentially a secular one aimed at establishing a common pause day. The ruling draws particular attention since the Supreme Court of Canada earlier struck down the Lord's Day Act used to restrict Sunday shopping in Alberta as unconstitutional because it had a religious purpose.

18 December
Deregulation—Financial Institutions

Minister of State for Finance Tom Hockin outlines the federal government's new rules governing financial institutions. The regulations mean that consumers will be able to deposit and withdraw money, buy stocks and bonds, arrange loans and mortgages and obtain investment advice and portfolio management all within the walls of one branch of a financial institution. The new rules require large trust, loan and insurance companies with non-financial owners to have at least 35 per cent of their voting shares publicly traded on stock exchanges and widely held by investors. Only the sale of insurance will remain out of the services offered under one roof. Ottawa will also consolidate its regulation of federally registered financial institutions under the control of a new super-agency to be called the Superintendent of Financial Institutions.

22 December
Language Policy—
Quebec; Quebec
Bill 101

The Quebec Court of appeal rules that the Quebec government went too far in enacting legislation in 1977 which required French-only commercial signs. The ruling invalidates four sections of *Bill 101* on the grounds that they contravene clauses in the Canadian and Quebec *Charters of Rights and Freedoms* guaranteeing freedom of expression. *Bill 101* had ordered that all commercial signs in Quebec be in French only.

The Quebec government requests time to study the ruling before deciding whether to amend the Quebec Language law to allow bilingual signs, or to appeal the case to the Supreme Court of Canada.

30 December
Canada-U.S. Trade
Relations—
Softwood Lumber;
Forestry—Exports

A deal is reached between the United States and Canada averting the imposition of countervailing duties of 15 per cent on the $4 billion worth of Canadian softwood lumber exports. The deal calls for the federal Government to impose a new 15 per cent export tax on Canadian softwood exports to the United States, which means that the revenues generated from such a tax will remain in Canada. Under the pact, the tax will eventually be replaced by higher fees charged by the provinces to lumber companies, although U.S. approval is needed for the calculation of the value of measures Canada uses to replace the tax. The pact may be cancelled by either side with 30 days notice.

1987

15 January
Northwest
Territories—
Division

After lengthy negotiations, a tentative agreement for the division of the Northwest Territories is reached by native groups at Iqaluit—formerly Frobisher Bay—Northwest Territories. The agreement is between the Dene Indians and Métis Association of the Northwest Territories on the one hand, and the Inuit, represented by the Nunavut Constitutional Forum, on the other. The new proposed territories are Denendeh, covering the western N.W.T. and Mackenzie Valley; and Nunavut in the East. The agreement has three main components: a consensus on the boundary between the two territories, principles for the development of their constitutions and the inclusion of the oil and gas-rich Beaufort Sea in the western territory. The agreement also contains a commitment to develop resource revenue-sharing mechanisms between the two territories.

21 January
Free Trade

United States Vice-President George Bush and Secretary of State James Baker arrive in Ottawa for a half-day meeting with Prime Minister Mulroney and Finance Minister Michael Wilson on free trade. Mr. Mulroney conveys his concern that the free trade talks have to be given a higher priority by the U.S. administration.

23 January
Canada-France
Relations—
Fisheries

France and Canada sign an "interim agreement" in Paris undertaking both to resolve their long-simmering dispute over boundaries and northern cod quotas and to send the dispute to international arbitration. Under the agreement, nine French factory trawlers from continental France are assigned quotas and given access both to the disputed waters off the French islands of St. Pierre and Miquelon and the Gulf of Saint Lawrence; ships from the French islands are allowed to take a quota of 3,500 tonnes from the Gulf. Newfoundland Premier Brian Peckford, furious that the federal government had not involved Newfoundland in the final negotiations, condemns the agreement, labelling it a sellout by the

federal government of Canadian fishermen, and calls
for a meeting of the premiers.

5 February
*Federal-Provincial-
Municipal Rela-
tions—Water
Delivery*

Federal Environment Minister Tom McMillan announces to Canada's municipal governments that
there will be no federal money for a proposed $12-
billion federal-provincial-municipal project to
rebuild the country's aging water-delivery infrastruc-
ture. Instead, he suggests that Canada's
municipalities increase the price of water they sell to
finance the massive expenditures required. Most of
the provinces had supported the Federation of
Canadian Municipalities plan.

9 February
*Premiers' Meet-
ings—Fisheries*

Eight provincial premiers meet in Toronto at the request of Newfoundland Premier Brian Peckford to
discuss the implications for the provinces of the controversial Canada-France fisheries deal. Provincial
delegates to the Canada-France negotiations were
absent when the interim agreement was put in final
form and signed. The premiers agreed that, although
Ottawa has exclusive rights in concluding treaties,
provinces have exclusive rights over natural resources. Since fish is a Newfoundland resource, they
argue, the province should have been involved.

18 February
Budgets, Federal

Federal Finance Minister Michael Wilson delivers
his 1987 budget, projecting a $29-billion deficit. In
what is considered by most to be a "stand pat" budget
designed to set the stage for his comprehensive tax
reform proposals later in the year, Mr. Wilson announces tax increases on a variety of items including
gasoline, cigarettes and snack foods. He projects a
deficit for the 1987-1988 fiscal year of $29.3 billion,
down from $32 billion in the current fiscal year.

*Language Policy—
Education—
Saskatchewan*

In a ruling hailed by the francophone groups of the
province as a great step towards reviving
Saskatchewan's French culture, a Saskatchewan
Court of Queen's Bench ruling gives the province's
francophones the right to "management and control"
of French-language schools in the province. In 1986
twelve "fransaskois" groups had asked the court to

decide if the province was complying with a Charter of Rights provision guaranteeing French language minorities schools and instruction where numbers warrant; the Court decided it was not. In his ruling, Justice Charles Wimmer holds that French education is essential to the development of French culture in the province, and that "Given management and control of their own schools, francophones will slowly start to assert their own rights." Justice Wimmer, however, leaves it up to the provincial government to decide how the new control given to francophones will be exercised. Wimmer's ruling also states:

• French language schools must match the quality of anglophone schools;

• anglophones who want French instruction must receive it in anglophone schools;

• the education minister cannot refuse to provide communities with French-language instruction on the grounds it will no longer be required in three years; and

• francophones applying for French language instruction do not have to live in the same school division.

26 February
Language Policy—
Quebec

Quebec Justice Minister Herbert Marx announces that Quebec will appeal the Quebec Court of Appeal ruling that struck down *Bill 101*'s French-only sign provision to the Supreme Court. According to Marx, the appeal will have no impact on the government's forthcoming decision about how to handle the thorny question of language on signs. Rather, the government is appealing the case for "technical reasons", namely, to test the scope of freedom of expression guarantees in commercial messages.

9 March
Environment—Acid
Rain—Federal-
Provincial Relations

The governments of Canada and Prince Edward Island sign an accord aimed at reducing sulphur dioxide emissions. Although the federal government and the seven provinces east of Saskatchewan had reached an oral agreement to reduce acidic emissions in 1985, this agreement, according to federal Environment Minister Tom McMillan, is the first between the federal Government and a province to follow it up. It calls for the province to reduce acidic emissions by 17 per cent by 1994.

The same day a similar pact is signed between the governments of Canada and Newfoundland and, the next day, with the government of Ontario. The agreements collectively require the three provinces to reduce acidic emissions by more than 1.3 million tonnes by 1994, and are part of Canada's commitment to reduce national sulphur dioxide levels from the 1980 level of 4.6 million tonnes per year to 2.3 million tonnes by 1994. The federal government was concerned that the 1985 agreement be honoured in writing before the Mulroney-Reagan meetings on 5-6 April.

11 March
Federal-Provincial
Fiscal Relations—
Equalization

Federal Finance Minister Michael Wilson tables the equalization figures for the upcoming fiscal year (31 March 1987 to 31 March 1988). The bill provides for $5.6 billion in payments to the seven poorest provinces—Newfoundland, Prince Edward Island, Nova Scotia, New Brunswick, Quebec, Manitoba and Saskatchewan; this represents a 5.7 per cent increase over the previous year. In 1988-89, payments are to increase by 6.2 per cent over this year.

Free Trade—
Federal-Provincial
Relations

Prime Minister Mulroney and the ten premiers meet with International Trade Minister Pat Carney and free trade negotiators to discuss progress in the Canada-U.S. free trade negotiations. The premiers are promised that the issue of provincial ratification of a free trade agreement would be addressed in June.

17 March
Canada-France
Relations—
Fisheries

Canada closes all its ports to French fishing vessels in response to alleged overfishing by the French in disputed waters off Newfoundland.

26-27 March
First Ministers'
Conference on
Aboriginal Constitu-
tional Matters

The First Ministers' Conference on Aboriginal Constitutional Matters convenes in Ottawa to attempt to reach an agreement on aboriginal self-government. This is the third and final meeting provided for in a 1983 constitutional agreement through which a decision by the federal and provincial governments on aboriginal self-government was to be reached. The conference had been preceded by lengthy discussions between both levels of government and native organizations seeking agreement on the wording of a constitutional amendment that would entrench aboriginal self-government in the Constitution.

Throughout the conference, argument centred upon the circumstances under which aboriginal self-government could be included in the Constitution. The provinces argued that self-government, like any other aboriginal right, can be entrenched in the Constitution only after its substance has been negotiated in advance, making it a contingent rather than an inherent right. Native groups, on the other hand, argued the opposite: that self-government, as an inherent right, should be included first, with the substance to be negotiated later.

The participants were unable to reach agreement on any of the substantive issues and the conference failed when four provinces—British Columbia, Alberta, Saskatchewan and Newfoundland—and native leaders rejected a compromise proposal by Prime Minister Mulroney.

2-3 April
Telecommunica-
tions—Federal-
Provincial Relations

Canada's federal and provincial communication ministers meet in Edmonton to discuss ways to develop a national telecommunications policy. Federal Communications Minister Flora MacDonald announces that she and her provincial counterparts had made some progress in that regard by agreeing to six principles which they hoped would form the basis of a new policy. The six are:

• a Canadian approach to the country's telecommunications problems and policies;

- there should be universal access to basic phone services at affordable prices;
- the international competitiveness of Canadian industry is to be maintained;
- technological progress in the field should benefit all Canadians;
- the goal of telecommunications policy should be fair and balanced regional development; and
- the need for government to assume responsibility for policy development.

She also announces the formation of a federal-provincial committee to determine how to put those principles into action.

3 April
Regional Development—Prince Edward Island

The governments of Canada and Prince Edward Island sign a five-year, $23.5 million agreement to attract new investment and strengthen the province's industrial base. The agreement is the thirteenth to be signed under the Prince Edward Island Economic and Regional Development Agreement (ERDA) since its inception in 1984.

5-6 April
Canada-U.S. Relations—Summits; Acid Rain; Arctic Sovereignty

United States President Ronald Reagan and Prime Minister Mulroney hold their third annual summit meeting in Ottawa. High on the agenda is acid rain; Mr. Mulroney makes a proposal for a binding, non-partisan treaty to deal with the problem, in which the Canadian government, the Reagan administration and the U.S. Congress would agree to targets and schedules for emission reduction in both countries. Mr. Reagan agrees to consider the proposal but makes no commitments.

In private session, Mr. Mulroney reiterates Canada's position on Arctic sovereignty: that the waters around the Canadian Arctic archipelago should be considered internal Canadian waters. Mr. Reagan, in his 6 April address to Parliament, states that he and Mr. Mulroney are "determined to find a solution based on mutual respect for sovereignty and our common security and other interests". In addition, the two leaders discuss Canada's proposal to license film and video imports, with Mr. Reagan questioning whether the proposed policy would impede the flow of American films into Canada.

In conjunction with the leaders' two-day summit, External Affairs Minister Joe Clark holds talks with U.S. Secretary of State George Shultz on matters of mutual interest.

6 April
Supreme Court—
Charter of Rights
and Freedoms

In a series of judgments widely interpreted as major blows to Canada's labour movement, the Supreme Court of Canada rules that the Constitution's guarantee of freedom of association does not include the right to strike or to bargain collectively. The court, in three separate 4-2 judgments, upholds federal, Alberta and Saskatchewan laws that limited workers' right to strike, arbitrarily set their wages and called for compulsory arbitration in certain cases. The unions had argued that Section 2(d) of the Charter of Rights and Freedoms, which guarantees "freedom of association", also includes the right to strike. The Court, however, rules that because those who drafted the Constitution make no reference to the right to strike, it cannot be deemed a right that requires constitutional protection. The judgment dealt with the following appeals: more than 50,000 Alberta workers, including hospital workers, municipal police and firefighters, had challenged a law that prohibited them from striking and forced them to submit to binding arbitration; the Public Service Alliance of Canada had asked the court to declare the federal wage restraint law of 1982, which imposed ceilings of six and five per cent, unconstitutional; the Saskatchewan government had asked the Supreme Court to overturn a lower-court ruling that declared unconstitutional a provincial law making it illegal for provincial dairy workers to walk off the job.

7 April
Interprovincial Relations—Quebec-Ontario

The Ontario Government officially opens an office in Quebec City in what is described as a bid to strengthen relations between the two provinces (Quebec set up an office in Ontario in 1971). The government office is to promote the image of Ontario and provide information on the province's laws, business contracts, income tax and French-language services.

10 April
Environment—Acid Rain—Federal-Provincial Relations

Manitoba becomes the fifth province to sign an agreement with the federal Government for the reduction of sulphur dioxide emissions. In the agreement, Manitoba agrees to reduce its acidic emissions by about 25 per cent over the next seven years—from 738,000 tonnes to 550,000 tonnes by 31 December 1994.

11 April
Crown Corporations—Privatization

The federal crown corporation Teleglobe Canada, which handles Canada's overseas telephone and Telex traffic, is sold to Memotec Data Inc. for $483 million, plus a $106-million special dividend.

15 April
Supreme Court—Appointments

Prime Minister Mulroney appoints Madame Justice Claire L'Heureux-Dubé of Quebec City to the Supreme Court. She joins Madame Justice Bertha Wilson as the Supreme Court's second woman justice.

19 April
Environment—Provincial-International Relations

Ontario Premier David Peterson and Michigan Governor James Blanchard sign a series of general co-operation agreements in the areas of transportation, agriculture, trade and investment, science and technology, environment, education and natural resources. The major section of the pact is the establishment of a joint Maritime Advisory Committee, under the auspices of state and provincial transportation departments, which will look at issues concerning the Great Lakes and St. Lawrence Seaway.

27 April
Regulation—Securities Industry—Ontario

The federal government and the government of Ontario reach an agreement respecting the regulation of the province's securities industry. For months, Ottawa and the provinces had been holding discussions over who has jurisdiction over what aspects of the financial industry. Ontario's regulations concerned ownership of securities firms, and required any firm participating in the securities market to register with provincial authorities. Ottawa was concerned because banks, which also deal in securities, are regulated solely by the federal government. Provincial initiatives by Ontario and British Columbia to regulate more closely the securities industries in their provinces were interpreted by the federal government as a threat to federal jurisdiction over financial institutions.

Under the terms of the agreement, Ontario will regulate securities and affiliates of federally chartered banks as well as those of trust and insurance companies operating in the province. It will also have control over such stock activities as share-trading, mutual funds and underwriting corporate securities. For its part, Ottawa is to regulate the securities activities that federally-chartered institutions carry on in-house. The deal will also enable banks, insurance and trust companies—"three pillars" of the Canadian financial system—to buy into the fourth: brokerage houses.

The Ottawa-Ontario deal is denounced by the other provinces—particularly Quebec—as a sellout of provincial jurisdiction over securities.

30 April
Constitution—
Meech Lake Accord

Meeting at Meech Lake, Quebec, Prime Minister Mulroney and the ten provincial premiers reach an agreement-in-principle, thereafter known as the Meech Lake accord, resolving Quebec's constitutional grievances. There are essentially five main points to the agreement:

• Constitutional recognition of Quebec as constituting a distinct society;

• newly-defined roles for all provinces in appointments to the Senate and the Supreme Court of Canada;

- provision for federal-provincial agreements relating to immigration policy;

- the right for all provinces to opt out of future shared-cost programmes with full financial compensation; and

- a promise from Mr. Mulroney to discuss further constitutional changes, including Senate reform, by the end of 1988.

3 May
Mining and Gas Industries—Tax Incentives

Federal Energy Minister Marcel Masse announces the $200 million-a-year Canadian Exploration Incentive Program (CEIP), which is to encourage activity in the mining and gas exploration sectors. The programme, which was developed by Finance Minister Michael Wilson to replace the much criticized removal of incentives like flow-through shares, is to begin as these cuts take effect on 1 October.

7 May
Deregulation—Financial Institutions

Federal Minister of State for Financial Institutions Tom Hockin tables legislation in the Commons to permit federally-regulated financial institutions, including banks, to own securities dealers. It also contains provisions that empower the minister to review transfers of ownership, broadening the supervisory powers of federal regulators and raising financial standards for insurance companies. The move is in response to the Ottawa-Ontario accord on financial institutions reached 27 April. Ontario has announced similar legislation for financial institutions under its jurisdiction. The federal legislation represents the first time banks will have been allowed to operate in securities markets since the stock market crash of 1929.

11 May
Constitution—Meech Lake Accord

Prime Minister Mulroney proposes to the House of Commons that the House fully endorse the Meech Lake Agreement of 30 April. All members, including the leaders of the three parties, support the agreement-in-principle.

26-27 May
Western Premiers'
Conferences; Con-
stitution—Meech
Lake Accord;
Agriculture

The premiers of the four western provinces gather in Humboldt, Saskatchewan, for the Western Premiers' Conference, where they reaffirm their support for the Meech Lake Constitutional Accord and reject former Prime Minister Pierre Trudeau's criticisms of the agreement. In another development, the premiers call on Ottawa to make an early announcement for "an increased and substantial deficiency payment" to western grain farmers, estimating that at least $1.6 billion is needed to bring Prairie farmers' incomes back up to 1981 levels. On western diversification, the premiers agree to set up a working group of ministers charged with reviewing the matter.

27 May
Constitution—
Meech Lake Accord

Former Prime Minister Trudeau lashes out at the proposed Meech Lake Constitutional Accord and those who signed it, charging that the changes the Accord would bring would render the Canadian state "totally impotent", adding "What a dark day for Canada was this 30 April 1987". In criticizing the federal government for giving up significant powers over appointments to the Supreme Court and Senate, he characterizes Prime Minister Mulroney as a "weakling" and the premiers as lacking the courage to stand up against Quebec nationalists. Mr. Trudeau saves special criticism for the designation in the Accord of Quebec as a "distinct society," and all that the designation entails. Those who never wanted a bilingual Canada, he says, get their wish "with the recognition of the existence of French-speaking Canadians and English-speaking Canadians... those Canadians who fought for a single Canada, bilingual and multicultural, can say goodbye to their dream".

Mr. Mulroney's response to the broadside was to characterize it as typical of a bygone era: "You can have the old style warring federalism or you can have genuine co-operative federalism on which we're trying to build a new country".

31 May
*Reform Association
of Canada*

Bound by their dissatisfaction with the political *status quo* in Canada, delegates to the founding convention in Vancouver of the Reform Association of Canada vote to support the idea of a broadly-based federal political party to advance the West's economic and constitutional concerns. According to key organizer Preston Manning, the party's aim will be to attract disaffected westerners from all three existing political parties.

2-3 June
*Constitution—
Meech Lake Accord*

After 19 straight hours of negotiations involving the Prime Minister and the Premiers at the Langevin Block in Ottawa, Mr. Mulroney announces that an agreement has been reached on the provisions and legal wording of the 1987 Constitutional Accord. The document, known as the Langevin text, contains unanimous agreement on the following points:

- that the Constitution would recognize the existence of French-speaking Canadians centred in Quebec but present elsewhere in Canada and English-speaking Canadians concentrated outside of Quebec but also present in Quebec, and recognition of Quebec as a distinct society within Canada;

- the provinces are granted the right to opt out of national shared-cost programmes and still receive financial compensation providing they supply a similar programme in the province that meets the national objectives;

- Senate appointments will be made by the federal Government but candidates will be chosen from lists submitted by the provinces;

- Supreme Court Justices will be chosen in the same manner, with Quebec guaranteed three justices;

- constitutional recognition of federal-provincial immigration agreements—such as those negotiated between the governments of Quebec and Canada since 1971—which allow the provinces a more active role in the process, is granted; and

- all amendments affecting the House of Commons, the powers of the Senate and the selection and residence qualifications of Senators, the Supreme Court of Canada, the extension of new provinces into the Territories, and the creation of new provinces, are to require the consent of Parliament and all provincial legislatures.

6 June
Regional Develop-
ment—Atlantic
Canada Oppor-
tunities Agency

Prime Minister Mulroney announces in St. John's the development of a new Atlantic development agency. The Atlantic Canada Opportunities Agency (ACOA), promised by the Prime Minister in October 1986, is to be based in Moncton, N.B. and will be headed by Donald McPhail, Canada's former ambassador to West Germany. The minister responsible for ACOA will be Senator Lowell Murray, Minister of State for Federal-Provincial Relations. With a budget of $1.05 billion over five years, the agency is to concentrate on promoting small and medium-sized businesses in the Atlantic region as well as coordinating all federal economic programmes in the region. According to Mr. Mulroney, ACOA will succeed where other agencies have failed because it will keep decision-making within the Atlantic region. Besides its own budget, ACOA will absorb a number of programmes and funding now administered by the Department of Regional Industrial Expansion (DRIE), such as the Atlantic Enterprise Program. DRIE is to continue to be responsible for national industrial policy and major industrial projects.

14-16 June
Eastern Canadian
Premiers and New
England Governors

The Eastern Canadian Premiers and New England Governors hold their annual conference in Halifax, Nova Scotia. Most of the discussions are about environmental issues, particularly acid rain; the six governors and five premiers agree to consult more closely on monitoring and on development projects that might cause acid rain. Also, the group reaffirms its commitment to offshore oil and gas development and the construction of a gas pipeline from Nova Scotia to New England.

18 June
Energy Regula-
tion—
Hydroelectricity

The National Energy Board announces that it has rejected an application by Hydro-Québec to export $13 billion in hydroelectricity to the New England states. The bid is rejected because the Quebec utility did not present enough evidence to convince the N.E.B. that all the power to be exported was surplus to Canadian requirements, as required by regulation. The Quebec plan had been opposed by the electrical utilities of Ontario, Newfoundland, New Brunswick and Prince Edward Island.

Tax Reform

Finance Minister Michael Wilson reveals his proposals for federal tax reform in a White Paper on Tax Reform as a prelude to the actual tax reform legislation. The general principles of the paper include a reduction of corporate taxes, while at the same time closing many corporate tax loopholes; the introduction of a minimum tax on financial institutions, including insurance companies; a reduction of personal income tax brackets from ten to three; an increase in child-tax credits; and a tightening of provisions for people or companies attempting to avoid paying taxes.

23 June
Constitution—
Meech Lake Accord

The Quebec National Assembly votes 95-18 to ratify the Meech Lake accord. The vote split along party lines, with Liberals supporting and Parti Québécois opposing the resolution.

24 June
Environment—
Regulation

Federal Environment Minister Tom McMillan introduces *Bill C-74*, his new Environmental Protection Act in the Commons, pledging $37 million over the next five years to enforce the law. The proposed act prescribes up to $1-million-a-day fines for corporate polluters and jail terms of up to five years. McMillan tells the Commons that previous federal governments have failed to keep environmental law in tune with growing demand for tough action against polluters and pollution. This new act, he asserts, is intended to redress this situation.

The most controversial aspect of the bill, however, is what its critics term its "Meech Lake sellout" of federal authority. The bill requires Ottawa to consult with the provinces before taking action against environmental polluters; this, it is charged,in effect gives the provinces sweeping new veto powers over federal action.

On 25 November Mr. McMillan, appearing before a parliamentary committee, announces that he will amend the legislation. The amended version allows Ottawa to bring in pollution controls but, if a province has its own plan that is just as strong, the two levels of government are to negotiate an agreement. This revision meets with renewed charges that the federal Government is abdicating its responsibility over the environment to the provinces.

25 June
Language Policy—
Official Languages
Act

Federal Justice Minister Ray Hnatyshyn tables a new Official Languages Act in the Commons. *Bill C-72* updates the 18-year-old *Official languages Act* that brought official bilingualism to the public service. The act requires the federal government not just to protect official-language minorities but to promote the vitality of their community life as well. In addition, the bill:

• provides for more flexibility in designating what federal services will be provided in both official languages;

• gives more authority to the Commissioner of Official Languages, including the right to go to the courts if his directives are not followed;

• broadens the legal recourse available to those who feel their rights are not being observed; and

• states that English and French are the official languages of the courts, and either language may be used by any person in any federal court.

Supreme Court—
Separate Schools—
Ontario

The Supreme Court of Canada rules unanimously that Ontario has the constitutional authority to extend full public financing to Catholic high schools, and that this extension does not violate the guarantee of religious freedom in the Canadian Charter of Rights and Freedoms. *Bill 30*, the plan to extend the funding, was announced by then Conservative Premier Bill Davis in 1984 and passed by the Liberal government in 1986. The main opponents of the bill—most notably the Metropolitan Toronto School Board—argued that *Bill 30* was unlawful because it contravened the Charter. Other groups, including the Canadian Jewish Congress, argued that the funding legislation can be constitutional only if it is extended to all religious schools. Both Alberta and Quebec intervened on behalf of Ontario in the case, supporting its successful claim that provinces have the right under section 93 of the Constitution to create or extend denominational education systems as they see fit.

30 June
Capital Punishment

Reflecting a major change in opinion among many Conservative Members of Parliament, the Commons decide by a substantial 21-vote margin not to reinstate the death penalty in Canada. The count for the free vote is 127 in favour of the death penalty, 148 against. During the process leading to the vote at least twenty-five Conservatives and six Liberals abandoned their pro-capital punishment stances since the last election in 1984. Prime Minister Mulroney had intervened strongly in the debates on the side of the abolitionists.

30 June
Deregulation—
Securities In-
dustry—Ontario

Access to Ontario's securities market is widened as the *Ontario Securities Act*, given cabinet approval 17 June, goes into effect today. Under the new regulations—nicknamed the "Big Bang" after similar changes in London's financial industry in 1986—companies that had previously been banned or restricted from parts of the securities market will be able to enter the market. Banks, trust companies and insurance firms are now allowed to own or operate an investment firm. Foreign dealers are granted limited access to the market for one year, and by 30 June 1988 will be on an equal footing with other Canadian dealers.

7 July
Free Trade

The provincial premiers gather in Ottawa to be briefed on the free trade negotiations. Ontario Premier Peterson announces, following the briefing, that there was "no way" he could give his approval-in-principle to Ottawa's position at this time.

11 July
National Parks—Federal-Provincial Relations

Prime Minister Mulroney and British Columbia Premier William Vander Zalm sign an agreement in Victoria creating a new 145,000 hectare national park in the South Moresby region of the Queen Charlotte Islands. The ceremony is the culmination of two years of negotiations between the federal and provincial governments. The plan was initiated in 1985 when federal Environment Minister Tom Mc-Millan proposed to create the park after a series of bitter confrontations between loggers and Haida Indians. Ottawa committed $106 million to the project, with both Ottawa and British Columbia sharing the costs of compensating the loggers and forestry companies.

13 July
Regional Development—Northern Ontario

Federal Solicitor General James Kelleher announces a programme to encourage the development of small and medium-sized businesses in Northern Ontario. The Special Northern Ontario Development Program will supply grants, loans, interest rate subsidies and loan guarantees worth $100 million over five years to the Northern region.

22 July
Telecommunications—Regulation

Communications Minister Flora MacDonald announces the government's new telecommunications policy. The new policy commits the government to promoting more competition in some segments of the telecommunications business and points towards the establishment of a more uniform regulatory structure in Canada. The policy proposes to establish two categories of telecommunications carriers. The first, called Type I, will include companies which own and operate interprovincial and international networks; these will be allowed to compete among themselves, but new entrants will be limited. Type II companies can lease facilities from the national carriers, and then sell services to the public. Unfettered competition will be allowed in this business with no foreign ownership restrictions.

The new policy, however, does not address the contentious issues of competition in the long-distance market and the allowing of competitors to provide services by hooking up to provincial monopolies, leaving those issues to be decided either through federal-provincial negotiation or, failing that, through the Supreme Court.

2 August
Regional Development—Western Diversification Office

Prime Minister Mulroney announces the establishment of a $1.2-billion fund to diversify Western Canada's economy. The new Edmonton-based Western Diversification Office (WDO) will provide grants to businesses, local governments and universities over five years to lessen the West's dependence on oil and agriculture. The WDO is to work together with the provinces in encouraging worthwhile development projects. Money for the programme is to come from unallocated funds already in the federal budget; in addition, approximately $200 million will be transferred from the Department of Regional Industrial Expansion. The WDO is to be headed up by Indian Affairs Minister Bill McKnight.

21 August
Canada-U.S. Trade Relations—Exports—Potash

The United States Department of Commerce hands down a preliminary ruling that Canadian potash producers are dumping their product in the United States and prescribes duties of up to 85.2 per cent on Canadian potash exports to the U.S. On 1 September, Saskatchewan Premier Grant Devine, whose province is the world's largest producer of potash, retaliates with the Potash Resources Act, which sets strict production quotas on the Saskatchewan industry, thereby sharply curtailing exports of Saskatchewan potash to the United States. Devine later travels to New York to warn the fertilizer industry that "The entire U.S. agriculture industry will pay through the nose for the potash ruling."

27-28 August
Annual Premiers'
Conferences; Con-
stitution—Meech
Lake Accord;
Senate Reform

Canada's premiers gather in Saint John for the Twenty-eighth Annual Premiers' Conference, where constitutional issues, international trade and federal-provincial fiscal relations dominate discussions.

The premiers agree not to seek any changes to the Meech Lake Accord until after the Accord is ratified. In addition, they decide to postpone until the 1988 Constitutional Conference formal discussion of requests by territorial leaders to retain the present formula required for constitutional amendment—the consent of seven provinces representing half Canada's population—for the admission of new provinces to Canada. (Yukon Government leader Tony Pennikett had urged the premiers not to adopt the Meech Lake amending formula which would require the approval of all ten provinces and the federal government for such amendments.)

The premiers also choose to delay any discussion of Senate reform until the upcoming Constitutional conference, despite efforts by Alberta Premier Donald Getty to push for his proposed "Triple E Senate" (Effective, Elected, Equal).

During the premiers' discussion on trade there is strong support for retaliatory action taken by Saskatchewan Premier Grant Devine against the proposed U.S. tariff on Canadian potash exports.

28 August
Transportation—
Deregulation

Two bills deregulating the country's transportation industry receive royal assent today. The legislative process behind the two—*Bill C-18*, the *National Transportation Act*, and *Bill C-19*, the *Motor Vehicle Transport Act* —began with publication of the 1985 policy paper "Freedom to Move," which advocated sweeping changes to transportation regulation in Canada.

The *National Transportation Act* deals with both rail and air transport. For the railways, it will allow for more competition between rail companies and allow them to abandon unprofitable lines more easily. Airlines which once had to prove that they were viable operations will now only have to show that they are willing and able to service the routes. The bill also makes it easier for airlines to abandon unprofitable routes.

The *Motor Vehicle Transport Act* relaxes the rules for granting interprovincial licenses to trucking firms. Companies will no longer have to prove that a new service is necessary before starting up. Instead, anyone objecting to the license has to show that competition is not in the public interest.

30 August
Canada-France Relations— Fisheries

Prime Minister Brian Mulroney meets with French Prime Minister Jacques Chirac at Meech Lake to explore ways out of deadlock between the two countries over boundaries and fishing quotas. The two agree to resume talks after Mr. Mulroney agrees to change Canada's negotiating team. Montreal lawyer Yves Fortier is named to represent Canada in the new talks.

2-5 September
Francophone Summit

Prime Minister Mulroney and Quebec Premier Robert Bourassa co-host the second Francophone Summit, which is attended by 41 countries, in Quebec City. Among the items of business conducted at the Summit, Canada agrees to forgive $325 million in outstanding loans to seven African countries and contribute more in aid to French-speaking Africa. Resolutions are passed condemning South Africa for its policy of apartheid and calling for a peace conference in the Middle East.

10 September
Elections—Ontario

David Peterson leads the Ontario Liberal party to a huge majority in Ontario election. The Liberals take 94 of the province's 130 ridings, the New Democratic Party wins 20 and the Conservatives 16.

13 September
Canada-France Relations— Fisheries

France and Canada resume negotiations over their boundary and fishing dispute in Paris.

14 September
Fisheries—Federal-
Provincial Relations

The Newfoundland delegation to the Canada-France fisheries negotiations in Paris abandons the talks and its advisory role to the federal negotiators. Later, Newfoundland Premier Peckford outlines his reasons for ordering the action: the federal government, he charges, was prepared unilaterally to offer France access to valuable northern cod stocks in indisputably Canadian waters in return for an agreement to settle the boundary dispute. The talks end without an agreement, but the two sides agree to resume discussions on 6 October.

Free Trade—First
Ministers' Meetings

Prime Minister Mulroney meets with the premiers in Ottawa to discuss the development of the free trade talks. At this meeting Chief Negotiator Reisman warns the premiers that, unless the U.S. made more substantive offers in the areas of trade remedy and dispute settlement, the free trade negotiations would fail. Premier Peterson of Ontario had learned officially from Mr. Reisman that the U.S. negotiators had waited until after the 10 September Ontario election before declaring their interest in having the Auto Pact part of the negotiations. Mr. Peterson expresses his surprise, as he claims that only two days earlier Canadian officials and members of the Canadian automobile industry had said that the Auto Pact would not be placed on the table.

21 September
Constitution—
Meech Lake
Accord; Special
Joint Committee on
the 1987 Constitu-
tional Accord

The Special Joint Committee of the Senate and the House of Commons on the 1987 Constitutional Accord releases its Report, giving its approval to the Meech Lake Accord, but suggesting that the Prime Minister move to rectify some minor flaws. In particular, the Committee was concerned about the Accord as it related to the Northwest and Yukon Territories. The report questions those aspects of the agreement that grant each existing province a veto over the creation of new ones and those that shut the Territories out of the nominating process for the Supreme Court and Senate. As well, the Committee notes a need for granting greater protection for francophones outside Quebec.

23 September
Constitution—
Meech Lake Accord

The Saskatchewan Legislative Assembly votes 43-3 to ratify the Meech Lake Accord. Three New Democrats oppose the bill.

Free Trade

Prime Minister Mulroney announces to the Commons that free trade negotiations with the United States have been suspended because of "unacceptable" American demands in the areas of dispute settlement, culture and regional development grants. Chief negotiator Reisman states: "As far as I'm concerned, it's over. I terminated the negotiations today."

25 September
Free Trade

Finance Minister Wilson and International Trade Minister Pat Carney travel to Washington to meet with U.S. Special Trade Representative Clayton Yeuter and James Baker to explore the possibilities of reviving the free trade negotiations. Marathon discussions towards this end began on 25 September between Canadian and U.S. officials.

2 October
Free Trade

Canada-U.S. free trade negotiations resume following new proposals by U.S. Treasury Secretary Baker on the nature and rules of the dispute-settlement mechanism. The Baker proposals are as follows:

• that the omnibus trade bill, if passed, would not retroactively undermine any terms of a free trade agreement;

• agreement that a new binational tribunal would settle trade disputes between the two countries;

• the new rules under which the tribunal would operate would be drafted and phased in over five years; and

• in the interim, the tribunal would base its discussions on the provisions of current trade laws of the country where the complaint was filed.

3 October
Free Trade

After what have been described as "cliff-hanger" negotiations, Canadian and American negotiators reach agreement on the free trade agreement after racing to meet a Congressional deadline of 3 October. Key elements of the agreement, as announced the next day, include the following:

- the creation of a continental energy market. Canada receives assured market access to the United States in return for giving the U.S. a secure energy supply in periods of shortage;

- the establishment of a new bilateral panel to settle trade disputes;

- a commitment to write new trade rules over five years with a possible three-year extension. The trade tribunal would operate under these new rules;

- each government agrees not to launch countervailing duties or other trade complaints against the other country's imports. However, Canada would still be vulnerable to countervailing actions brought by U.S. industries;

- Canada would benefit from an exemption from the retroactive application of the omnibus trade bill being considered in Congress;

- Canada's regional development subsidies remain protected, but could be affected when the new rules are written;

- Canada would be limited in its ability to screen foreign investment, with the phasing out of scrutiny of indirect takeovers;

- a phased elimination of all tariffs between the two countries;

- an end to all tariffs on agricultural products and the elimination of grain transportation subsidies between the two countries;

- no changes to the Canada-U.S. Auto Pact; and

- a limited agreement on government procurement that would allow firms in each country to compete for federal government contracts in the other country.

6 October
Free Trade—
Federal-Provincial
Relations

Prime Minister Mulroney meets with the premiers to discuss the just-concluded Free Trade Agreement. Within two days, provincial positions are announced: British Columbia, Alberta, Saskatchewan, Quebec and New Brunswick support the agreement; Ontario, Manitoba and Prince Edward Island oppose it; Newfoundland and Nova Scotia request more time to study the agreement. Both the latter eventually support the agreement.

6-9 October
Canada-France
Relations—
Fisheries

Canadian and French negotiators meet to continue their talks over boundaries and fish. After two days of talks, however, France recalls its negotiators, claiming that the two parties are too far apart and that French fishermens' interests were being "seriously jeopardized" by the low fishing quotas offered by the Canadians.

7 October
Hydroelectricity

Manitoba Energy Minister Jerry Storie announces an agreement between Manitoba Hydro and Ontario Hydro which would send 200 megawatts of Manitoba power to Northwestern Ontario under a five-year, $500,000 deal to begin in 1998. This is to be in addition to the 80 megawatts of power annually purchased by Ontario from Manitoba Hydro.

8 October
Environment—Acid
Rain—Federal-
Provincial Relations

New Brunswick becomes the sixth province to sign a joint agreement with the federal Government on the reduction of sulfur dioxide emissions. The agreement, signed in Fredericton, requires the province to reduce allowable emissions from 215,000 tonnes to 185,000 tonnes by 1984. Premier Hatfield notes that the province is still negotiating with Ottawa over funding for the conversion and anti-pollution equipment necessary for the province to reach the agreed-to limits.

11 October
Deregulation—
Financial
Institutions—
Quebec

Quebec releases its White Paper on the reform of financial institutions. The White Paper mounts a rigorous defence of provincial jurisdiction over securities markets; condemns the Ontario-Ottawa agreement of June 1986 which recognized a measure of federal jurisdiction over securities; and states

Quebec's intention to impose no limits on the ownership of financial institutions, including those groups involved in business activities.

The same day, Quebec Associate Minister for Finance and Privatization Pierre Fortier announces a major Quebec initiative to lighten regulations on the province's financial sector, with the aim of encouraging the growth of financial supercompanies better able to compete within modern international markets. He announces plans to table four bills toward this end within the year: the first will allow trust and savings companies to diversify into the securities field; the second will allow foreign-owned insurance companies to incorporate and raise capital in Quebec; another bill is to deal specifically with allowing the huge Desjardins credit union movement to diversify its activities; the fourth bill will allow insurance agents and brokers to form groups or conglomerates to sell all types of insurance, and not have to limit themselves to only one type. These initiatives represent an aggressive incursion by Quebec into the world of regulation of financial institutions and most run contrary to federal guidelines set out by Federal Minister of State for Finance Tom Hockin in 1986.

13 October
Elections—New
Brunswick

Richard Hatfield's political dynasty ends as Frank McKenna's Liberals sweep the Conservative Party from power in the New Brunswick election, scoring one of the greatest electoral victories in Canadian history. The Liberals, who had not been in power for 17 years, return with a vengeance, capturing all of the province's 58 seats.

25 October
Constitution—
Meech Lake Accord

The House of Commons votes 242 to 16 to ratify the Meech Lake Accord. Eleven Liberals and two New Democrats break ranks with their leaders to oppose the Accord, together with one Independent. The Accord moves on to the Senate, where it is to be debated and voted on.

30 October
Reform Party of Canada

The Reform Party of Canada holds its founding convention in Winnipeg, attended by nearly 400 delegates, and announces its intention to contest the next federal election. Main planks in its platform will be the call for a reformed Senate to provide greater representation for Western Canada and the freeing of Members of Parliament from the bonds of party discipline. The delegates adopt a constitution which calls for a "free enterprise economy," and elect Preston Manning, son of former Alberta Premier Ernest Manning, as the party's first leader.

5 November
Regulation—Water Exports

Federal Environment Minister Thomas McMillan announces his government's long awaited policy on the export of water. In a policy paper tabled in the Commons, the Government announces that it will use its constitutional authority to prohibit large-scale water exports, the largest of which is the proposed $100-billion Grand Canal project—supported by Quebec Premier Bourassa—which was to bring water from James Bay, through the Great Lakes, to the U.S. Southwest. Although small-scale exports are to be allowed, the federal Government announces its intention to begin negotiations with the provinces to create a system that ensures that such sales do not go against the national interest.

10 November
International Trade—Beer and Liquor—GATT

A panel of the General Agreement on Tariffs and Trade rules against Canada and the discriminatory policies of its provinces in the pricing of beer and wine. The panel, acting on a complaint by the European Community, rules that Canada should impose "national treatment standards" on foreign beer, wine and liquor. This would mean, for example, that Canadian provinces might have to drop regulations requiring breweries to produce beer in the province where it is sold. The decision is non-binding, but if Canada does not act upon the finding, it is to go to the full GATT Council.

16 November
Supreme Court—
Language
Policy—Quebec;
Quebec Bill 101

Hearings begin in the Supreme Court of Canada over the constitutionality of Quebec's controversial *Bill 101*. The Court is to hear arguments on three cases which will more closely define both Quebec's constitutional right to legislate in language matters and provincial powers to exempt legislation from the protection of the Canadian Charter of Rights and Freedoms.

The three cases involve Allan Singer, a Montreal stationer who refused to take down an English-only sign over his stationery store and had been fighting the Quebec language law virtually since its inception in 1977; the footwear company La Chaussure Brown's Inc., which won the right in Quebec Appeal Court in 1986 to post bilingual signs, a ruling being challenged by the Quebec Government; and Irwin Toy Co., which succeeded last year in overturning a Quebec consumer law banning advertising directed at children younger than 13.

During the hearings, provincial government lawyers argue that it is within Quebec's rights to issue a blanket exemption from the Charter. They cite section 33 of the Charter, which allows certain laws to be passed "notwithstanding" constitutional guarantees. For their part, lawyers for Brown, Singer and Irwin question Quebec's right to exempt its consumer protection legislation and its language law from the guarantees of freedom of expression contained in the Charter. The Court reserves judgment.

Regional Develop-
ment—Prince
Edward Island

Federal Public Works Minister Stewart McInnes announces that tenders will be received for the construction of a fixed link by bridge or tunnel between Prince Edward Island and the mainland, to be built by 1993. Seven construction companies had been invited to bid on the 14-kilometre $900-million link. Premier Ghiz offers tentative support for the project, allowing that "the voices of Islanders must be heard first." A year-round link to the mainland was a condition of Prince Edward Island's entry into Confederation in 1873.

18 November
Environment—
Canada-U.S.
Relations

Federal Environment Minister Tom McMillan and Mr. Lee Thomas, his American counterpart, sign a Great Lakes Cleanup Agreement, updating a similar 1978 agreement. Among its provisions, the agreement pledges the two countries to step up efforts to track down and eliminate sources of toxic chemicals in the water and underground and also calls for both governments to produce "action plans" for the cleanup of 42 of the most polluted areas in the Great Lakes region. Left out of the accord is the contentious issue of acid rain.

22 November
Hydroelectricity—
Exports—Quebec

Hydro-Québec and New Brunswick Hydro sign a six-year energy deal by which the New Brunswick utility may purchase as much as 3-billion kilowatt/hours of electricity per year from 1988 to 1992, and as much as 2-billion kilowatt/hours per year from 1992 to 1994. In signing the agreement, New Brunswick drops its objection to a Hydro-Québec plan to export 70-billion kilowatt/hours of electricity to New England beginning in 1990. A similar Hydro-Québec plan had been rejected earlier by the National Energy Board on the grounds that the Quebec Utility had failed to offer the electricity to Ontario and New Brunswick.

26-27 November
Annual Conference
of First Ministers;
Free Trade; Con-
stitution—Meech
Lake

Prime Minister Mulroney meets with the ten provincial premiers in Toronto for the Annual Conference of First Ministers, where the proposed Canada-U.S. free trade agreement and the Meech Lake Accord dominate discussions.

Responding to the known opposition to the free trade agreement by Premiers Ghiz of Prince Edward Island, Pawley of Manitoba and Peterson of Ontario, Mr. Mulroney makes it clear that he will not let their objections to the pact either stop or impede his government in its drive to implement the agreement by 1989.

In apparent recognition of the differences around the table on free trade, the First Ministers discuss domestic trade issues, including the elimination of barriers to interprovincial trade, and Premier Peterson of Ontario presents six components of a national economic plan as an alternative to free trade with the United States.

Notwithstanding the nearly unanimous agreement of conference participants on the Meech Lake Accord, Premier McKenna of New Brunswick expresses his strong reservations about the pact. In addition to his criticism that the agreement does not address the concerns of women and aboriginal peoples, he seeks Ottawa's assurances that the federal government's power to help the have-not provinces would in no way be jeopardized by the Accord.

26 November
Regional Development;
Federal-Provincial
Task Force on
Regional Development

The Federal-Provincial Task Force on Regional Development Assessment produces its report to the Annual Conference of First Ministers in Toronto. The report is critical of the federal Government's regional development policies, asserting that Ottawa's transfers of funds to poorer regions have more often served to compensate them for underdevelopment than for raising their level of industrial development. The report calls for sharper federal and provincial targeting in the allocation of funds, together with the establishment of areas of specialization, where particular industries can be encouraged. As well, both levels of governments are encouraged to place more emphasis on education and retraining.

1 December
Multiculturalism

Secretary of State David Crombie introduces *Bill C-93*, his Government's multiculturalism policy, in the Commons declaring that "the rights of ethnic people are the rights of all Canadians". The intent of the bill is to encourage the "full and equitable participation ... in the continuing evolution and shaping of all aspects of Canadian society".

3 December
Day Care

Federal Health Minister Jake Epp announces the details of his government's child care policy. Ottawa is to spend $5.4 billion between 1988-1995 and $1 billion thereafter on a three-part programme that includes increased funding for day care spaces, tax breaks and a research fund to help children with special needs. Of the $5.4 billion, $3.1 billion will be for the provinces to spend on the establishment of new non-profit day care centres and subsidization of new non-profit and commercial centres. The plan also calls for $2.3 billion over seven years to provide tax breaks for families with small children.

According to Epp, day care spaces in Canada are to double to 400,000 by the end of the programme under a cost-sharing plan with the provinces. Poorer provinces are to get a proportionally larger share, and it is to be up to each province to decide whether to fund commercial or non-profit centres or both. The overall programme is to be administered under a proposed Canada Child Care Act that will set national standards for child care after negotiations with the provinces.

7 December
Hydroelectricity—
Exports—Quebec

Quebec Premier Bourassa announces the sale of hydroelectricity worth as much as $8.6 billion to Vermont Joint Owners, a consortium of nine New England utilities. Having completed its public hearings into the matter 1 December, the National Energy Board is to render its decision in the new year.

Constitution—
Meech Lake Accord

The Alberta Legislative Assembly votes unanimously to support the Meech Lake Accord, although 43 of the Assembly's 83 members are absent. The snap vote caught the Liberals, who had planned to vote against it, off-guard, finding them in caucus when the vote was taken.

8 December
Financial Institu-
tions—International
Banking Centres

Bill C-56, the federal Government's legislation designating Montreal and Vancouver as international banking centres, is approved by the Commons. The most controversial clause of the legislation is the one allowing banks in the two cities to accept deposits from, and make loans to, foreign firms without paying any tax on their profits from the transactions.

Ontario Treasurer Robert Nixon, concerned that his province might lose business to the new international banking centres, announces that the province will reluctantly offer tax breaks or other financial incentives to banks if it becomes apparent that the federal government's banking legislation hurts Toronto's competitive position as a banking centre.

11 December
Free Trade

Prime Minister Mulroney tables the final text of the Canada-U.S. free trade agreement in the Commons.

15 December
Agriculture—Assistance

The federal government announces a farm assistance programme expected to cost $2.8 billion by the end of 1991, making it the largest aid package yet offered to the agricultural sector. Major components of the package include the Special Canadian Grains Program, a $1.1-billion cash payout to grain farmers; a $1-billion debt write-off programme; and fuel tax rebates each worth about $500 million over the next two years. It is estimated that 250,000 farmers—90 per cent of the nation's total—will benefit from the programme in 1988.

Education— Quebec; Constitution—Separate Schools—Quebec

Quebec Education Minister Claude Ryan tables *Bill 107*, a reform of the *Quebec Education Act*, that announces the province's intention to reorganize Quebec's school boards along the lines of language rather than denomination. The plan is similar to a bill adopted under the Parti Québécois in 1984 and later struck down by the Quebec Superior Court on grounds that it violated the constitutional rights of Catholics and Protestants to control their own education systems. In order to allay concerns that this might happen again, Ryan announces that he will not put the plan into action until he receives a ruling from the courts on whether such an action would be constitutional. The legislation leaves intact for the present the four denominational school boards whose existence the Superior Court ruled were protected under the *British North America Act, 1867* and upon which the PQ's earlier reorganization attempts foundered: the Montreal Catholic School Commission, the Protestant School Board of Greater

Montreal, and two Catholic School Boards in Quebec City.

16 December
Tax Reform

Finance Minister Michael Wilson introduces *Bill C-39*, his long-awaited tax reform proposals into the Commons. Mr. Wilson claims that the changes to the tax structure are designed to make the federal tax structure simpler and to reverse the trend toward greater government reliance upon personal rather than corporate income taxes. The changes affect both the personal and corporate income tax systems. Mr. Wilson adheres to the spirit and most of the letter of his 18 June White Paper on taxation. His tax reform plans include the following:

* reduction of corporate taxes to stimulate the economy and the elimination of many tax breaks and broadening the scope of taxation to raise revenue;

* the reduction of personal income tax brackets from ten to three;

* the conversion of many exemptions and deductions to tax credits and the elimination of many tax breaks;

* an increase in the refundable child-tax credit;

* an increase in federal sales tax on alcohol and cigarettes;

* introduction of a tax on the capital of large financial institutions, which has the effect of a minimum tax without being one; and

* the introduction of a three-per-cent tax on life insurance companies in 1988, rising by stages to 15 per cent in 1992.

17 December
Free Trade—First Ministers' Meetings

At a meeting of the First Ministers on Canada-U.S. free trade agreement, seven of the ten provincial governments voice their support of the deal. Following the meeting, the premiers of the three provinces opposed to free trade—Peterson of Ontario, Pawley of Manitoba, and Ghiz of Prince Edward Island—concede that they are unable to stop the Canada-U.S.

Free Trade Agreement. The three back away from earlier threats of a court challenge to the deal, stating instead that only the Canadian people, voting in a national election, can stop the free trade deal from taking effect.

18 December
Regional Develop-
ment—Atlantic
Canada Oppor-
tunities Agency

Federal Minister of Transport John Crosbie introduces into the Commons the legislation required to establish officially the Atlantic Canada Opportunities Agency (ACOA).

Government
Procurement—
Defence

Defence Minister Perrin Beatty announces that Saint John Ship-building of St. John, New Brunswick has been awarded the contract to build the second group of six frigates in the new series of warships for the Canadian navy. The nine-year programme will be worth about $3.5 billion. The contract was the subject of intense lobbying by the governments of Quebec and New Brunswick, with MPs from both regions seeking at least a share of the work for their constituencies. According to Beatty, it is Saint John Ship-building Ltd.'s experience and knowledge, together with their lower bid—almost $200 million lower—that won them the entire contract, although the Government's regional development concerns for the eastern region certainly played a part.

23 December
Constitution—
Meech Lake
Accord—Yukon

The Yukon Court of Appeal rejects the Yukon government's attempts to challenge the Meech Lake Accord. Counsel representing the Yukon Government had argued that the federal Government infringed upon the rights of Yukoners in signing the Meech Lake Accord. Tony Pennikett, Yukon Government leader, does not rule out a challenge to the Supreme Court.

Chronology:
List of Recurring Entries

Aboriginal Peoples: 21 May 1986, 17 June 1986, 26-27 March 1987.

Acid Rain: 8 January 1986, 18-19 March 1986, 9 March 1987, 5-6 April 1987, 10 April 1987, 10 October 1987.

Agriculture: 29 May 1986, 9 December 1986, 15 December 1987.

Alberta: 8 May 1986, 20 August 1986, 1 October 1986.

Budgets (federal): 26 February 1986, 18 February 1987.

British Columbia: 7 September 1986, 22 October 1986.

Canada-U.S. Summit: 18 March 1986, 5-6 April 1987.

Canada-U.S. Trade: 22 May 1986, 23 May 1986, 29 May 1986, 2 June 1986, 26 June 1986, 7 September 1986, 16 October 1986, 18 November 1986, 21 November 1986, 30 December 1986, 21 January 1987, 11 March 1987, 7 July 1987, 21 August 1987, 14 September 1987, 23 September 1987, 25 September 1987, 2 October 1987, 3 October 1987, 6 October 1987, 26-27 November 1987, 11 December 1987, 17 December 1987.

Constitution: 6 March 1986, 9 May 1986, 21 July 1986, 10-12 August 1986, 30 April 1987, 11 May 1987, 27 May 1987, 2-3 June 1987, 23 June 1987, 27-28 August 1987, 21 September 1987, 25 October 1987, 26-27 November 1987, 15 December 1987, 23 December 1987.

Council of Maritime Premiers: 10 September 1986, 2-3 December 1987.

Crown Corporations: 31 October 1986, 31 January 1987, 11 April 1987.

Deregulation: 4 July 1986, 10 September 1986, 2-3 December 1986, 4 December 1986, 18 December 1986, 27 April 1987, 7 May 1987, 30 June 1987, 28 August 1987, 11 October 1987.

Eastern Canadian Premiers and New England Governors: 12-13 June 1986, 14-16 June 1987.

Education: 18 February 1987, 25 June 1987, 15 December 1987.

Elections: 21 April 1986, 8 May 1986, 20 October 1986, 22 October 1986, 10 September 1987, 13 October 1987.

Environment: 8 January 1986, 18-19 March 1986, 9 March 1987, 10 April 1987, 19 April 1987, 24 June 1987, 8 October 1987, 18 November 1987.

Equalization Payments: 19 June 1986, 20 June 1986, 11 March 1987.

Financial Institutions: 4 December 1986, 18 December 1986, 27 April 1987, 7 May 1987, 11 October 1987, 8 December 1987.

First Ministers' Meetings: 2 June 1986, 26-27 March 1987, 14 September 1987, 26-27 November 1987, 17 December 1987.

Fisheries: 7 February 1986, 23 January 1987, 9 February 1987, 17 March 1987, 30 August 1987, 13 September 1987, 14 September 1987, 6-9 October 1987.

Francophone Summit: 17-18 February 1986, 2-5 September 1987.

Free Trade: 2 June 1986, 10-12 August 1986, 21 January 1987, 11 March 1987, 7 July 1987, 14 September 1987, 23 September 1987, 25 September 1987, 2 October 1987, 3 October 1987, 6 October 1987, 26-27 November 1987, 11 December 1987, 17 December 1987.

GATT: 19 June 1986, 10 November 1987.

Government Procurement: 31 October 1986, 3 November 1986, 18 December 1987.

Health: 19 April 1986, 19 June 1986, 1 October 1986.

Hydroelectricity: 14 February 1986, 18 June 1986, 7 October 1987, 5 November 1987, 22 November 1987, 7 December 1987.

Language Policy: 1 May 1986, 22 December 1986, 18 February 1987, 26 February 1987, 25 June 1987, 16 November 1987.

Lumber/Forestry: 22 May 1986, 23 May 1986, 29 May 1986, 26 June 1986, 7 September 1986, 16 October 1986, 18 November 1986, 21 November 1986, 30 December 1986.

Meech Lake Accord: 30 April 1987, 11 May 1987, 27 May 1987, 2-3 June 1987, 23 June 1987, 27-28 August 1987, 21 September 1987, 25 October 1987, 26-27 November 1987, 7 December 1987, 23 December 1987.

Ontario: 19 June 1986, 4 December 1986, 18 December 1986, 7 April 1987, 27 April 1987, 30 June 1987, 13 July 1987, 10 September 1987.

Premiers' Conference: 10-12 August 1986, 27-28 August 1987.

Privatization: 31 January 1986, 31 October 1986, 11 April 1987, 11 July 1987.

Quebec: 6 March 1986, 1 May 1986, 9 May 1986, 4 July 1986, 21 July 1986, 10-12 August 1986, 22 December 1986, 26 February 1987, 15 April 1987, 2-5 September 1987, 11 October 1987, 16 November 1987, 22 November 1987, 7 December 1987, 15 December 1987.

Regional Development: 1 February 1986, 3 April 1987, 6 June 1987, 13 July 1987, 2 August 1987, 16 November 1987, 26 November 1987, 18 December 1987.

Saskatchewan: 20 October 1986, 18 February 1987.

Supreme Court: 1 May 1986, 18 December 1986, 5-6 April 1987, 15 April 1987, 25 June 1987, 17 November 1987.

Tax Reform: 18 June 1987, 16 December 1987.

Telecommunications: 2-3 April 1987, 22 July 1987.

Transportation: 24 June 1986, 10 September 1986, 2-3 December 1986, 28 August 1987.

Western Premiers' Conference: 29 May 1986, 26-27 May 1987.

List of Titles in Print

Peter M. Leslie, *Rebuilding the Relationship: Quebec and its Confederation Partners/Une collaboration renouvelée: le Québec et ses partenaires dans la confédération*, 1987. ($8)

A. Paul Pross and Susan McCorquodale, *Economic Resurgence and the Constitutional Agenda: The Case of the East Coast Fisheries*, 1987. ($10)

Bruce G. Pollard, *Managing the Interface: Intergovernmental Affairs Agencies in Canada*, 1986. ($12)

Catherine A. Murray, *Managing Diversity: Federal-Provincial Collaboration and the Committee on Extension of Services to Northern and Remote Communities*, 1984. ($15)

Peter Russell et al, *The Court and the Constitution: Comments on the Supreme Court Reference on Constitutional Amendment*, 1982. (Paper $5, Cloth $10)

Allan Tupper, *Public Money in the Private Sector: Industrial Assistance Policy and Canadian Federalism*, 1982. ($12)

William P. Irvine, *Does Canada Need a New Electoral System?*, 1979. ($8)

Canada: The State of the Federation

Peter M. Leslie, editor, *Canada: The State of the Federation 1986.* ($15)

Peter M. Leslie, editor, Canada: The State of the Federation 1985. ($14)
Volumes I and II ($20)
Canada: L'état de la fédération 1985. ($14)

The Year in Review

Bruce G. Pollard, *The Year in Review 1983: Intergovernmental Relations in Canada.* ($16)

Revue de l'année 1983: les relations intergouvernementales au Canada. ($16)

S.M. Dunn, *The Year in Review 1982: Intergovernmental Relations in Canada.* ($12)

Revue de l'année 1982: les relations intergouvernementales au Canada. ($12)

S.M. Dunn, *The Year in Review 1981: Intergovernmental Relations in Canada.* ($10)

R.J. Zukowsky, *Intergovernmental Relations in Canada: The Year in Review 1980, Volume I: Policy and Politics.* ($8) (*Volume II not available*)

Research Papers/Notes de Recherche (formerly Discussion Papers)

24. Peter M. Leslie, *Ethnonationalism in a Federal State: The Case of Canada*, 1988. ($4)
23. Peter M. Leslie, *National Citizenship and Provincial Communities: A Review of Canadian Fiscal Federalism*, 1988. ($4)
22. Robert L. Stanfield, *National Political Parties and Regional Diversity*, 1985. (Postage Only)
21. Donald Smiley, *An Elected Senate for Canada? Clues from the Australian Experience*, 1985. ($8)
20. Nicholas R. Sidor, *Consumer Policy in the Canadian Federal State*, 1984. ($8)
19. Thomas O. Hueglin, *Federalism and Fragmentation: A Comparative View of Political Accommodation in Canada*, 1984. ($8)
18. Allan Tupper, *Bill S-31 and the Federalism of State Capitalism*, 1983. ($7)
17. Reginald Whitaker, *Federalism and Democratic Theory*, 1983. ($7)
16. Roger Gibbins, *Senate Reform: Moving Towards the Slippery Slope*, 1983. ($7)
14. John Whyte, *The Constitution and Natural Resource Revenues*, 1982. ($7)

Reflections/Réflexions

3. Peter M. Leslie, *Federal Leadership in Economic and Social Policy*, 1988. ($3)
2. Clive Thomson, editor, *Navigating Meech Lake: The 1987 Constitutional Accord*, 1988. ($4)
1. Allan E. Blakeney, *Canada: Its Framework, Its Foibles, Its Future*, 1988. ($3)

Bibliographies

Bibliography of Canadian and Comparative Federalism, 1980-1985. ($39)
Aboriginal Self-Government in Canada: A Bibliography 1986. ($7)
A Supplementary Bibliography, 1979. ($5)
A Supplementary Bibliography, 1975. ($10)
Federalism and Intergovernmental Relations in Australia, Canada, the United States and Other Countries: A Bibliography, 1967. ($9)

Aboriginal Peoples and Constitutional Reform

Background Papers

16. Bradford W. Morse, *Providing Land and Resources for Aboriginal Peoples*, 1987. ($10)
15. Evelyn J. Peters, *Aboriginal Self-Government Arrangements in Canada*, 1987. ($7)

14. Delia Opekokew, *The Political and Legal Inequities Among Aboriginal Peoples in Canada*, 1987. ($7)
13. Ian B. Cowie, *Future Issues of Jurisdiction and Coordination Between Aboriginal and Non-Aboriginal Governments*, 1987. ($7)
12 C.E.S. Franks, *Public Administration Questions Relating to Aboriginal Self-Government*, 1987. ($10)
11. Richard H. Bartlett, *Subjugation, Self-Management and Self-Government of Aboriginal Lands and Resources in Canada*, 1986. ($10)
10. Jerry Paquette, *Aboriginal Self-Government and Education in Canada*, 1986. ($10)
9. Marc Malone, *Financing Aboriginal Self-Government in Canada*, 1986. ($7)
8. John Weinstein, *Aboriginal Self-Determination Off a Land Base*, 1986. ($7)
7. David C. Hawkes, *Negotiating Aboriginal Self-Government: Developments Surrounding the 1985 First Ministers' Conference*, 1985. ($5)
6. Bryan P. Schwartz, *First Principles: Constitutional Reform with Respect to the Aboriginal Peoples of Canada 1982-1984*, 1985. ($20)
5. Douglas E. Sanders, *Aboriginal Self-Government in the United States*, 1985. ($12)
4. Bradford Morse, *Aboriginal Self-Government in Australia and Canada*, 1985. ($12)
3. (not available).
2. David A. Boisvert, *Forms of Aboriginal Self-Government*, 1985. ($12)
1. Noel Lyon, *Aboriginal Self-Government: Rights of Citizenship and Access to Governmental Services*, 1984. ($12)

Discussion Papers

David C. Hawkes, *The Search for Accommodation*, 1987. ($7)
David C. Hawkes, *Aboriginal Self-Government: What Does It Mean?*, 1985. ($12)

Position Papers

Inuit Committee on National Issues, *Completing Canada: Inuit Approaches to Self-Government*, 1987. ($7)
Martin Dunn, *Access to Survival, A Perspective on Aboriginal Self-Government for the Constituency of the Native Council of Canada*, 1986. ($7)

Workshop Reports

David C. Hawkes and Evelyn J. Peters, *Issues in Entrenching Aboriginal Self-Government*, 1987. ($12)

David C. Hawkes and Evelyn J. Peters, *Implementing Aboriginal Self-Government: Problems and Prospects*, 1986. ($7)

Bibliography

Evelyn J. Peters, *Aboriginal Self-Government in Canada: A Bibliography 1986.* ($7)

Publications may be ordered from:

Institute of Intergovernmental Relations
Queen's University
Kingston, Ontario, Canada
K7L 3N6